Corpus Linguistics for Grammar

Corpus Linguistics for Grammar provides an accessible and practical introduction to the use of corpus linguistics to analyse grammar, demonstrating the wider application of corpus data and providing readers with all the skills and information they need to carry out their own corpus-based research.

This book:

- explores the kinds of corpora available and the tools which can be used to analyse them;
- looks at specific ways in which features of grammar can be explored using a corpus through analysis of areas such as frequency and colligation;
- contains exercises, worked examples and suggestions for further practice with each chapter;
- provides three illustrative examples of potential research projects in the areas of English Literature, TESOL and English Language.

Corpus Linguistics for Grammar is essential reading for students undertaking corpus-based research into grammar, or studying within the areas of English Language, Literature, Applied Linguistics and TESOL.

Christian Jones is Senior Lecturer in TESOL at the University of Central Lancashire, UK.

Daniel Waller is Senior Lecturer in ELT, Testing and TESOL at the University of Central Lancashire, UK.

Routledge Corpus Linguistics Guides
Series consultants: Ronald Carter and Michael McCarthy
University of Nottingham, UK

Routledge Corpus Linguistics Guides provide accessible and practical introductions to using corpus linguistic methods in key sub-fields within linguistics. Corpus linguistics is one of the most dynamic and rapidly developing areas in the field of language studies, and use of corpora is an important part of modern linguistic research. Books in this series provide the ideal guide for students and researchers using corpus data for research and study in a variety of subject areas.

Ronald Carter is Research Professor of Modern English Language in the School of English at the University of Nottingham, UK. He is the co-series editor of the Routledge Applied Linguistics, Routledge Introductions to Applied Linguistics and Routledge English Language Introductions series.

Michael McCarthy is Emeritus Professor of Applied Linguistics at the University of Nottingham, UK, Adjunct Professor of Applied Linguistics at the University of Limerick, Ireland and Visiting Professor in Applied Linguistics at Newcastle University, UK. He is co-editor of the Routledge Handbook of Corpus Linguistics and editor of the Routledge Domains of Discourse series.

Corpus Linguistics for Grammar
Christian Jones and Daniel Waller

Corpus Linguistics for ELT
Ivor Timmis

Corpus Linguistics for Discourse Analysis
Michael Handford

Corpus Linguistics for Sociolinguistics
Bróna Murphy

Corpus Linguistics for the Social Sciences
Tony McEnery, Amanda Potts, Vaclav Brezina and Andrew Hardie

Corpus Linguistics for Grammar

A guide for research

Christian Jones and
Daniel Waller

Routledge
Taylor & Francis Group

LONDON AND NEW YORK

First published 2015
by Routledge
2 Park Square, Milton Park, Abingdon, Oxon OX14 4RN

and by Routledge
711 Third Avenue, New York, NY 10017

Routledge is an imprint of the Taylor & Francis Group, an informa
business

British Library Cataloguing-in-Publication Data
A catalogue record for this book is available from the British Library

Library of Congress Cataloging-in-Publication Data
Jones, Christian (Linguist) author.
Corpus linguistics for grammar : a guide for research / Christian Jones,
Daniel Waller.
pages cm. — (Routledge corpus linguistics guides)
Includes bibliographical references and index.
1. English language—Grammar—Study and teaching (Higher)—Foreign
speakers. 2. English language—Study and teaching (Higher)—Foreign
speakers. 3. English language—Grammar—Research. 4. Second language
acquisition—study and teaching—Foreign speakers. 5. Vocabulary—Study
and teaching (Higher) 6. Corpora (Linguistics) I. Waller, Daniel
(Linguist) II. Title.
PE1128.A2J6423 2015
420.1'88—dc23
2015006152

ISBN: 978-0-415-74640-3 (hbk)
ISBN: 978-0-415-74641-0 (pbk)
ISBN: 978-1-315-71377-9 (ebk)

Typeset in Baskerville
by Swales & Willis Ltd, Exeter, Devon, UK
Printed in Great Britain by Ashford Colour Press Ltd.

Contents

Figures

Tables

Acknowledgements

We would like to thank colleagues past and present for help, inspiration and support:

Svenja Adolphs, Gülfem Aslan, Stephen Bax, Shelley Byrne, Ronald Carter, Jane Cleary, John Cross, Honor Dargan, Teresa Doğuelli, Isabel Donnelly, James Donnithorne, Andy Downer, Tony Green, Nick Gregson, Nicola Halenko, Patrycja Golebiewska, Tania Horak, Douglas Hamano-Bunce, Simon Hobbs, Stuart Hobbs, Josie Leonard, Dan Lumley, Michael McCarthy, Fergus Mackinnon, Alan Milby, Carmel Milroy, John O'Dwyer, Linda Bruce Özdemir, Sheena Palmer, Simon Pate, Raymond Pearce, Keith Richards, Karen Smith, Carole Thomas, Ivor Timmis, Nicola Walker, Cyril Weir, Andy Williams, and Jane Willis.

Thanks to all our BA TESOL/MOLA and MA TESOL with Applied Linguistics students past and present.

Thanks to Rachel Daw, Nadia Seemungal and Helen Tredget at Routledge for clear guidance and help throughout.

Finally, thanks to our families for all their support.

The author and publishers would like to thank the following copyright holders for permission to reproduce the following material:

Extract from the Collins COBUILD online dictionary CollinsDictionary. com, reproduced with kind permission of Harper Collins.

Extract from the *Guardian*, 22 December 2011, 'We can't afford the bosses' crazy unearned pay' taken from www.theguardian.com/commentisfree/ 2011/nov/22/cut-executive-pay. Reproduced with kind permission of Deborah Hargreaves, Director of the High Pay Centre.

Extracts from speeches by Ed Miliband as party leader from 2011–13 from www.britishpoliticalspeech.org/index.htm, reproduced with kind permission of the Labour Party.

Extracts from speeches by David Cameron as party leader from 2011–13 from www.britishpoliticalspeech.org/index.htm, reproduced with kind permission of the Conservative Party.

Extracts from speeches by Nick Clegg as party leader from 2011–13 from www.britishpoliticalspeech.org/index.htm, reproduced with kind permission of the Liberal Democrats.

Sample exercise on 'area' from www.nottingham.ac.uk/alzsh3/acvocab/exercises.htm reproduced with kind permission of Sandra Haywood.

Extract from Jones, C. and Waller, D. (2011). If only it were true: the problem with the four conditionals. *ELT Journal*, 65, 1, 24–32. By permission of Oxford University Press.

While the publishers have made every effort to contact copyright holders of material used in this volume, they would be grateful to hear from any they were unable to contact.

Abbreviations

AdjP	Adjective phrase
AdvP	Adverb phrase
BYU-BNC	Brigham Young University and the British National Corpus
CEFR	Common European Framework of Reference for Languages
COBUILD	Collins Birmingham University International Language Data base
COCA	Corpus of Contemporary American English
DDL	Data-driven learning
EAP	English for academic purposes
EFL	English as a foreign language
ESL	English as a second language
GloWbe	Corpus of Global Web-Based English
HKCSE	Hong Kong Corpus of Spoken English
KWIC	Key word in context
MALU	Mobile-assisted language use
MI score	Mutual Information score
MICASE	Michigan Corpus of Academic Spoken English
NP	Noun phrase
PrepP	Prepositional phrase
VOICE	Vienna-Oxford International Corpus of English
VP	Verb phrase
WebCorp LSE	WebCorp Linguist's Search Engine

Introduction

The word 'grammar' conjures up all kinds of associations, many of them fairly negative. We hear or read of 'bad grammar' (which, we are assured, many of us have) and how we can transform this into 'good grammar'. All too often then it is used to describe a 'correct' way of saying or writing something based on a particular view of language. What is neglected in this kind of viewpoint is that grammar, alongside other aspects of language, is part of a communicative system. It is not a closed system and is composed of patterns of use; patterns that change over time. It is not the preserve of Plato's elite guardians or a matter of standards but just another resource we use when communicating. In the words of Halliday (1975), when children are learning grammar, they are 'learning how to mean'. We believe that the investigation of grammar, alongside other features, can tell us how people use language to make sense of the world around them.

This book was written to fill what we saw as a gap in the literature currently available on the use of corpora to investigate language. While there are many excellent books for teachers and academics, we felt that there was little that catered to those new or relatively new to the field. We wanted to produce a book that would not only provide guidance on the sorts of things corpus data can tell us, but that would also show people how to go about carrying out their own investigations. We also wanted to point learners in the direction of freely available resources we hope they will find useful. To this end, we have used open-access corpora and corpus analysis tools throughout the book so that readers can practise with these on their own.

There are many excellent corpus-informed grammars of English and this book does not attempt to describe the main grammatical features of English. We have acknowledged and referenced some grammar resources that can assist learners who are less confident in talking about grammar. There are also many excellent introductions to corpus linguistics. This book is not intended to replicate these. While we do introduce certain approaches to analysing language, the book does not comprehensively cover everything we can use a corpus for. Again, we have referenced some useful books for those who wish to read a more general introduction to corpus linguistics.

This book is essentially a 'how-to' guide for those who are interested in using corpora to research grammar. We have tried to show the different tools and issues that confront anyone who wishes to use corpora in this way. In doing so, we have presumed a basic knowledge of and interest in grammar including common metalanguage. We also take as read that the reader has an interest in exploring grammar!

The book is divided into three parts. The first part deals with the basics and introduces what corpora are, which ones are available and what kinds of things they can tell us. In Part 1 we also set out our view of grammar and how we intend to treat it throughout the book.

Part 2 explores three important ways in which corpus data can be explored: frequency, chunks and colligation, and semantic prosody.

Part 3 provides examples of different applications of research into grammar through corpora and finally gives examples of short research projects to show possible areas for exploration.

Each chapter contains a number of exercises. These are divided into two types. The first are labelled 'sample exercise'. These are tasks we hope the reader will undertake for themselves but they may also simply wish to read along and check the answers, which follow immediately after the task. The second type of tasks are labelled 'try it yourself' and are intended as slightly longer activities for the reader to undertake. The answers for the 'try it yourself' tasks are at the back of the book. These exercises and 'try it yourself' tasks are intended to give the reader an opportunity to engage with some of the data and methods we outline in this book. Chapters also contain suggestions for further practice which readers can take up as well as a list of references for further reading. The book also has a glossary and terms which we have identified as being technical. These are bolded on first mention in the text.

References

Halliday, M.A.K. (1975). *Learning how to mean: explorations in the development of language*. London: Edward Arnold.

Chapter 1

What is a corpus? What can a corpus tell us?

1.1 Introduction

Suppose you had an argument with a friend as to whether Sherlock Holmes ever said 'elementary, my dear Watson' (he didn't!) and you wanted to prove your case; how would you go about doing it? One option would be to read all of the novels and short stories, but presumably you would have to get your friend to do the same to verify the truth of what you find. The other would be to turn to an electronic database that contained all of the Holmes stories and then search for the phrase. Essentially, this is how a corpus can help you.

This chapter will explain what a corpus is and why we may wish to consult one when trying to analyse grammatical and **lexico-grammatical** patterns. We will demonstrate what different types of corpora exist, including examples of various spoken and written corpora with different designs. We will then move on to an explanation of what information a corpus can provide us with and why we might want to use one to analyse areas such as frequency or grammatical patterns, to provide robust evidence of language in use. We will also examine how corpora have been used within the development of corpus-informed dictionaries and grammars. All the samples we use will be taken from **open-access** corpora (corpora on the internet that are free to access). By using resources that anyone can access, we aim to encourage the reader to look at these corpora for themselves.

1.2 What is a corpus?

A corpus is simply an electronically stored, searchable collection of **texts**. These texts may be written or spoken and may vary in length but generally they will be longer than a single speaking turn or single written sentence. They are normally measured in terms of the number of words they contain or to use a word common in most corpora, the number of **tokens**. Consider an analysis of the sentence above:

They are normally measured in terms of the number of words they contain or to use a word common in most corpora, the number of tokens.

This sentence has a total of twenty-six tokens in it.

We can also measure a corpus by the number of different word **types** it may contain, i.e. how many adjectives, how many verbs, etc. If we look at the sentence above, we can see how many different types there are in the sentence.

Pronouns:	they × 2
Verbs:	are, measured, contain, use
Nouns:	terms, number × 2, words, word, corpora, tokens
Adjectives:	common
Adverbs:	normally
Determiners:	the × 2, a, most
Prepositions:	in × 2, of × 3, to
Conjunction:	or

Therefore there are twenty different types in the text.

Types and tokens can also be compared by dividing the number of types by the number of tokens, giving us a type:token ratio. In this case that is 20 divided by 26 × 100, which is a type token ratio of 76%. Obviously, in this example we have used only one sentence, which is a sample size that most researchers would not use. When looking at a corpus the type-token ratio simply allows a researcher to see how varied a collection of texts may or may not be; in general, the more types there are in comparison to the number of tokens, the more lexically varied the text.

Corpora vary enormously in size and there is no minimum limit on how many tokens they should contain or indeed no set maximum size. In general, written corpora tend to be larger due to the relative ease of locating and storing electronic texts and the time-consuming nature of transcribing spoken data. It is also fair to say that a small corpus can be just as effective as a large one, depending on the purpose for which it is used and the principles behind its construction, a point we shall go on to discuss in 1.3. However, at this stage, it is instructive to compare the size of many of the corpora we will use in this book, alongside some others that are commonly used by publishers. These details are shown in Table 1.1 and there is more information given on the open-access corpora in Chapter 2.

1.3 Different types of corpora and good corpus design

Corpora can be **mono-modal** (through one medium, typically text) or **multi-modal** (through more than one medium, typically text and video), as described by Adolphs and Carter (2013). Due to costs, most corpora are mono-modal, although increasingly multi-modal corpora are being developed (see Adolphs and Carter, 2013 for examples). According to Sinclair

Table 1.1 Examples of corpora

Corpus name	Spoken/written or both	Number of tokens	Text types	Availability	Dates
Brigham Young University-British National Corpus (BYU-BNC) (Davies, 2004)	Both	100 million	Newspapers, fiction, journals, academic books, published and unpublished letters, school and university essays, unscripted conversation, meetings, radio phone-ins and shows	Open-access (registration needed)	1980s–1993
Corpus of Contemporary American English (COCA) (Davies, 2008)	Both	450 million	Fiction, newspapers, magazines, academic texts, unscripted conversations	Open-access (registration needed)	1990–2012
Corpus of Global Web-Based English (GloWbe) (Davies, 2013)	Written	1.9 billion	Web pages from 20 English-speaking countries	Open-access (registration needed)	2013
Vienna-Oxford International Corpus of English (VOICE) (Seidlhofer et al., 2013)	Spoken (English used as a Lingua Franca)	1 million words	Interviews, press conferences, service encounters, seminar discussions, working group discussions, workshop discussions, meetings, panels, question-answer, sessions conversations	Open-access (registration needed)	2008–2011
Cambridge English Corpus (CEC)	Spoken and written	Multi-billion words	Learner English, business English, academic English, unscripted conversations	No general access	No dates given
The Cambridge English Profile Corpus (CEPC)	Spoken and written (learner data)	10 million words	Spoken and written texts from English language tests	Access to the English vocabulary profile available. Once complete, parts of the CEPC will be open-access	2005–present

(1991), a corpus should consist of a principled collection of texts. This means that a corpus should contain texts that can provide answers to questions we want answers to.

By way of example, if we wished to analyse the performance of learners in a set of English language tests, we would need samples of their written and spoken work from the tests to be able to make realistic statements about the language in use. We would also need to make decisions about whether to include students who pass or fail tests with a particular mark. Other variables we would need to acknowledge and control for are the age and nationalities of the candidates. If the test is taken by a range of nationalities, for example, we would need a sample of tests that give a representative sample of those nationalities. We would also need to make a decision about how many words (or tokens) to include. This should be based upon two aspects: what we intend to use the corpus for and, practically, how many texts we can collect in the time available to us.

In the hypothetical example of the corpus of tests, should we wish to make statements about how a grammatical pattern is used across different levels, then clearly we would need a lot more words than if we wished to investigate how a particular pattern was used only in a written test at one particular level. Finally, we would need to decide upon the type of corpus we need. For example, a mono-modal corpus of texts would give us information about candidates' writing and speech but in the case of speech, we would be unable to comment upon their use of body language and how this acts to reinforce their message.

Try it yourself 1.1

Imagine you wish to construct a corpus to represent the following types of English and purposes. What types of texts would you need and approximately how large would each corpus need to be? A suggested answer is available at the back of the book.

1   A corpus of British spoken academic English. Purpose: to discover the most frequent words used by lecturers.
2   A corpus of Dickens' fiction. Purpose: to discover the way lexical and grammatical patterns are used to reinforce themes.
3   A corpus of written requests made by colleagues in a UK university. Purpose: to discover the most common patterns used by colleagues in requests made to each other.

1.4 What a corpus can tell us

As mentioned in 1.2, the reason we wish to use a corpus is that we can analyse large quantities of language and uncover patterns of usage which our intuitive sense about language may miss. This then allows researchers to make clearer and better descriptions of language which can inform practice or simply develop our understanding of language in use. When looking at a corpus to make statements about grammar, we are taking a **descriptive**, as opposed to **prescriptive**, stance. In other words, we are seeking to show how the language is used and from this make statements about it, such as the rules that are followed. The opposite approach is to formulate a rule, often based on intuition, set this as a 'standard' and then attempt to suggest that deviations from this are not correct. This is a prescriptive stance (see Freeborn, 1995 for a useful discussion of this area). We will say more about this when we describe and define our view of grammar in Chapter 2.

The first thing we can use a corpus for is to test and challenge our intuitions about language. A corpus may underline or refute an idea we have about language use. To give an example, we may wish to uncover how speakers report what others are saying in conversation. We may assume that speakers always use 'backshift' to report speech and employ a 'rule' often given in grammars of English (for example, Murphy, 2012), where the common 'formula' is 'He/she said that + backshift' e.g. 'He said that he was going' to report 'I'm going'. However, when this aspect of language has been investigated using corpora, it has been found that this does not always follow. McCarthy and Carter (1995), for instance, looked at the five million-word CANCODE corpus of spoken English and found that 'X was saying + summary with or without backshift' e.g. 'She was saying she's starting a new job' was also a very frequent way of reporting what others have said in conversations. Carter and McCarthy (2006) describe reporting using the Cambridge English Corpus and suggest that while backshift is common in conversations, it is also the case that reported and direct speech are often mixed together to make more vivid stories.

Try it yourself 1.2

Using your intuition, look at the patterns in Table 1.2, which can be used to express judgements and opinions in speech or writing. Try to decide the order of frequency (1–4) in each of the four different corpus types. Then check with the answer key.

Table 1.2 Opinion and judgement patterns in different corpora

Pattern	Fiction corpus	Spoken corpus	Newspaper corpus	Academic English corpus
We can assume that . . .				
I'd say that . . .				
You can be sure that . . .				

Analysing corpora to identify the usage of pieces of language has direct application to areas such as language teaching. When you begin a teaching career in English Language Teaching (ELT), you tend to assume that the language patterns that appear in the textbook you are given are the most frequent and potentially useful for learners. After all, it is obvious that no teacher will ever have the time to teach everything. Sadly, when we began teaching, it was still relatively rare for textbook writers to consult a corpus because they were not generally available. Instead, they relied upon a mix of intuition and (we suspect) observing what other textbooks tended to teach! While this is not in itself a bad thing, it can lead to a focus on grammatical patterns that are given more prominence than perhaps they deserve.

Sample exercise

The following patterns featured heavily in textbooks we used to teach from:

> 'Going to' e.g. 'I'm going to have lunch at 1 pm'
> 'Able to' e.g. 'I've been able to swim since I was five'
> 'was/were + v + ing' e.g. 'I was watching TV at six yesterday'

In the textbook, they were presented in the order given above, meaning students were first expected to master 'going to' before moving on to 'able to' and 'was/were + v + ing'. Would you predict this same order of frequency if we searched a corpus? Think about the potential order. Then have a look at the results in Table 1.3, drawn from the British National Corpus (BYU-BNC) (http://corpus2.byu.edu/bnc):

Table 1.3 Frequency of 'going to', 'able to' and 'was + v + ing'

Grammatical pattern	Number of occurrences
Going to	32557
Able to	28015
Was + V + ing	76780

Even a very simple analysis such as this suggests that the greater frequency of the pattern 'was + v + ing' suggests that there is at least an argument for teaching it before the other patterns.

We can also of course use a corpus to explore language and uncover aspects of usage or patterns that have previously been under-described or perhaps even misunderstood, as Sinclair (1991, 2004) has suggested. McCarthy and Carter (1995), for example, point to the very high frequency of 'tend to' used to describe habitual action in a spoken corpus, something that at that point had been neglected in some grammars. Carter and

McCarthy (2006) also show how certain patterns are used in academic texts to avoid directness and to 'hedge' statements and thus render them less definitive and more considered, objective and academic. They give examples of passive constructions such as 'it is widely accepted' and 'it is generally agreed', which are frequent in the academic corpus used to inform their reference grammar. We can use a corpus to further investigate such patterns and to build a clearer picture of how they are used in actual texts. To take 'it is generally agreed' as an example, a search in the BYU-BNC academic corpus reveals the patterns shown in Table 1.4.

Table 1.4 'It is generally agreed' in an academic corpus

Number of occurrences	Most frequent word that follows 'it is generally agreed'	Most frequent words that follow 'it is generally agreed that'	Most frequent position in sentence (front, mid or end)	Function
14	'that'	'the + noun phrase' followed by a verb phrase	Front (9 out of 14 examples)	To 'hedge' an authoritative statement
		Examples:		
		'it is generally agreed that the method works only for highly constrained tasks'		
		'However, it is generally agreed that industrial structure plays no general part in the urban-rural shift.'		

Sample exercise

Think about another phrase that Carter and McCarthy (2006) identify as being common in academic discourse, 'in most cases', which is also used to hedge a statement in academic written discourse. Consider how this is patterned in texts. What words and patterns are likely to follow it? Is it likely to be more or less frequent than 'It is generally agreed'? Is it likely to be positioned in the front, mid or final position in a sentence? Look at the suggested answers in Table 1.5 once you have considered these questions.

This data suggests that for those wishing to use this pattern in a more proficient way, it will mainly be used in the front and mid position and be followed by 'the + noun phrase'. For those learning English as a second language, this is a useful, generalisable pattern and for those simply looking

Table 1.5 'In most cases' in an academic corpus

Number of occurrences	Most frequent word that follows 'in most cases'	Most frequent words that follow 'in most cases the'	Most frequent position in sentence (front, mid or end)	Function
288	'the' It is most often followed by a comma but the most frequent word is 'the'	Noun phrases. Example: 'They will be incorporated. However, **in most cases** the **crucial question** will be whether the person seeking to rely on the terms'	Front and mid position. Examples: whereas nationals of other member states would, **in most cases**, have to move their residence and domicile (mid) enactment by a legislature, and judicial precedents. **In most cases,** provision is made for possible conflict by ranking these criteria (front)	To 'hedge' an authoritative statement

to improve their own academic writing, the data can be used to raise aware-ness of how this pattern can be used.

1.5 The use of corpus linguistics in language description: dictionaries

As the examples above show us, corpora help us to explore language. Although they are not a new phenomenon, it is only in the last forty years that they have begun to more strongly influence language description. The establishment of the Collins Birmingham University International Language Database (COBUILD) corpus in 1980 heralded a revolution in the use of cor-pus data in language description. The work of researchers including Sinclair and colleagues provided new information on language that subsequently influenced much description of language. This included information on fre-quency and patterning of words into **chunks** including **collocation** and **col-ligation**. In other words, they began to tell us about the grammar of words, sentences and texts. This resulted in the COBUILD dictionary, grammars and English language textbooks, which used evidence from the corpus both in the information given about language and the examples used.

Figure 1.1 (on p. 13) shows a simple example of this, with the first entry for 'go'.

go[1] (gǝʊ ◁») *(moving or leaving)*

Word forms: goes ◁») , going ◁») , went ◁») , gone ◁»)

Definitions

In most cases the past participle of **go** is *gone*, but occasionally you use 'been': see <u>been</u>.

I. verb

1. When you **go** somewhere, you move or travel there. ⇒ [v prep/adv] We went to Rome. ⇒ [vprep/adv] Gladys had just gone into the kitchen. ⇒ [v prep/adv] I went home at the week-end. ⇒ [vamount] It took us an hour to go three miles.

Figure 1.1 Entry for 'go' from the Collins COBUILD dictionary

The COBUILD dictionary marked a major upheaval in dictionary design, resulting in all major dictionaries now making extensive use of corpus data to inform their language description. Now frequency data and information on grammatical patterning is included as standard practice and dictionaries are excellent, evidence-based resources for information about language. Naturally, the information they contain will vary slightly between dictionaries according to the corpus they employ, but it will generally be the case that a dictionary will contain information on frequency, collocations and colligation. In other words, it will show us how often a word is used, the common contexts of use, the other words it commonly forms partnerships with and the grammatical patterns it is part of.

1.6 The use of corpus linguistics in language description: grammars

Following the revolution in dictionary design begun by the COBUILD project, grammars began to be produced based on corpus data. As with learner dictionaries, such description made use of corpus data to provide information on aspects of language such as frequency and collocation/colligation patterns. Looking at corpus data also allowed patterns to be analysed that may have received less attention in those based more on intuition about language. The *Collins COBUILD grammar of English* (Sinclair, 1990, now in a fourth edition) was probably the earliest of such books and used corpus data to give a fresh perspective on grammatical description. It was followed by a number of other descriptive grammars, all using corpus data to inform their analysis. These have included *The Longman grammar of spoken and written English* (Biber et al., 1999) and the *Cambridge grammar of English* (Carter and McCarthy, 2006). Some of the findings naturally simply confirm the frequency of certain aspects of grammar, such as the tendency of English to add the 's' morpheme to pluralise countable nouns. However, such grammars have also revealed the following:

1 Corpora have given us information about the frequency of grammatical patterns in particular contexts. Grammar varies according to contexts of use so that academic English, to take an example, often employs certain grammatical forms more frequently than English used in other contexts. Carter and McCarthy (2006: 272) give an example of 'nominalisation' being used more commonly in academic English; that is, noun phrases being used to replace clausal constructions made with verb phrases. They give the following example:

> 'The time lag between marking and first recapture was higher than the lag between second and third recapture' vs. 'The time lag between when we marked the animals and when we first recaptured them'.

In this book we will refer to language according to the contexts it is used in.

2 There is a distinct grammar of spoken English, which cannot always be analysed using the same labels and terms as we may wish to describe written grammar. For example, when a speaker replies with 'absolutely' to the question 'are you going to the party?', it is difficult to classify this precisely, raising questions regarding how 'absolutely' functions here and whether we could describe this reply as a sentence. This has also led to some features that predominantly occur in spoken grammar being described. Carter and McCarthy (2006) give the example of 'headers' such as 'My brother, he lives in London', which are very common in the spoken corpus data they examine but do not really exist in written forms. In this book, we examine spoken examples in isolation and more frequently in contrast with language in written contexts.

3 Lexico-grammar is an important feature of language because words cluster together in predictable rather than random patterns. Biber et al. (1999: 12–13) suggest that '**syntax** and lexicon are often treated as independent components of English. Analysis of real texts shows, however, that most syntactic structures tend to have an associated set of words or phrases that are frequently used with them'. They give examples such as the following: 'In conversation, the subject of the main clause in constructions with those clauses is frequently "I" referring to the speaker. In contrast, the norm in news reports is for subject noun phrases to refer to third person entities, usually humans'. For example, 'I realise that there's been something on your mind recently' (conversation) vs. 'Mr Sisulu said that it was a draft plan' (news). Carter and McCarthy (2006) show how clusters (which we have termed 'chunks' in this book) such as 'I don't know' are very common in spoken English. Such chunks are examined in more detail in Chapter 7.

We will reflect on these features throughout the book and look at each in more depth when we outline our view of grammar in Chapter 2.

Try it yourself 1.3

Here is an example of what a corpus can tell us about the frequency of grammatical patterns in different contexts. Look at the modal verb forms in the questions in Table1.6. Use your intuition and consider the frequency of each question form in each of the contexts given. The answer can be checked at the back of the book.

1.7 What a corpus cannot tell us

As defined by Sinclair (1991), a corpus is a principled collection of texts. It can provide us with data of many types but it cannot tell us why a particular pattern is used. Cook (1998), for example, suggests that a corpus cannot tell us how speakers process language in the mind or what the intention behind the use of a common pattern may be. This simply means that we, as researchers, will always have a role in interpreting the data a corpus can provide. We have shown above, for example, how 'in most cases' is frequent in academic discourse but its function is only made clear when we examine the data ourselves. To do this we must train ourselves in looking at samples of language and using them to discover language patterns, which may be based on intuition or may lead us in completely new directions. Providing that we acknowledge that a corpus contains data that we, as researchers, interpret (and not an absolute truth), it seems we can treat corpora in the same way we would other collections of data.

It is also the case that no corpus can incorporate the totality of language, however many words it contains. Cook (1998: 39) suggests:

> Corpora are only partial authorities. The cumulative experience of an individual, though less amenable to systematic access, remains far larger and richer. Even a three hundred million word corpus is only around three thousand books, or perhaps the language experience of a teenager.

Therefore, we must see that a corpus is a partial snapshot of the language it has captured and one taken at the time the data was collected. A news

Table 1.6 Modal forms in three corpora

Question	Frequency order (1–4)	General spoken	Academic English	Fiction
Do I have to...?	2			
Must I...?				
Should I..?				
Do I need to..?				

corpus, based on the data available as we write this in 2014, would contain a great many patterns that would differ from a news corpus of twenty years ago, for example. This means that we have to accept that any corpus, once compiled, is partial and immediately dated. This does not invalidate what we find but means we must acknowledge that our results are never definitive, as they are not, of course, in any research we conduct.

1.8 Conclusion

In this first chapter, we have attempted to explain why we may wish to use a corpus, how we can compile one in a principled way and how we can use the data we find within it. We have also looked briefly at how corpora have been used to inform dictionaries and grammars. A corpus does not simply provide us with all the answers about language in use, but it does give us an evidence base on which to provide better descriptions of language. These descriptions can be based on intuition or analysis. Some of the ways we can use the data are objective (nobody can dispute the number of times a pattern occurs), but there will always be an element of subjectivity in how we describe and interpret the data. This is where the role of the researcher is key: using the corpus in a principled way to provide clearer answers in a bid to better describe language.

Further practice

1 Think of an aspect of language you would like to investigate further. This could be a simple grammatical pattern of the type we have described in this chapter. What type of corpus would you need to access to investigate this piece of language?
2 Take an aspect of grammar you feel reasonably familiar with but which you feel unclear about. Using corpus data, what would you like to find out about this aspect of language? What type of corpus would you need to use?

References

Adolphs, S. and Carter, R. (2013). *Spoken corpus linguistics: from monomodal to multimodal*. London: Routledge.
Biber, D., Johansson, S., Leech, G., Conrad, S. and Finegan, E. (1999). *Longman grammar of spoken and written English*. London: Longman.
Cambridge University Press (2014). *Cambridge English Corpus 2014*. [Online], Information available: www.cambridge.org/gb/cambridgeenglish/about-cambridge-english/cambridge-english-corpus [25 August 2014].
Carter, R. and McCarthy, M. (2006). *Cambridge grammar of English*. Cambridge: Cambridge University Press.

Collins COBUILD advanced learners' dictionary (2015). [Online], Available: www. collinsdictionary.com/dictionary/english-cobuild-learners [4 July 2014].

Common European Framework of Reference for Languages (2014). *The Cambridge English Profile Corpus.* [Online], Information available: www.englishprofile.org/ index.php/corpus [25 August 2014].

Cook, G. (1998). The uses of reality: a reply to Ronald Carter. *ELT Journal,* 52, 1, 57–63.

Davies, M. (2004). *BYU-BNC* (based on the British National Corpus from Oxford University Press). [Online], Available: http://corpus.byu.edu/bnc [20 October 2013].

Davies, M. (2008). *Corpus of contemporary American English: 450 million words, 1990– present* (COCA). [Online], Available: http://corpus.byu.edu/coca [20 October 2013].

Davies, M. (2013). *Corpus of global web-based English: 1.9 billion words from speakers in 20 countries* (GloWbe). [Online], Available: http://corpus2.byu.edu/GloWbe [20 July 2014].

Freeborn, D. (1995). *A course book in English grammar.* Basingstoke: Palgrave Macmillan.

McCarthy, M. and Carter, R. (1995). Spoken grammar: what is it and how can we teach it? *ELT Journal,* 49, 3, 207–218.

Murphy, R. (2012). *English grammar in use.* Cambridge: Cambridge University Press.

Sinclair, J. (1990). *Collins COBUILD grammar of English.* London: Collins.

Sinclair, J. (1991). *Corpus, concordance, collocation.* Oxford: Oxford University Press.

Sinclair, J. (2004). *Trust the text. Language corpus and discourse.* London: Routledge.

VOICE (2013). The Vienna-Oxford International Corpus of English (version 2.0). Director: Barbara Seidlhofer; Researchers: Angelika Breiteneder, Theresa Klimpfinger, Stefan Majewski, Ruth Osimk-Teasdale, Marie-Luise Pitzl, Michael Radeka. [Online], Available: www.univie.ac.at/voice [20 July 2014].

Chapter 2

Definitions of a descriptive grammar

2.1 Introduction

As we explained in Chapter 1, we take a descriptive view of grammar in this book. This means we suggest looking at examples in use from a corpus or corpora and then commenting on aspects such as rules and the frequency of patterns, rather than providing rules and then trying to find examples to fit them. The examples we have used so far also show the importance of context (either spoken or written) and looking beyond an isolated single sentence example when making statements about grammar. Although we do look at grammar in sentences in this book, we aim to also look at these in wider contexts of use, whether written or spoken. Also, although grammar allows us to create an infinite number of possible sentences, we are more interested, in this book, in what Lewis (1993, 1997) described as language that is probable; that is, the patterns that most commonly occur in corpora. To illustrate these points, we begin this chapter with a brief exploration of a prescriptive view of grammar contrasted with a descriptive, corpus-informed one. We then move on to giving a definition of 'grammar', which we explain with the help of exercises and examples. Finally, we demonstrate what we believe to be the benefits of analysing grammar with the aid of a corpus before briefly outlining the analysis covered in Part 2 of this book.

2.2 Views on grammar

The word 'grammar' tends to evoke strong feelings among linguists and non-linguists alike. An internet search containing the words 'good grammar' provides numerous links to guides about the correct usage and several articles in popular newspapers which debate the subject. In the UK, it is a subject never very far from the news. For instance, the recent government decision to introduce a spelling, grammar and punctuation test at primary schools produced a whole series of opinion pieces and online 'tests' for readers to check their own knowledge of grammar. The debate, in the popular press at least, tends to crystallise around notions of correctness.

Knowledge of grammar, particularly its rules, is equated with the ability to use English correctly. A 2014 article in the *Daily Telegraph*, for example, asked readers to decide which sentence or sentences were grammatically correct and to name various parts of speech. Here is one example:

> Which of these sentences is grammatically correct?
>
> A) Do you see who I see?
> B) Do you see whom I see?
>
> > (www.telegraph.co.uk/education/educationquestions/
> > 9987757/Good-grammar-test-can-you-pass.html)

The answer given as correct is the second one, the reason being that:

> 'Who I see' should be 'whom I see'. This is because 'whom' is the object in the subsidiary **clause** 'whom I see', and must therefore be in the accusative or objective case.
>
> > (www.telegraph.co.uk/education/educationquestions/
> > 9990622/Good-grammar-quiz-the-answers.html)

Such an answer is fairly typical of such stories. A 'rule' is given in semi-technical language, usually with some reference to Latin. A closer look at this pair of sentences, however, raises some interesting questions:

1   Intuition suggests that, at least in spoken contexts, the first sentence feels correct. Is the suggestion that everyone saying sentence A is wrong?
2   Intuition suggests that sentence B is not as frequent as sentence A and usage is likely to be restricted to specific contexts. Is this the case?

When we check this in a corpus-informed grammar (Carter and McCarthy, 2006: 566–71) we find a lot of information about these patterns. The grammatical structures used in these sentences are both commonly referred to as defining relative clauses. They can define the noun phrase which precedes them and act as the subject, e.g. 'The guy *who shouted* must have been on the seventh floor' or as the object in a clause, e.g. 'Have you seen those people *who we met last night?*'. When we further check the usage of 'who' and 'whom', we find the following:

> In most styles, except very formal ones, *who* may also refer to the object of the relative clause. . . . *Whom*, which was traditionally used to refer to the human object of a relative clause or complement of a preposition, is now confined to very formal styles and mostly to writing. . . . *Whom* is many times more frequent in writing than in speech.
>
> > (Carter and McCarthy, 2006: 569–70)

They give examples, drawn from the Cambridge International Corpus, such as the following:

> 'It was from a woman *who I know slightly*' (who as object)
> 'It appeared she had struggled with her attacker, *whom she almost certainly knew*' (written newspaper story)

This shows that, as we had suspected, the use of 'who' in the relative clause within the question 'Do you see who I see?' is actually commonly used, particularly in a spoken style. It also shows us that the use of 'whom' is often confined to more formal, written contexts. It is therefore misleading to suggest that only 'Do you see whom I see?' is correct. Both examples are possible, with the first 'who' being much more likely to be used in this type of construction and both related to contexts of use. Whether the entire question 'Do you see who I see?' is a probable realisation of this type of relative clause is also worth considering. A quick search of the spoken section of COCA (http://corpus2.byu.edu/coca), which consists of largely unscripted television programmes such as chat shows, reveals the following:

Table 2.1 Occurrences of 'Do you see who/whom I see?' in COCA

Occurrences	More frequent patterns
Do you see who I see? = 2	Who I am = 598
Do you see whom I see? = 0	know who I am = 136
Who I see = 8	I know who I am = 40
Whom I see = 2	They know who I am = 26

This shows that in this spoken corpus 'I know who I am' is twenty times more frequent than the target sample 'Do you see who I see?', and the cluster 'who I am' is more likely to occur than 'who I see'. Therefore, the example itself, 'Do you see who I see?', is fairly rare, at least in this corpus and 'Do you see whom I see?' does not occur at all.

2.3 What is grammar?

As we have explained in our introductory chapter, this book is not intended to be an introduction to grammar but rather a guide to how we can use corpora to analyse grammar. It is of course still important that we define what we mean by the term 'grammar' and what our view is, so that the chapters that follow show the theoretical stance we are taking. It is simplest if we take each aspect of our definition in turn, with exercises and examples to illustrate, before summarising. Although we reference each of these in the sections below, it is worth acknowledging at this stage that the way we view grammar has been influenced by Biber et al. (1999), Carter and McCarthy (2006), Halliday and Matthiessen (2004, 2013), Hoey (2005), Hymes (1972) and Sinclair (1991).

(A) Our view of grammar is descriptive rather than prescriptive.

This means, as we have stated, that we seek to base our ideas on evidence of actual language use, which we can find in corpora. This does not mean that 'anything goes' but rather that we use corpora to help define such aspects of grammar as rules.

Sample exercise

Let us look at an example of this descriptive stance in practice. Look at the **concordance lines** in Figure 2.1 (taken from the BYU-BNC, http://corpus2. byu.edu/bnc) featuring the use of the determiners 'some' and 'any'. Look at the rules given below the examples and decide which ones best fit the examples given. The context is given for reference after each sample.

1   cassettes, then picked up a transistor radio.' Would you like **some music** or a story for company while I wrestle with my old adversary? (conversation)

2   supposed to are we all supposed to write this out? (unclear) **some music?** Nothing interesting's happened. (conversation)

3   He felt a new bond between them. He liked **some music** but generally wasn't musical and was always slightly put off to find himself in (fiction)

4   was bored to tears! I thought they were gonna play **some music** and let them dance! (conversation)

5   the pedals." I haven't decided yet. Do you have **any music** you could play?" (conversation)

6   said I don't know (pause) boogie, boogie (pause) she dances to **any music** don't she? (conversation)

7   and records like that depressing. I find Buck's Fizz depressing ... or **any music** that expresses no humanity. And also I've just got tired of the group (music writing)

8   music on that. (SP:PS556) Ooh look there's Nick! (SP:PS6R3) Is there **any music** on that? ey stopped it. (SP:PS02H) there is, they stopped it. (conversation)

9   There **isn't any** more. (SP:PS02G) Mm. (SP:PS02H) No, I'm sort of I think he confused (conversation)

10 SP:PS03T) Well you want to save your eyes. (SP:PS03S) No, there **isn't any** (unclear). (conversation)

11 Er (SP:PS03T) Well they were there. (SP:PS03S) Mm mm. (SP:PS03T) Mm. (pause) all together. (SP:PS07E) He's retired. (laugh) (SP:PS07J) Although, there **isn't any** at Marseilles (conversation)

Figure 2.1 Concordance lines for 'some' and 'any'

Possible rules for the use of 'some' and 'any':

1   We use 'some' in affirmative sentences and 'any' in negative sentences and questions.
2   We use 'some' and 'any' in questions, affirmative sentence and negative sentences, depending on context. 'Some' is less frequent in negative sentences.
3   Both 'some' and 'any' indicate an indefinite amount of an object they are referring to when unstressed in speech, e.g. 'Would you like some music?' and not 'that's <u>some</u> car you've got!'
4   'Some' does not normally follow 'not' in the negative construction 'There isn't . . . ' to describe the complete absence of something.

You should have found that all the rules *except* rule 1 are correct, based on this set of examples. Rule 1 is one that is often given in prescriptive grammars or those that are based upon intuition. For example, an internet search for the difference reveals definitions such as the following:

> In general 'some' is used in positive sentences. In general, 'any' is used in negatives and questions. We can use 'some' when offering or requesting (e.g. 'Would you like some tea?') and 'any' in positive sentences when the meaning is 'it doesn't matter which . . . ' (e.g. 'ask for help any time').
> (http://esl.fis.edu/grammar/rules/some.htm).

While this is not entirely incorrect, it oversimplifies the actual usage of these items and it is easy to find contradictions when we look at corpus data. Biber et al. (1999: 176–7, 277), for example, make a distinction between assertive and non-assertive forms and label 'some' as assertive and 'any' as non-assertive. They then suggest that non-assertive forms are used in negative clauses (e.g. 'There aren't any crisps') and that assertive forms can be used in a clause before the negative form (e.g. 'For some reason it did not surprise him') or in some cases after the negative form e.g. ' I don't mind talking, not to some people'. They also give information about frequency, such as showing that 'some' is the most common determiner in their corpus when indicating a small amount, and is most frequent in academic prose. This type of information helps us to build a more realistic picture of how the language is used. It is more complex and less convenient than some rules but also, we would argue, more accurate. For a more detailed explanation of the use of 'some' and 'any', see Biber et al. (1999) and Carter and McCarthy (2006).

(B) Grammar can be defined on a basic level as being concerned with the internal structure of words and phrases (**morphology**) and the way in which words are arranged into sentences and texts (syntax) (Carter and McCarthy, 2006).

Within this broad definition, we are concerned with what is possible or probable and accepted as correct within context and what is considered impossible, improbable and incorrect within context. To take a simple example such as 'My brother goes shopping every weekend', we can analyse this as correct and probable within a spoken context, whereas 'Goes weekend every my brother shopping' would be considered incorrect. This is because the standard syntax of English is normally subject (My brother), predicator (goes shopping), plus either an object, adjunct (as in this case – every weekend) or complement. Analysing the morphology of this example, we can also see how word forms help to make the meaning. For example, 'goes' indicates a present time, and the final 's' indicates that we are talking about a subject related to 'he', 'she' or 'it'.

(C) Grammar is the analysis of **form** and **function**.

When we focus on grammar we are interested in words, phrases, clauses, sentences, utterances and texts in terms of both the forms used and how these make meaning in context. Words have their own grammar because they can be marked to show number or tense. For example, Carter and McCarthy (2006: 1) give the example of 'I gave my sister a sweater for her birthday', where the word 'gave' is marked to show past time and 'sweater' does not have the 's' morpheme and is therefore marked as singular. The use of 'a' marks the fact it is a countable noun. Words are used together to form noun (NP), adjective (AdjP), verb (VP), adverb (AdvP) and prepositional (PrepP) phrases (see Halliday and Matthiessen, 2004, for more detail) which themselves form clauses, sentences, **utterances** and texts. A phrase can consist of a single word or several together. For example, 'I gave my sister a sweater' consists of I (NP) gave (VP) my sister (NP) a sweater (NP). Clauses consist of a subject and predicate (a verb phrase and any other elements, as distinct from a predicator, which describes the function of a verb phrase) and can be subordinate or main. They may also be interrogative, declarative or negative in form. Carter and McCarthy (2006: 486) give the following example: 'We (subject) baked some potatoes in the fire (predicate)'. This is one main clause. Should we add 'and they were nice', there would be two main clauses, joined by the conjunction 'and'. Should we add 'We baked some potatoes in the fire, which was getting a bit hot by that time' then we have a main clause, followed by a subordinate clause, both in declarative form.

Clauses make sentences, which need at least one main clause and of course are recognisable in writing by the use of full stops. 'Which was getting a bit hot', for example, would not be accepted as a sentence because there is no main clause to help us make sense of it. Sentences can be simple (with one clause), compound (with two clauses joined by a conjunction) or complex (a main clause and a subordinate clause). The term 'utterance' is used because spoken language is distinct from written language and 'sentence' is not always an adequate way to describe it. Carter and McCarthy (2006) suggest that this is because much spoken language has a distinct grammar of its own, as we shall discuss below. Therefore, they suggest that an utterance must be **pragmatically** and communicatively complete but may not be grammatically accepted as sentences, if we apply the rules introduced above. For example, a reply to a question such as 'Are you going?' with 'Absolutely' cannot be said to be a clause or a sentence but it is certainly a complete utterance. Although the sentence is often seen as the largest unit of grammar, we also wish to see how grammar operates in texts, at the level of **discourse**, to explore how all the aspects are used together to make a cohesive whole. The forms used in clauses can also be analysed to examine how they function in context. This will either be as Subject (S), Predicator (P), Object (O), Complement (C) or Adjunct (A). For example, 'We (S) baked (P) some potatoes (O) in the fire (A)', 'They (S) seem (P) nice C)'.

(D) The different 'levels' of grammar are linked together.

Although sentence and clause length examples can be useful for illustrative purposes, we are not simply interested in isolated sentences in this book because looking at corpus data means we are always attempting to look at language in context. This means that we are interested in viewing grammar at the word, sentence and text level. We will seek to isolate particular features and how they are arranged at one level but will also seek to show how the language can be linked simultaneously at different levels. This idea is influenced by the notion of 'rank scale' (Halliday and Matthiessen, 2004, 2013), which suggests that different aspects of grammar are linked:

> There is a scale of rank in the grammar of every language. That of English (which is typical of many) can be represented as:
>
>   clause
>   phrase/group
>   word
>   morpheme
>
> Each consists of one or more units of the rank next below. For example, 'Come!' is a clause consisting of one group, consisting of one word, consisting of one morpheme.
>
> (Halliday and Matthiesen, 2004: 9)

This idea of rank scale shows that different aspects of grammar work together to make meaning.

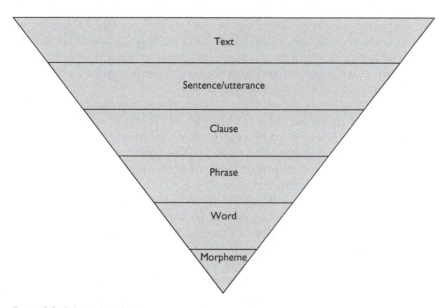

Figure 2.2 Adapted rank scale

In this book, we have adapted this idea slightly so that it reads as set out in Figure 2.2, to reflect how we wish to view grammar and to acknowledge the role of spoken language.

This model seeks to show that we see how grammar works together from the smallest unit (a morpheme such as the 's' in 'two chairs') to the largest unit, which we feel is a text. Although it can be suggested that texts are not units of grammar (Carter and McCarthy, 2006), we include the term to show how grammatical forms combine to make meaning at the level of discourse, beyond sentence or utterance level. The example below illustrates this idea.

Sample exercise

Look at the text below (taken from *The Guardian* newspaper (www.guardian.co.uk).

What do you notice about the way the choices of words, clauses and sentences work together to help form the grammar of the text? Why were these choices made in this case? There is a suggested answer which follows the text.

We can't afford the costs of bosses' crazy unearned pay

British business is facing a crisis. The public has lost faith in the corporate sector, which it sees as monolithic, money-grabbing and uncaring. Excessive pay for company bosses has added to the malaise. As those on middle and low incomes face a sharp squeeze in their living standards, corporate leaders are awarding themselves 49% pay rises. These bosses see little irony in then lobbying to repeal the 50p top rate of tax paid by those on £150,000 or more. These are the same leaders who are arguing for real-term cuts to the minimum wage, because, after all, aren't we all facing times of unparalleled austerity?

Directors' hypocrisy over pay reinforces the view among the public that businessmen are "in it for themselves". It is worrying that trust in big business has sunk to this extent when there is so much emphasis on the private sector leading us out of the economic crisis. In polling for the High Pay Commission, 79% of those questioned said pay and bonuses were out of control.

Our year-long inquiry has led us to believe that excessive top pay levels are not only corroding trust in business but also damaging society and the economy as a whole. In the last 30 years we have seen rewards channelled upwards. The top 0.1% of earners have pulled away from the rest at a rapid pace. In 1980, for instance, the boss of Barclays was earning 14.5 times average pay at the bank; the current boss, however, is on 75 times the average, representing a 4,899% rise over that 30 years.

During the same period average UK wages have gone up threefold and pay for a senior policeman or schoolteacher has risen sixfold. Of course, leading Barclays today is a different proposition, but the lives of a policeman and headteacher have also changed beyond recognition in that time.

Some features of this text we may wish to look at are as follows:

1   This text makes extensive use of complex sentences, containing main and subordinate clauses. Very often these complex sentences follow simple (one clause) sentences, to expand upon and illustrate a point in more depth. For example, 'British business is facing a crisis' (simple sentence), 'The public has lost faith in the corporate sector, which it sees as monolithic, money-grabbing and uncaring (complex sentence)'. Complex sentences allow the writer to 'pack' a great deal of information into the text without losing the reader as they may if more simple sentences were used.

2   There are a number of nouns that are heavily pre- and post-modified, which again allow the writer to build a lot of information into a short text. Examples of this (head of noun phrases in italics) are 'Excessive *pay* for company bosses', 'real-term *cuts* to the minimum wage'.

3   Tense choice is either present simple/continuous for the current situation or present perfect when the problem is viewed over a period of time but is still current. The text achieves a structure partly by choosing present forms to highlight the current problem in focus and the last two paragraphs to analyse this historically. The choice of present forms allows

the writer to write opinions with a 'factual' sounding tone (as they read as if universal truths) and to give the reader the feeling that the issue is current and therefore pressing, as in the example 'As those on middle and low incomes face a sharp squeeze in their living standards, corporate leaders are awarding themselves 49% pay rises'. The present perfect forms allow the writer to show that this is not a new issue; for example, 'During the same period average UK wages have gone up threefold and pay for a senior policeman or schoolteacher has risen sixfold'.

4   Adjective phrases are often used in the text to express the opinions of the writer. They add 'colour' to what otherwise may seem too factual a tone. Compare the use, for instance, of 'excessive pay' with alternatives such as 'high wages' or 'a sharp squeeze' compared to 'a large reduction'.

Of course, to make more definitive statements about the use of grammar in texts of this type, we would need to look at a larger corpus of similar newspaper articles, but this example serves to illustrate how we can analyse the different levels or 'ranks' of grammar to show how they work together to make meaning in texts.

(E) Speech has a grammar that is often distinct from writing.

We have already noted that when a speaker replies with 'absolutely', it is difficult to classify this as a sentence or clause or define it as subject, predicator, object or complement. There are also many features of spoken grammar that have not traditionally been described in grammars based on written forms. Carter and McCarthy (2006) give the example of 'headers' such as 'My brother, he lives in London', which are very common in the spoken corpus data they examine but do not tend to exist in written forms. Biber et al. (1999) suggest that although spoken language shares many grammatical features with written language, it is worth analysing features that are particularly characteristic of conversational language. In this book we try to display and contrast spoken and written examples wherever possible and draw distinctions between usage in these different modes where applicable.

Try it yourself 2.1

Look at the samples from the Corpus of Contemporary American English (COCA) below. They all contain the word 'nice'. Which examples would you say are from a spoken language corpus and which are from a written corpus? What helped you decide?

1   I mean **nice** that it was a good storyline
2   By the way, there are a lot of things in Belgium that are very **nice**
3   It was **nice** seeing you again, she said softly

4   This place offers clean bathrooms, hot showers, a **nice** and reasonably priced restaurant
5   A **nice** balance is two parts calcium to one part magnesium, says nutritionist Shawn Talbott
6   I'm just being **nice**

You probably decided fairly quickly on which samples are spoken English. This is likely to be (at least in part) because they contain features that are common within spoken grammar. Sentence 1, for example, features the **discourse marker** 'I mean', which is often used to rephrase or clarify an utterance in conversation. While this feature may occur in written texts that are reasonably similar to spoken discourse (e.g. text chatting online), we would be unlikely to see this feature in a written news article or more scripted spoken texts such as news reports. The other samples contain features that are much less likely to be heard in spoken discourse. Sentence 3, for example, contains an adverb of manner ('softly') which speakers would not normally feel the need to report to each other. This is probably because most speakers simply wish to report (or summarise) the content of what another person says rather than how they say something. In fiction, this description becomes necessary to add 'colour' to the reporting and build an atmosphere without the reader being able to actually hear the characters.

(F) Grammar operates in context and is a system to make meaning.

We are also interested in how grammar functions in context. Halliday and Matthiessen (2004, 2013) suggest that all texts can express **ideational, interpersonal** and **textual metafunctions**. The ideational metafunction means that language is used to help us understand and express our ideas and perceptions of the world. The interpersonal metafunction suggests that it is used to enable us to participate in communicative acts with other people, to maintain, build and establish relationships, and the textual language is used organisationally to relate what is said (or written) to the text itself and the 'real world' outside the text. To take a simple example we have already used, the following spoken exchange between two friends can be analysed in this way:

A: Are you going out tonight?
B: Absolutely!

Ideationally, the text expresses the idea that yes, speaker B is going out. Interpersonally, the choice of 'absolutely' expresses enthusiasm for the idea and this helps maintain or establish a relationship. We might also argue that the use of ellipsis here (a key feature of spoken grammar, Carter and

McCarthy, 2006) also marks the informality. Compare this answer to one such as 'Yes, I am going out tonight'. Finally, the answer 'absolutely' makes a cohesive answer to the interrogative form and so the exchange works on a textual level. Imagine if the speaker had answered 'I had a cup of tea this morning' or some other unrelated response. Textually, the conversational exchange would not work.

Try it yourself 2.2

Look at the grammatical forms used in the simple text in Figure 2.3. How do these work to fulfil the three metafunctions? Why were they chosen for this text? There is a suggested answer at the back of the book.

Here are Hansel and Gretel. This is Hansel and Gretel's stepmother. The stepmother says to the woodcutter 'we have no food'. Hansel and Gretel have to go.

Figure 2.3 Hansel and Gretel simplified text (Grimm, Grimm and Hunia, 1978: 3)

Halliday (1975) famously described the way a child acquires the grammar of their first language as a process of 'learning how to mean'. The reason we are interested in using a corpus to analyse grammar in context is to observe how grammar makes meaning. Therefore, although we look at specific grammatical and lexico-grammatical forms in this book, we are simultaneously interested in how they function.

(G) Grammar and vocabulary are difficult to separate.

Many of the examples used above show that it is difficult to separate words and grammar. As we have noted, single words have their own grammar. For example, we have to indicate possession by saying 'my brother' as opposed to 'I brother', for example, because 'my' is a determiner that indicates possession of a noun that follows it, while 'I' is a personal pronoun that does not indicate possession. Words also cluster together in predictable ways to make units which have their own internal grammar. To recognise this, in this book we often use the term 'lexico-grammar' after Halliday and Matthiessen (2004: 43). They suggest that lexico-grammar is a term we can use to refer to 'patterns which lie somewhere in between structures and collocations, having some of the properties of both. Consider patterns of wording such as . . . 'take + pride/pleasure/delight + in + . . . –ing' (Halliday and Matthiessen, 2004: 45). Sinclair (1991) termed this phenomenon the '**idiom principle**' and suggested that much language is learnt and used as prefabricated wholes, in the way we would learn an idiom such as 'I'm over the moon'. This was in contrast to the '**open choice**' principle, by which we use grammar to generate unique utterances, sentences and clauses. Sinclair's suggestion and that of other researchers such as Pawley and Syder (1983) proposed that these pre-fabricated chunks are very common features of the language. Rather than being random collections of words, many words form chunks packaged with a particular syntax and morphology. To take one example which Pawley and Syder give, 'Will you marry me?' is the socially sanctioned chunk we use when asking somebody to marry us. Speakers do not normally use the grammatically correct 'Will you be wedded to me?'. The syntax is also fixed so that 'Will you me marry?' is not considered possible and the word forms chosen are fixed so that, for example, 'will' is generally favoured above the equally possible 'would', perhaps because 'would' seems too distanced and polite and because 'will' can indicate volition. So words are not put together with grammar in random ways but instead often have predictable partners and grammatical patterns which form chunks with predictable meanings. Hoey (2005) suggests that words are '**primed**' for particular collocations (words that **co-occur**) and colligations (grammatical patterns such as tense) so that hearing a word or reading it in a particular context brings with it particular and predictable chunks. This does not mean that grammar is not used to create original language or that words do not exist as single lexical items outside of any of these chunks, but simply that the idiom principle does the bulk of the work when we produce language.

   (H) Grammar is choice.

Speakers and writers make choices within context. Looking at a corpus can tell us which choices seem the most probable within a given context and also how they are formed. All the examples above make this point implicitly by linking the use of grammar to the context and text in which they are produced. It seems obvious, but grammar is not a set of absolutes. Speakers or writers can often make different choices for different intended meanings.

2.4 What can a corpus tell us about grammar?

Looking at grammar and lexico-grammar in a corpus can tell us about how words, clauses, sentences and utterances operate in texts to shape meaning. Specifically, it can tell us about frequency, chunks and **semantic prosody**; that is, whether a pattern has negative, neutral or positive shading in context. A corpus can be used for more purposes than this (for example, to trace the historical development of a form) but we consider these to be the key areas of language use for which a corpus can be examined. The benefits of analysing grammar with the aid of a corpus, as we outlined in Chapter 1, are that it allows us to check or refute our intuitions about language and to explore/discover new language patterns. Halliday and Matthiessen (2004: 34) suggest that a corpus also allows us to look at grammar in authentic (as opposed to contrived) contexts and to study patterns in a **quantitative** as well as **qualitative** sense, as we will demonstrate in Chapter 3. For these reasons, it is these aspects we explore in Chapter 4 (frequency), Chapter 5 (chunks and colligation) and Chapter 6 (semantic prosody). A simple example (below) highlights these benefits.

Let us consider the verb forms 'marry', 'marries' and 'married'. Which form of the verb would you consider to be most frequent in newspaper texts and a spoken corpus? Which other words and wider patterns would you imagine it is used within in each context? An example of this in spoken language, as we mentioned above, is the chunk 'will you marry me?'. Think of possible combinations and larger patterns and then check the suggested answers in Table 2.2 and Table 2.3. The newspaper corpus consists of 10,466,422 words and was compiled from data occurring from the 1980s to 1993. The spoken corpus is compiled from American TV shows, the majority of which are not scripted. It was compiled from data from 1990 to 2012.

Table 2.2 Results for 'marry, married, marries' from a newspaper corpus (http://corpus2.byu.edu/bnc). Number of occurrences followed by the occurrences per million words in brackets

Word forms	Verb collocations with 'married'	Patterns with 'married'	Samples
Married – 858 occurrences (81.98) Marry – 163 (15.57) Marries – 25 (2.39)	1 IS MARRIED 55 (5.25) 2 BEEN MARRIED 47 (4.49) 3 WAS MARRIED 44 (4.20) 4 GET MARRIED 32 (3.06)	'Who is married' 16 (1.53) 'He is married' 13 (1.24) 'Is married with' 24 (2.29) 'Is married to' 21 (2.1) NP + who is married with + numeral + NP e.g. 'A, who is married with two children, has ...' NP + who is married to + NP e.g. 'A, who is married to B, is ...'	1 Lady Teresa Waugh, the novelist, **who is married to** Auberon Waugh. 2 The woman, **who is married and lives in Formby,** Sefton, said: 3 Sgt Window, 39, **who is married with two children**, was attacked when ... 4 Mark, 27, **who is married with two children**, has been a soldier for nine years

In summary, by exploring this word and linking this to different 'levels' of our adapted rank scale, we find the following:

1 'Married' is the most common word form in both corpora (morpheme level). It is most often used as an adjective rather than as the past form of the verb 'marry'. 'Married' is more frequent as a form (if we take the per million words figure) in the spoken corpus. A **log-likelihood** comparison gives the figure of 4726.40, which shows that the greater usage in the spoken corpus is **statistically significant**.

Table 2.3 Results for 'marry, married, marries' from the COCA spoken corpus (http:// corpus.byu.edu/coca). Number of occurrences followed by the occurrences per million words in brackets

Word forms	Verb collocations with 'married'	Patterns with 'married'	Samples
Married – 10298 (107.76) Marry – 1774 (18.56) Marries – 83 (0.87)	1 GET MARRIED 1192 (12.47) 2 GOT MARRIED 856 (8.96) 3 BEEN MARRIED 832 (8.71) 4 WAS MARRIED 556 (5.82)	'going to get married' 108 (1.13) 'when you get married' 24 (0.25) 'if you get married' 16 (0.17) 'want to get married' 220 (0.21) 0.21 NP + be + going to get married NP + be + going to get married + AdvP	1 So, you're **going to get married** and he says, 2 I had a boyfriend and I thought we were **going to get married** 3 But you know what's sad? They're **going to get married** 4 and instead of telling him that she is **going to get married** once again

2   It commonly collocates with forms of the verb 'to be' e.g. 'is married', 'been married' and 'get married' in newspapers and most commonly with 'get married' in the spoken corpus (word level).

3   In the newspaper corpus, it is part of a pattern often used within a non-defining relative clause e.g. 'NP, who is married with + numeral + NP' or 'NP, who is married to + NP'. For example, 'Mark, 27, **who is married with two children**, has been a soldier for nine years'. In the spoken corpus, the pattern 'NP + be + going to get married' is more frequent e.g. 'I had a boyfriend and I thought we were **going to get married**'. It is occasionally followed by an adverb such as 'soon' to indicate time.

4   In newspaper texts it takes a present form (most often 'is married') as it is used as part of factual information when describing subjects of stories. The non-defining clause shows that the pattern is primed to provide additional background information about someone. For example, 'Lady Teresa Waugh, the novelist, who is married to Auberon Waugh'. The clause is marked by a comma before it, which shows us it is extra information rather than defining who Teresa Waugh is as we might in the invented example 'No, I mean the Teresa Waugh who lives in Bristol, not in Birmingham' (clause and text level).

Look at the short extract in context below to see how this works within a text.

Lady Onslow, widow of Sir Richard Onslow. For the last 30 years of her life Lady Onslow lived at Notting Hill Gate, and in the mid-1970s she led her neighbours in a rates protest against the Royal Borough of Kensington and Chelsea. She also kept up a vigorous campaign against the expansion of Geale's fish and chip restaurant near her house: she said the smells made her garden unusable. Lady Onslow is survived by a son, the present Earl of Onslow, and a daughter, Lady Teresa Waugh, the novelist, **who is married to Auberon Waugh**. Pamela's major qualities were courage, humour and broadmindedness, although the last of these was put to the test, first when her only brother became a Roman Catholic, then when her only daughter married one. However, these qualities enabled her to win the trust and friendship of many ex-convicts. Although her house was frequently burgled, she maintained a high standard of hospitality. While tending to keep her two worlds separate, she made the literary, political and family circles she inhabited . . .

Daily Telegraph, 1992

In the spoken corpus, 'married' seems primed to co-occur with 'get' and in the wider pattern 'going to get married', and this is used to indicate a future event or a future in the past event e.g. 'we were going to get married'. Many of the samples are based on chat shows or news shows. This suggests, as we would expect, that guests often discuss their future plans and at times reflect on past decisions. The samples below show this:

File number: 19991126

Source CNN_Event

PICKLER: Yeah, there he is. Yeah. KOTB: Wow, that's a great wedding picture. PICKLER: Yeah, we went to the Caribbean. KOTB: Yeah. PICKLER: This little place called Jumby Bay. KOTB: Uh-huh. Mm. PICKLER: And we got married in the water on a sandbar and it was the most amazing thing ever. It was the most incredible . . . KOTB: How did you know that this was going to be the guy for you, Kellie? PICKLER: You know, it's funny because I was never **the girl that was going to get married**, I just . . . KOTB: Mm-hmm. PICKLER: . . . I didn't believe in it, I'd never seen the right marriage. KOTB: Mm-hmm. PICKLER: And so I just didn't know that it was out there. KOTB: Yeah. PICKLER: And God placed Kyle in my life and, you know, he completely just swept me off my feet. KOTB: Wow. PICKLER: And I just – I fell head over heels for him. I did. And he's a keeper, so I . . . KOTB:

File number: 120323

Source: NBC Today

As a dialysis patient, you know, we don't regulate the chemicals in our body. We also can't regulate fluid so we have to stand on a scale and we have to use other devices to kind of figure out where I am. I'm the only one who is riding of course. But I have Heather (ph), who is the head of my road crew, my fiancée, and she, you know, she is fantastic. She keeps me going. A few weeks after the ride **we are going to get married** and we're planning a big wedding. Let's see: California, Arizona, New Mexico, Texas, Louisiana – this is Mississippi. WALL: Have you become an expert on road kill? VOGA: Road kill has becomes some of my specialty along the way.

Although we could not claim that this is a comprehensive study of all aspects of the word form 'married' in all contexts, we at least have a clearer picture of how it is commonly used in each corpus chosen and how the usage differs in each case. We can see some clear grammatical patterns and make some initial observations about why they are used in the texts as a whole. Some of this information may confirm intuitions (such as the high frequency of 'get married' in spoken texts) but other aspects may be less obvious. We may believe, for example, that 'marries' would be more frequent in newspapers than it is here, because it could form part of headlines.

2.5 Conclusion

This chapter has outlined the approach to grammar we are taking throughout this book and attempted to show how we will use corpus data to analyse grammar. We have also outlined the ways in which corpus data has been used to inform our descriptions of grammar. Using a corpus does not tell us everything about grammar or how to interpret the information, but it does provide an evidence base which is often more reliable than intuition alone. In the following parts of the book, we intend to show how you can put these insights to use, with specific sections on each area and guidance on how to undertake your own analysis. Chapter 3 considers what corpora are available and how to search them. Chapter 4 explores the notion of frequency, Chapter 5 collocation, colligation and chunks and Chapter 6 semantic prosody. We then move on, in Part 3 of the text, to show how these can be applied to particular studies.

Further practice

1   Try looking in an online dictionary and check a noun you commonly use such as 'bread'. What does the entry tell you about this word's grammatical patterning? What does this add to your intuition about how the word is used?

2   Look in an online dictionary (such as the ones we have given examples from in this chapter) and check a noun you commonly use such as in the example 'bread'. What does the dictionary tell you about its frequency and grammatical patterning?

References

Biber, D., Johansson, S., Leech, G., Conrad, S. and Finegan, E. (1999). Longman grammar of spoken and written English. London: Longman.

Carter, R. and McCarthy, M. (2006). *Cambridge grammar of English*. Cambridge: Cambridge University Press.

Dzierzek, A. and Hunia F. (1993). *Hansel and Gretel (Ladybird read it yourself level 1)*. London: Ladybird Books.

Grimm, J. Grimm, W. and Hunia, F. (1978). *Hansel and Gretel (Read it yourself series)*. Loughborough: Ladybird Books.

Gywnne, N. (2014a). Good grammar test: can you pass? [Online], Available: www. telegraph.co.uk/education/educationquestions/9987757/Good-grammar-test-can-you-pass.html [2 July 2014].

Gywnne, N. (2014b). Good grammar quiz: the answers. [Online], Available: www. telegraph.co.uk/education/educationquestions/9990622/Good-grammar-quiz-the-answers.html [2 July 2014].

Halliday, M.A.K. (1975). *Learning how to mean: explorations in the development of language*. London: Edward Arnold.

Halliday, M.A.K. and Matthiessen, C. (2004). *An introduction to functional grammar* (3rd edition). London: Routledge.

Halliday, M.A.K. and Matthiessen, C. (2013). *Halliday's introduction to functional grammar* (4th edition). London: Routledge.

Hargreaves, D. (2011). *We can't afford the costs of bosses' crazy unearned pay*. [Online], Available: www.theguardian.com/commentisfree/2011/nov/22/cut-executive-pay [30 November 2011].

Hoey, M. (2005). *Lexical priming: a new theory of words and language*. London: Routledge.

Hymes, D.H. (1972). On communicative competence, in J.B. Pride and J. Holmes (eds.) *Sociolinguistics. selected readings*. Harmondsworth: Penguin, 269–293.

Lewis, M. (1993). *The lexical approach: the state of ELT and a way forward*. Hove: Language Teaching Publications.

Lewis, M. (1997). *Implementing the lexical approach*. Hove: Language Teaching Publications.

Pawley, A. and Syder, F.H. (1983). Two puzzles for linguistic theory: nativelike selection and nativelike fluency, in J.C. Richards and R. Schmidt (eds.) *Language and communication*. London: Longman, 191–226.

Shoebottom, P. (2014). *A guide to learning English*. [Online], Available: http://esl.fis.edu/grammar/rules/some.htm [11 July 2014].

Sinclair, J. (1991). *Corpus, concordance, collocation: describing English language*. Oxford: Oxford University Press.

Sinclair, J. (2004). *Trust the text: language, corpus and discourse*. London: Routledge.

Chapter 3

What corpora can we access and what tools can we use to analyse them?

3.1 Introduction

In the first two chapters, we examined the reasons why we may wish to make use of corpora to analyse grammar and our view of grammar. In this chapter, we will explore the different types of corpora we will make use of in this book. This will include a description of each corpus and a discussion of the advantages of each. We will also show how we can use these corpora to analyse grammar, which will then be demonstrated with exercises to allow you to conduct a basic analysis. Following this, we will explore two pieces of free software which can be used to construct and search your own corpora. Each type of analysis introduced in this chapter will be expanded upon in subsequent chapters.

3.2 Open-access corpora

As mentioned previously, our intention in this book is to use only open-access corpora, namely those that are freely available on the internet. The term 'open-access' itself is the subject of some debate, as there have been recent calls for UK higher education research to be openly available to all. The discussion in relation to this regards how this can be done while allowing quality to be maintained and people to receive payment (see www.theguardian.com/higher-education-network/open-access for some examples of this). We do not wish to deny this debate; our choice of open-access corpora is simply to allow readers to explore these for themselves. We also reference several other corpus-informed resources, which make use of corpora that are not open-access.

A number of the open-access corpora we use require registration but they are free to use. We listed some of these in Chapter 1 but this was in comparison with those that are not available. Table 3.1 gives a list of the corpora used throughout this book and some advantages of each.

Table 3.1 Open-access corpora

Corpus name	Spoken/written or both	Number of tokens	Text types	URL	Dates	Advantages
Brigham Young University-British National Corpus (BYU-BNC) (Davies, 2004)	Both	100 million	Newspapers, fiction, journals, academic books, published and unpublished letters, school and university essays, unscripted conversation, meetings, radio phone-ins and shows	http://corpus.byu.edu/bnc	1980s–1993	Useful for comparing language in several contexts
Corpus of Contemporary American English (COCA) (Davies, 2008)	Both	450 million	Fiction, newspapers, magazines, academic texts, unscripted conversations	http://corpus.byu.edu/coca	1990–2012	Useful because of the amount of tokens. Contains more recent data than the BYU-BNC and in a similar range of contexts
Corpus of Global Web-Based English (GloWbe) (Davies, 2013)	Written	1.9 billion	Web pages from 20 English-speaking countries	http://corpus2.byu.edu/GloWbe	2013	Useful for comparing language used in e-contexts and in Lingua Franca contexts
Corpus of American Soap Operas (Davies, 2012)	Spoken	100 million	22,000 transcripts form 10 different American soap operas	http://corpus2.byu.edu/soap	1990–2012	Useful for making comparisons between the language of soaps and spoken English and for exploring this in its own right
Hong Kong Corpus of Spoken English (HKCSE) (Cheng et al., 2008)	Spoken	907,657	Academic lectures, tutorials, presentations, job interviews, office talk, workplace presentations, speeches, public interviews, press briefings, unscripted conversations	http://rcpce.engl.polyu.edu.hk/HKCSE	1997–2002	Useful for exploring spoken language used in the Hong Kong context

(Continued)

Table 3.1 (Continued)

Corpus name	Spoken/written or both	Number of tokens	Text types	URL	Dates	Advantages
Michigan Corpus of Academic Spoken English (MICASE) (The University of Michigan English Language Institute, 2014)	Spoken	1,848,364	Advising session, colloquium, dissertation defence, discussion sections, interviews, lab section, lectures, meetings, office hours, seminars, study groups, student presentations, service encounters, tour	http://quod.lib.umich.edu/m/micase	No information given	Useful for exploring spoken English in an American academic context. Researchers are able to search by speech act, subject, speaker
Vienna-Oxford International Corpus of English (VOICE) (Seidlhofer et al., 2013)	Spoken (English used as a Lingua Franca)	1 million words	Interviews, press conferences, service encounters, seminar discussions, working group discussions, workshop discussions, meetings, panels, question-answer sessions, conversations	www.univie.ac.at/voice	2008–2011	Useful for exploring English used as a Lingua Franca
WebCorp Linguist's Search Engine (Research and Development Unit for English Studies. Birmingham City University, 2014)	Written	Various	Contains a synchronic web corpus (470 million words) A diachronic web corpus (130 million words) The Birmingham blog corpus (630 million words) Anglo-Norman letter corpus (150 letters) Novels of Charles Dickens (16)	http://wse1.webcorp.org.uk/home	2000–2010 (web and blog corpora)	Useful for e-language and comparisons between literary vs e-language

Building your own corpus

In addition to these corpora, it is also a fairly simple task to compile your own corpus. This can easily be done from resources on the internet and by making use of the corpus analysis tools we will explore in sections 3.3, 3.4 and 3.5. To use your own resources (such as student essays), you need permission to use the texts and to ensure they are anonymised, where appropriate. In spoken transcripts, for example, this would involve (at least) removing speakers' names. It may also be necessary to remove proper nouns that identify particular places and speakers. Should you choose to use texts from an online source, you need permission to use the texts, provided they are under copyright. The simplest way to obtain permission to use a text or set of texts is to contact the author(s) and request permission for educational use. It is also possible to locate open-access resources. One particularly useful source of literary texts, for example, is Project Gutenberg (www.gutenberg.org) which contains e-copies of books that are no longer under copyright. These texts can be used fairly quickly to compile a corpus, as we will demonstrate later in this chapter and in Chapter 9. As discussed in Chapter 1, your choice of corpus will depend upon what you are attempting to analyse and how you wish to analyse it. For more details on how to construct your own corpus, see O'Keeffe et al. (2007).

3.3 Conducting a basic search

The simplest way to use a corpus is to search for a word or longer stretch of language. Corpora vary a little in the information they provide but will always give us the number of occurrences of the target form and samples of the language being used in context. This is demonstrated in the bullet-pointed steps below which allow you to undertake the search yourself.

Sample exercise

To take a simple search, let us imagine we wish to check which grammatical form of a word is more frequent – the singular or plural form.

- Type the words 'example' and 'examples' into the search bar in the following corpora listed above: MICASE, VOICE and HKCSE. (MICASE allows you to specify the type of speaker and speech etc., but do not specify the search in this way for this initial exercise.)
- Check the number of occurrences of each form of the word. You should have found results as in Table 3.2.

Table 3.2 Occurrences of 'example' and 'examples' in three spoken corpora

	MICASE	VOICE	HKCSE
Example	996	952	516
Examples	215	75	65

Although these are only basic results and we would not want to rely on raw frequency results alone, they indicate that the singular form is more frequent in each corpus, which can at least prompt further investigation. We could look at this in a number of ways to search for larger patterns in which the word occurs. These include looking for collocations and clause or **sentence-level patterns** and by exploring samples of the word 'example' in context.

Corpora vary in the manner in which they allow us to look for collocations. For instance, the HKCSE allows us to search for an additional word or phrase alongside the target word, but we need to specify what this word is, while VOICE allows us to simply put an asterisk (*) before the target word and look at the results in a set of concordance lines. Other corpora such as the BYU-BNC allow a more detailed search. We will explore these in detail as we progress through the book but at this stage we will look at fairly simple searches.

We are now going to use the corpus to investigate why the singular form is more frequent.

Sample exercise

- Look in the HKCSE and type 'example' in the first box and 'for' and then 'an' in the box marked 'additional word or phrase'. This will give the frequencies for 'example' and its co-occurrence with 'for' and 'an'.
- In VOICE type '* example' and then 'for example' into the search box. This will first give instances of anything that comes before the target word and then instances of 'for example' will be highlighted in the concordance lines.

You should find the following results:

Table 3.3 Collocations with 'example' in two spoken corpora

	VOICE	HKCSE
Collocates with 'example'	952 occurences of '* + example'	519 occurrences of 'for + example'
	774 occurrences of 'for example'	92 occurrences of 'an + example'

These results suggest that the occurrence of the singular form 'example' is more frequent than the plural 'examples'. This is because it occurs in the collocation 'for example' and the need to exemplify is likely to be frequent in many types of speech.

To investigate larger, sentence-level patterns in which the word occurs, we can either use intuition and search for the occurrences of the target word as we believe it may be used or we can search for particular parts of speech, if the corpus allows. In this exercise, we will search for particular parts of speech using the BYU-BNC corpus.

Try it yourself 3.1

- Look at the BYU-BNC spoken corpus (specify spoken corpus in 'sections').
- Click on 'list' view at the top of the page.
- Using the 'POS list' click verb all [v*] and then type 'for example'.
- Following this, type '* [v*] for example' into the search bar.
- Now click on the 'search' button.
- The search should look as shown in Figures 3.1 and 3.2 below.

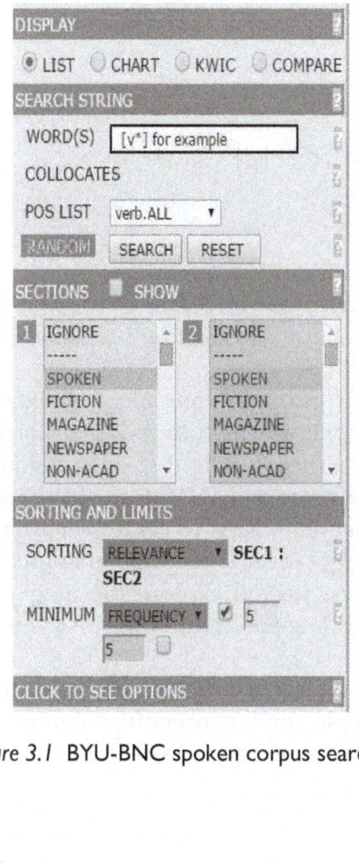

Figure 3.1 BYU-BNC spoken corpus search for '[v*] + for example'

Figure 3.2 BYU-BNC spoken corpus search for '*+ [v*] + for example'

Results can be found at the back of the book.

The results show us that both 'say for example' and 'I mean for example' are ways in which the collocation can occur at clause and sentence level, in this corpus.

Finally, we can look at samples of 'for example' in context by examining concordance lines and the original texts in which they occur. Corpora will produce these with the target form either highlighted or in bold and normally display examples as **key word in context** (KWIC) files so the target form is in the middle of the concordance line. Next to each concordance line, it is normally possible to see the target form in its original context by clicking where indicated. In this instance, we will explore the usage in a spoken academic context. Figure 3.3 shows some samples of this from the MICASE corpus.

These samples allow us to see how the target form operates in context. We can see that in these samples 'for example' tends to occur in mid-utterance position, as opposed to at the start of the **turn**. This is likely to be because

elf. and it comes up all the time you know there are certain things that he will not give up. uh, so	**for example**	he has this paper i think i mentioned, maybe not in this class mentioned it before called religious
of lumpers or splitters i mean they wanna divide species or (xx) but, it seemed to me if i looked at	**for example**	your two n- papers in uh, nineteen eighty-five in one case you're setting up a new genus on the othe
some, less, defined maybe ethical considerations PAUSE duration :05 about the acceptability	**for example**	of putting antibiotic resistance markers, in food products. now, there's an article, they comment,
compounds but you do need to know how to write a, uh formula. oh and we have on camera some formulas,	**for example**	, uh here's your N-A-C-L and these are all chloride salts, so you want to be able to, figure out what
yes it make sense to do this. mathematically you can always take these tables and make this, but, say	**for example**	no i mean
can help us to be better writers. we can we can look at them we can look at,	**for example**	the sonnet as a form of, as a means of conducting an argument. um, it can be very instructive to us
standard, but we're not there yet, because of other problems. so that this, is, a way to measure,	**for example**	transitions between hyperfine states . . . now what if we did have a monoenergetic beam? what would this
here's other, constructs which work perfectly well and pro- properly regulated high level expression	**for example**	they had the switch region and, they had the same amount of promoter, so i i don't think that
daries with so in the master planning, that we're going through as a campus um, (xx) meet constantly	**for example**	with, people in the city in the community and have a sense of what what it would mean for them if we

Sample context

S1: right that's because you know he would [S2: yeah] be thinking about this [S2: right] uh [S5: correct] and may have i- some ideas that, that so

S2: yeah well we've certainly talked about that

S1: yeah. so, you know us having someone who does Hinduism **for example** we_ whi- which White does, [S2: yeah] would be, [S2: and if] would be good [S5: we'd actually talked] [S2:yeah] right. and then having maybe someone who is more on the Taoist side of things, [S2: right yeah] um, i can't think right now of a name but you know we can, start thinking about it. there are a number of people, um, (who) would probably be better. and you have everything you need?

R1: mhm

S1: well i don't think you have any papers from John, so, you can, you can go ahead without his consent um <LAUGH>

Figure 3.3 Sample concordance lines and target form in context

the MICASE corpus consists of spoken academic English such as lectures and seminars and it is used to immediately illustrate or clarify what you have just said, whereas in written language, we may use 'for example' at the start of a clause to signal a new step in the writing and clearly separate the point we are making from the illustration of it. Further investigations of the spoken MICASE data may also reveal whether there is a different frequency of occurrence of noun phrases following 'for example' such as 'for example transitions' as opposed to verb phrases in clauses such as 'for example he has this paper'. We may then wish to investigate which types of noun phrases are most common in this spoken academic context and how this differs from other spoken contexts.

3.4 Analysing open-access corpora

As mentioned, any open-access corpus will give us data on the frequency of individual word forms or larger patterns such as collocations. We can then analyse these using quantitative or qualitative methods of data analysis. Bond and Fox (2007: 217) suggest that 'both quantitative and qualitative approaches have the same starting point: observation', and we would argue that this is the fundamental point about analysing corpus data. We make choices about the type of data analysis we undertake based upon what we, as researchers, can see in the data.

We will start with a brief exploration of quantitative corpus data analysis. Once we search for grammatical patterns, they can be analysed using statistical analysis, which will either provide evidence to support the ideas we may have about the occurrences of a particular grammatical form or provide evidence we had not expected to uncover.

Searching for frequency

To take a simple example which we have already explored in chapter 2, we may wish to check the relative frequency of the word form 'married' in a spoken and literary corpus. A search of the BYU-BNC corpus (http://corpus.byu.edu/bnc) reveals the following:

Table 3.4 'Married' in a fiction and spoken corpus

Fiction corpus (15,909,312 words)	Spoken corpus (9,963,663 words)
2796 occurrences (175.75 per million words)	959 occurrences (96.25 per million words)

Clearly, the raw frequency shows us that 'married' occurs more often in this fictional corpus.

Using log-likelihood

As we have mentioned, raw frequency is a very crude measure and as the corpora are of different sizes, we cannot be sure whether this difference is worth further investigation. Therefore, to understand whether this difference is significant, it is helpful to use some form of statistical measure. One common means of checking for this is to use log-likelihood, which can be used to check whether the greater occurrence of an item in one corpus can be suggested to occur by chance (see Rayson and Garside, 2000 for a more detailed explanation). Should we find that the greater frequency of a word or larger grammatical pattern does not occur by chance or there is less than a 5% chance it does, then we can suggest the greater occurrence is statistically significant. This can be calculated online using a log-likelihood calculator. We have used one created by Rayson and Garside (2000), available here: http://ucrel.lancs.ac.uk/llwizard.html. You can simply type in the number of occurrences in each corpus and the size of each corpus and the calculator will do the rest, taking into account the different-size corpora. Results for 'married' are shown in Table 3.5 below:

Table 3.5 Log-likelihood scores for 'married' in two corpora

Fiction corpus (15,909,312 words)	Spoken corpus (9,963,663 words)	Log-likelihood
2796 occurrences (175.75 per million words)	959 occurrences (96.25 per million words)	282.57

The calculator provides a number with a plus or minus symbol to indicate overuse in one corpus compared with the other or underuse in one compared with the other. In this case, the results showed + 282.57, indicating much 'overuse' in corpus one, the fiction corpus, when compared with the spoken corpus. According to Rayson's explanation (provided on the web page alongside his calculator and in Rayson and Garside, 2000), provided the log-likelihood for the result is greater than 6.63, the probability of the different scores between the two corpora happening by chance is less than 1%. This is expressed as probability (p), $p < 0.01$. If the log-likelihood is 3.84 or more, the probability of it happening by chance is less than 5%. This is normally written as $p < 0.05$. The minimum score for statistical significance is generally accepted as $p < 0.05$ (Dörnyei, 2007). In the case of 'married' we can see that on this measure, the greater occurrence of the form in the fiction corpus is highly significant and Rayson suggest that such a score (above 15.13) can be expressed as $p < 0.0001$. Although we have demonstrated this example on grammar at the word level, we can easily extend this to larger patterns of language.

Try it yourself 3.2

Try the same process as the one above for the chunk 'I mean', something we would expect to be significantly more frequent in a spoken corpus. Go to http://corpus.byu.edu/bnc and look at the results from the fiction corpus and spoken corpora, then feed these into the log-likelihood calculator (http://ucrel.lancs.ac.uk/llwizard.html). Use the fiction corpus as corpus one and the spoken corpus as corpus two. You can check the answers in the back of the book.

We may also wish to look for longer patterns than this. To take another simple example, we may wish to investigate patterns around the verb 'want' in two similar spoken corpora of the BYU-BNC. A search for 'pronoun + want to + verb' reveals that the most common pattern is 'you want to go' and the fifth most common pattern is 'I want to go'. It may be useful to investigate, at least initially, if 'you want to go' differs in frequency between two spoken corpora and whether this difference has any **statistical significance**. The results for this search are given below, using the BYU-BNC spoken corpus and the spoken corpus from COCA.

This suggests that the greater occurrence of 'you want to go' is highly significant using this measure in the BYU-BNC spoken corpus (the score given was + 67.90, indicating overuse in the BYU-BNC corpus in comparison to COCA) and from a research perspective, it may merit further investigation to understand why this is the case.

Table 3.6 Log-likelihood score for 'You want to go' in two spoken corpora (BYU-BNC and COCA)

Spoken corpus (BYU-BNC) (9,963,663 words)	Spoken corpus (COCA) (95,565,075 words)	Log-likelihood
'You want to go' 180 occurrences (18.07 per million words)	'You want to go' 828 occurrences (8.66 per million words)	67.90

T-tests

Another way we can analyse frequency statistically is to use a T-test to compare two sets of scores. A T-test simply measures whether there is a significant difference between the mean scores of two groups. It is often used in instructed second language acquisition research to check on the difference between the test scores of two experimental groups, e.g. those who have received a particular type of instruction in comparison with those who have received another (Dörnyei, 2007). According to Oakes (2004), we may wish to use a T-test in corpus studies to compare independent samples or matched pairs. An independent samples test could be used to compare data from a learner corpus where we wished to compare a form in the essays of a learner group taught in one way in comparison to one taught in another way (Oakes, 2004: 14). A matched pairs T-test might be used to compare the same form in a set of spoken corpora in comparison to those in written corpora because we are attempting to observe the same thing under different conditions and not the different impact of types of instruction on different groups (Oakes, 2004: 15). We can use a T-test to compare sets of frequency data from different corpora, such as several spoken and several written corpora. Compleat Lexical Tutor (commonly called LexTutor) has a calculator which allows you to conduct a simple T-test. This simply means you input the data for two groups (for example, three spoken corpora and three written corpora). Access the calculator via the 'vocab stats' section of LexTutor (www.lextutor.ca/stats/t-test/xtutor) and input the number of times the target form occurs per million words, as this T-test calculator cannot take into account the different sizes of the corpora. Click on 'correlated samples' after inputting the data (used for matched pairs). Here is an example of the results for the word form 'married'.

Table 3.7 T-test for 'married' in six corpora

Written corpora (sample A)	Spoken corpora (sample B)
Occurrences per million words	Occurrences per million words
175.75 (BYU-BNC fiction)	96.25 (BYU-BNC spoken)
66.51 (BYU-BNC magazine)	107.77 (COCA spoken)
81.98 (BYU-BNC newspaper)	29 (HKCSE)

$p < 0.25$ (not statistically significant – indicated by 'n.s.d' on the calculator)

Try it yourself 3.3

Try the same process with 'I mean'. Search for this chunk in the corpora above and feed the occurrences per million words into the T-test calculator given above. Use the written corpora for sample A and the spoken corpora for sample B. Results are shown in the answers section of the book. Again, we need to use a 'matched pairs' T-test so click on 'correlated groups'.

Mutual Information

Another way to check on the significance of frequency figures is to look at **Mutual Information** (MI) scores. This is a measure used particularly when looking at collocations: words that co-occur with other words or patterns in greater than random frequency. MI seeks to calculate whether the co-occurrence of a word with a target word happens by chance. It is suggested that the higher a MI score is from zero, the more evidence there is that the words have a strong association (McEnery and Wilson, 2001; Oakes, 2004). To take a very simple example, if I search for any collocates that occur immediately to the left of 'paper' in the whole BYU-BNC, I get 'white' as the most frequent collocate (1,100 occurrences) with a MI score of 8.10. This suggests that the chance of these items co-occurring is fairly high in this corpus. Words with a high MI score may not always be those that are most frequent as the results also show that the word 'consultation' occurs before 'paper' only thirty-nine times but has a MI score of 8.28. In contrast, if I search for 'thick' coming immediately before 'paper', there are only thirteen occurrences and the MI score is 4.01. This suggests that the items do collocate but are less likely to do so than 'white' or 'consultation' in this corpus. The BYU-BNC and COCA corpora calculate MI scores automatically when you search for collocates of words and have a default cutoff point of MI 3 for calculations. We can also do this with larger patterns beyond single words. Let's look at another example.

Try it yourself 3.4

Imagine we wish to investigate patterns around 'You want to go', which we mentioned above in section 3.4. Type this pattern into the search bar of the BYU-BNC (http://corpus2.byu.edu/bnc) and then click 'collocates' below this. Type * in this box (which means any collocates) and then set the right-hand dropdown bars to '0' for the left and '1' for the right. This will give you only collocates immediately to the right of 'You want to go'. At the bottom of the page, change 'frequency' to 'mutual information' on the dropdown bar. Repeat the same process using the COCA corpus (http://corpus2.byu.edu/coca). The search should look as shown in Figure 3.4 below.

You should find similar results to these in the answers section at the back of the book.

We can use MI scores to help us look for patterns of co-occurrence, which we can then investigate using other measures, such as the suggestions given for

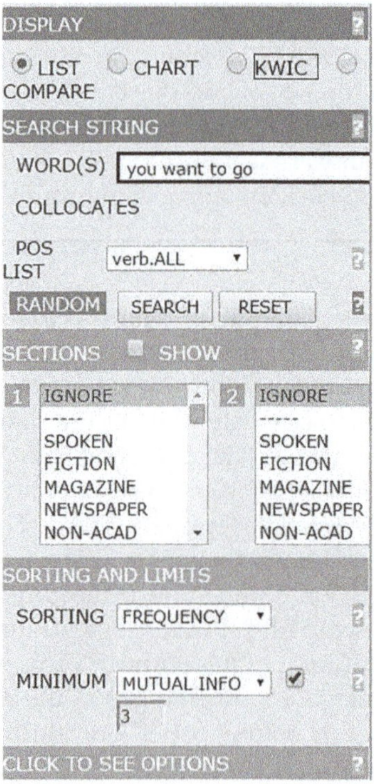

Figure 3.4 Search for 'You want to go + collocate' in the BYU-BNC

frequency searches above. We could, for example, check a pattern for frequency of occurrence in different corpora and then use a log-likelihood score to check for statistical significance when comparing occurrences in two different corpora.

Qualitative analysis

Statistical measures such as log-likelihood and MI are of course only one way to look at grammatical patterns in a corpus. They are useful in helping us to provide support for our own observations or evidence we did not expect to find. However, quantitative measures such as these do not tell us why a grammatical pattern occurs often or how it is being used. To find this out, we need to look at the data qualitatively, using the context to help us. This can be done as the starting point of an investigation or as a follow-up to interrogate quantitative findings. The most common way to do this is to extract a number of **concordance lines** for a particular word or pattern. These show the target form in bold and give some immediate contexts for it. Clicking on these to the left of each line allows us to see the broader text from which each example is taken. Here is an example of some of these patterns for 'You want to go' from the spoken section of the BYU-BNC (http://corpus2.byu.edu/bnc).

1	You know it says book forty, do you have to know which books	**you want to go**	into? (SP:PS007) Yes (pause) erm (pause) er, it's on a
2	and I says why don't you, no, but like (SP:PS01V) If	**you want to go**	to Skeggy it's a lot. (SP:PS01T) Well what's the rush
3	minutes darling. What do you want? (SP:PS14A) Go outside! (SP:PS147) Do	**you want to go**	outside? (SP:PS14A) (unclear) (SP :PS147) Do you want your coat? Well let
4	from school in a few minutes. He will! (SP:PS14A) (unclear) (SP:PS 147) Do	**you want to go**	outside (unclear) now? (SP:PS1 4A) (unclear) (SP:PS147) Good girl! (pause) Mummy put
5	from school in a few minutes. He will! (SP:PS14A) (unclear) (SP:PS 147) Do	**you want to go**	outside (unclear) now? (SP:PS1 4A) (unclear) (SP:PS147) Good girl! (pause) Mummy put
6	SP:PS149) I thought you might (unclear) put you in jail for that (SP:PS147) Do	**you want to go**	outside? (SP:PS149) (unclear) oh you're going outside? (SP:PS148) (shouting) Dad
7	trees up there. (SP:PS14M) I wan na go in the tunnel. (SP:PS14B)	**you want to go**	in the tunnel? (SP:PS14M) Yeah. (SP:PS14B) You mean underneath the bridge
8	thought we were walk-ing? (SP:PS14C) Well do you want to walk or do	**you want to go**	in the car? (SP:PS14B) Well I'll have to go (pause) to
9	about (pause) when is this? It's in June. (SP:PS14B) Well do	**you want to go**	(pause) take some of the other patients that day and I'll go
10	I said no. I said mark the ones on that thing. (unclear)	**You want to go**	to. (pause) That's when I (unclear) (SP:PS14B) It's a bit

Figure 3.5 Sample concordance lines for 'you want to go'

We can observe from this sample that in conversations 'you want to go' is predominantly used in questions either with 'do' or in an ellipted form 'you want to go?' as opposed to a declarative form such as the imperative 'You want to go there'. We can confirm this with a quick check of '* you want to go' in the BYU-BNC spoken corpus, which shows that 'do' is the most frequent (eighty occurrences) word that comes before 'want to go', followed by 'if' with thirty-four occurrences. Such findings can be followed up with statistical analysis of the type we have described above. A quick search for the MI score of 'do' when used as a collocate of 'you want me to' gives a score of 6.15, which shows that there is a fairly strong co-occurrence of this word with this pattern in the corpus.

We can also suggest, by looking at these samples, that 'you want to go' has a neutral shading in terms of its semantic prosody. This term simply refers to the idea that grammatical patterns can have positive, negative or neutral connotations. In this case, 'You want to go' does not seem to suggest any particular positive or negative meaning. We can use such samples to follow up on frequency data or as a 'way in' to the data. We may wish, in this example, to investigate more carefully the use 'you want to go' in question forms and check the relative frequency of ellipted as opposed to non-ellipted forms, for example. We can of course also use concordance lines to illustrate points we have made already in regard to corpus data.

Look at the concordance lines in Figure 3.6. They show samples of 'in Hong Kong' from the HKCSE. Does it tend to have a negative, neutral or positive shading? Think about aspects of this you may wish to follow up with frequency analysis as described above. There are some suggestions given below this exercise.

We can observe the following from this data:

1   'In Hong Kong' has a neutral shading in these examples
2   It seems to regularly occupy the end position in a clause, sentence or utterance e.g. 'asked if erm are they coming to have any crew to stay in Hong Kong but she said that it hasn't concluded yet and for the'
3   NP + in Hong Kong is clearly a pattern e.g. 'trend in Hong Kong'. This needs further investigation to understand which (if any) NPs are most frequent and why.

In addition to looking at co-occurrence and semantic prosody, we can use qualitative analysis to discover how particular forms function in context. This also involves searching for patterns and looking at concordance lines and, if needed, the use of the form in its original context. We can observe the concordance lines or look at the KWIC for a more focused view. Such searches allow us to comment upon the pragmatic use of a particular form in context and may also show us patterns of usage which we can relate to different contexts. One form which is often highlighted in textbooks for English language learners (for example, Soars and Soars, 1996) is present

		in Hong Kong	
1	Hong Kong girls are very hard-working but Hong Kong girls stay	**in Hong Kong**	a: mm B: er I think it is worth trying to travel abroad
2	um we we will be getting perma-nent ((laugh)) residency	**in Hong Kong**	a: oh really (.) * oh that * is ((inaudi-ble)) A1:*
3	Hong do it in Hong Kong or overseas a3: I will do it	**in Hong Kong**	and I may like to apply for like linguistics (.) er in
4	regulatory measures will there-fore still be necessary	**in Hong Kong**	and my colleagues in the Department are working on the
5	ign domestic helpers should be given the right to live	**in Hong Kong**	and whether that would really affect the population b2
6	3: yes cos I've been working as er editorial assistant	**in Hong Kong**	Arts Festival and that covers part of proofreading and
7	ness children is is a big group of the minorities *	**in Hong Kong**	as b1:
8	ions is already an offence under the existing law both	**in Hong Kong**	as well in other common law juris-dictions (.) but I can
9	ecause the minimum salary in Japan is three times that	**in Hong Kong**	B: yes but the cost of living b: no the cost of living
10	t have additional resources to live on * while they're	**in Hong Kong**	b1:
11	is actually the the how we control development density	**in Hong Kong**	b1: mm okay (.) let me er bring H W here (.) H W has g
12	ng is er maintain at the same level as private housing	**in Hong Kong**	b2: well I think our public housing is is a problem in
13	d out the trend the community language attitudes trend	**in Hong Kong**	before nineteen ninety seven (.) that's the end of our
14	is highlight of Chinese New Year celebrations not only	**in Hong Kong**	but also among Chinese communi-ties around the world it
15	asked if erm are they coming to have any crew to stay	**in Hong Kong**	but she said that it hasn't concluded yet and for the

Figure 3.6 Samples of 'in Hong Kong'

perfect ('have and past participle' e.g. 'I have been to Spain'). This is because the perfect aspect, which allows a speaker to refer to two times as connected (in this case the past and the present), is said to be expressed dif-ferently in many languages and therefore causes difficulty for many English language learners. Therefore, it is a form we may wish to investigate to see which patterns are most frequent and how the form is used in particular contexts, as this is likely to be helpful for learners. For English language learners, we can guess that it could be useful to understand how the form can be used as we speak and also how they may encounter it in magazine articles. The task below explores the form in these contexts.

Try it yourself 3.5

- Open the BYU-BNC corpus (http://corpus.byu.edu/bnc)
- Specify the spoken corpus where you are given a list of 'sections'

- Search for 'have and past participle' in the search box (have [v?n*])
- Look in the 'list' view for the most common two patterns with this form
- Search again but this time input the pattern with * before and * after it. For example, you might input * have met *
- Find the most common two patterns
- Look at the concordance lines for the most common patterns used. Can you say any more about them by looking at these lines? For instance, which type of words occur around the main pattern?
- How does the form seem to function in each context?
- Repeat the process above but switch to the magazine corpus, in the 'sections' box.

Check the answers in the back of the book.

When we explore the language by looking at concordance lines, we can suggest the following:

1   In both contexts, the most common use of 'have and participle' is that it co-occurs with 'been' and in larger patterns with the modal verb 'would'. It is most commonly used in this larger pattern to hypothesise about possible outcomes of past events which did not occur. For example, 'Do you think Elvis would have been a good character to have lived into his old age?' (magazine corpus) and 'Well it would have been a hell of a lot of money' (spoken corpus).

2   In the spoken corpus 'have and past participle' is also commonly used with 'would' as a way for speakers to offer opinions, often of a speculative nature. For example, 'I would have thought that would have been your cup of tea' (spoken corpus). This usage does not seem to occur in the magazine corpus.

3   In the magazine corpus, 'have and past participle' is also used in the pattern 'VP + to have been a + NP' often to speculate or offer tentative opinions on past events. For example, 'In those days, simply being British seems to have been a passport to the higher circles' (magazine corpus). This usage does seem to occur in the spoken corpus.

This section has introduced some ways in which we can analyse corpus data using quantitative statistical measures to look at grammar at the word, sentence and text level. It has also shown that we often need to supplement this with more qualitative analysis, using concordance lines. The next section will show how we can use these measures when constructing our own corpora.

3.5 Using open-access corpus analysis software

As well as using available corpora to analyse language, it is also possible to use open-access tools to analyse corpora you have created yourself. This may be because the data you wish to analyse is not available or because you wish to make comparisons with data already accessible. The tools we will use throughout this book are LexTutor (www.lextutor.ca) and AntConc (www. antlab.sci.waseda.ac.jp/software.html). We will look at each in turn and then compare the features of each.

LexTutor (2013) allows the researcher to analyse large amounts of text and produce data based on aspects such as frequency. It also allows us to produce concordance lines for qualitative analysis of data. Although the aim is to examine language in terms of lexis, it can also be used to inform us about grammar and lexico-grammar and is a very useful piece of software. We will not examine every possible feature of LexTutor here but simply outline what we consider to be major features.

Should we choose to use our own corpus data, we can simple copy and paste in small texts online but in most cases we will want to examine larger amounts of data. To do this, corpus data is saved as plain text files. It is also important to remove words you may not wish to be in the text, such as proper nouns. LexTutor can help with this process. Simply click on the 'text tools' section and there is guidance given for 'cleaning up' texts. Once the data is ready, it can simply be uploaded and analysed. The simplest analysis available is a frequency list, which can help us see which words and in which forms are being used most often in our data. To explore this option, simply click on 'frequency' and 'English' and either paste in or upload a text. The output produced will look similar to the sample in Figure 3.7, which was produced using our own sample of Sherlock Holmes texts taken from Project Gutenberg (www.gutenberg.org). Using *The Valley of Fear, The Lost World, The Sign of The Four, The Hound of The Baskervilles, The Adventures of a Dying Detective, The Memoirs of Sherlock Holmes, His Last Bow, The Adventures of Wisteria Lodge, The Adventures of the Cardboard Box, The Adventures of the Red Circle,* and *The Adventures of the Devil's Foot,* we created a corpus of 372,841 words. The frequency function includes an automatic calculation of types and tokens and an individual and cumulative score for frequency, showing the percentage of a text a word or set of words takes up. The results are not stored by LexTutor so must be copied from the website for use.

Although much of the initial frequency data is obvious (for example, we would expect 'the' to be very high in almost any frequency list), this list also gives us indications of grammar at the word level which we may wish to investigate further. For instance, it is clear that 'had' has greater frequency than the base form 'have' and it may be worth checking what patterns and functions 'had' and 'have' occupy in these texts and if that can tell us anything of note. We can also undertake the type of statistical analysis discussed in section 3.3, to compare the number of occurrences of different word forms and if the difference is significant. What is likely to also be of interest is which words in our corpus are **keywords**; that is, they occur many more times in our data than in comparison with a **general reference corpus**. To find this list click on 'keywords' and input or upload a text. This will generate a list in comparison to the BNC spoken corpus. Figure 3.8 shows the first five keywords from the Sherlock Holmes data.

```
Tokens: 371637
Types:  18075
Ratio:  0.0486
```

RANK	FREQ	COVERAGE		WORD
		individ	cumulative	
1	20820	5.60%	5.60%	The
2	10160	2.73%	8.33%	Of
3	9916	2.67%	11.00%	And
4	8900	2.39%	13.39%	I
5	8801	2.37%	15.76%	A
6	8744	2.35%	18.11%	To
7	6146	1.65%	19.76%	That
8	6047	1.63%	21.39%	In
9	5971	1.61%	23.00%	It
10	5400	1.45%	24.45%	Was
11	5285	1.42%	25.87%	He
12	4985	1.34%	27.21%	You
13	4167	1.12%	28.33%	His
14	3472	0.93%	29.26%	Had
15	3343	0.90%	30.16%	Is
16	3036	0.82%	30.98%	With
17	2976	0.80%	31.78%	Have
18	2916	0.78%	32.56%	My
19	2851	0.77%	33.33%	We
20	2786	0.75%	34.08%	As

Figure 3.7 Sample frequency list – Sherlock Holmes corpus

1) 1717.00 jack
2) 1163.00 weight
3) 720.00 fellah
4) 720.00 pterodactyl
5) 650.50 baronet

Figure 3.8 Top five keywords in Sherlock Holmes data

The figure on the left shows the 'keyness' of the word and is calculated, according to LexTutor, as follows:

The number accompanying each word below represents the number of times more frequent that word is in your text than in bnc_speech_fams_per10mill, proportionally. For example, the first item in the output **1717.00 jack** means that **jack** has **1** natural occurrence in 10000000 words, but **62** occurrences in your 361194-word text, which would work out to (62/361194) x 10000000 =**1717** occurrences if your text were the same size as the corpus. The word is thus 1717/1 = **1717.00 times** more frequent in your text than it is in the reference corpus. This probably means that the word plays quite an important (or 'key') role in your text.

(LexTutor, 2014)

Although this is not a statistical measure, it is a calculation that has been used in lexical studies, with the suggestion that a **keyness factor** of fifty and above is likely to mean the word has an importance in the data you are examining (Chung and Nation, 2004). For us as researchers, a keyword can indicate something we may wish to investigate further in terms of how it is 'grammaticalised' in our data and how it functions. We can also, of course, conduct statistical analysis on the frequency of a keyword and its patterns. In the data above, we may wish to look further at the word 'weight' as one example. To examine how words combine into chunks and thus lexico-grammatical patterns, LexTutor allows us to analyse **N-Grams**. The software allows us to check for two, three, four, five etc. word combinations which occur in the data. This results in output that can produce recognisable whole sequences and also strings of words that commonly co-occur. An example of this is shown in Figure 3.9 below.

```
4-word
001.[12]          BUT THERE WAS NO
002.[12]          ON THE OTHER HAND
003.[11]          THAT HE WAS A
004.[11]          I DON'T KNOW WHAT
005.[10]          OF ONE OF THE


3-word
001.[86]          IT WAS A
002.[56]          IT IS A
003.[53]          THERE WAS A
004.[43]          OUT OF THE
005.[42]          WHICH HAD BEEN
```

Figure 3.9 Five most common four- and three-word N-Grams in Sherlock Holmes data (number of occurrences in brackets)

These chunks can prompt further investigation and analysis. We might ask, for example, what other language occurs around 'I don't know what', what contexts it occurs in and who says it in the stories. We may also wish to find out whether 'which had been' occurs in defining or non-defining relative clauses and again which characters tend to say it and how it functions.

Once we have investigated further, we can then begin to explore the data in other ways – for example, through looking at concordance lines. These can be produced in LexTutor by clicking the 'concordance' tab. Upload your own texts via the 'text-based concordance option'. It is also possible to produce concordance lines from a number of other corpora by clicking 'corpus-based concordances'.

Finally, as mentioned above in section 3.4, we can also use LexTutor for some statistical analysis, such as T-tests. Inputting different frequency figures from different corpora here allows us to check whether there is a significant difference between their occurrences. For example, I may wish to compare the number of occurrences of 'It was a' in the Sherlock Holmes corpus with its occurrences in several other corpora. Try using each of the features above with a text or texts of your own in LexTutor. Alternatively, there are sample texts provided for use with each feature. What does this tell you about the grammar of your chosen texts?

AntConc is free to download to your computer and comes with a detailed user's guide, which is also free to download. It has many of the same features as LexTutor, including the ability to compose frequency lists and N-Grams. To use these, you must upload a plain text file – unlike LexTutor, it is not possible to paste in texts. There are also some additional features which differ from LexTutor and it is these we explore here.

One difference between the tools is that AntConc allows us to investigate collocations using a MI score. By clicking the 'collocates' tab we can specify how many items left or right of a word (1L, 1R etc.) or stretch of words we wish to check. This is the same function available in the BYU-BNC and other corpora. The 'tools preference' tab also allows us to display the MI score and data can be displayed by frequency of collocate and strength of MI. For example, if we run a check for 'had' to discover what may come after it (1R) in the Sherlock Holmes data, we find that, as we would presume, words in past participle form are common. These include 'been' (465 occurrences, MI score = 5.23968), 'come' (eighty-six occurrences, MI score = 3.90764) and 'gone' (forty-two occurrences, MI score = 4.73051). While we would expect many novels to feature 'had' in a past perfect form (e.g. 'He had gone'), it may be worth investigating whether these instances are more frequent in the Sherlock Holmes data than in other fiction corpora and if so, why this is. We can do this with qualitative analysis by simply clicking on the display of 'had been' etc and seeing concordance lines instantly, but as there are a great number of occurrences of 'had been', it may also be useful to make comparisons with other corpora using quantitative measures. A comparison of 'had been' with the BYU-BNC fiction corpus, for example, reveals the following:

Table 3.8 'had + been' in Sherlock Holmes data and the BYU-BNC fiction corpus

Sherlock Holmes data (372,841 words)	BYU-BNC (fiction) (15,909,312 words)	Log-likelihood
465 occurrences	21,001 occurrences	Log likelihood = 2.36 (not statistically significant)

This suggests that 'had been' is a very frequent realisation of a past perfect form, in both fictional corpora. There are no statistically significant differences between the corpora, which suggests it is likely to occur in many texts and is not a special feature of Sherlock Holmes texts.

Another key difference between AntConc and LexTutor is that AntConc allows us the ability to use log-likelihood scores when undertaking keyword comparisons. To do this, you must upload your own reference corpus or wordlist. Use the 'tool preferences' tab and upload a reference list or corpus. Then use the keywords tab to check a target word and the software will automatically calculate the log-likelihood. To demonstrate this, we have run a keyword list using one Sherlock Holmes story (*The Valley of Fear*) as a reference point. Running a keyword list produces some of the following keywords:

	Occurrences	Keyness (Log-likelihood)	Word
1	2925	94.711	my
2	1397	60.105	our
3	606	56.617	sir
4	1592	38.174	upon
5	231	35.923	challenger

Figure 3.10 Five most common keywords in Sherlock Holmes data

As we suggested in section 3.3, these may then point the way towards larger grammatical patterns. A quick check of 'my' in this data, for example, reveals that the word it collocates most commonly with is 'friend' (130 occurrences, MI score = 5.99431) and that the most common word to follow 'my friend' with a meaningful MI score is 'here', of which there are seventeen occurrences (MI score = 5.43086). We could see this as a possible cue to examine the concordance lines for this pattern, looking at its position in clauses, who tends to say it and how it functions in the story. We may also wish to undertake a comparison with other corpora, as we have done in the examples above.

Try using each of the features above with a text or texts of your own in AntConc. What does this tell you about the grammar of your chosen texts?

Table 3.9 LexTutor and AntConc features compared

	Frequency	Keywords	Collocation	N-Grams
LexTutor Data can be exported	Individual and cumulative scores produced for each word list Type-token ratio produced Text files or pasted texts	Produced in comparison to the BNC spoken corpus Keyness factor given	No specific feature for collocation	Produced for 2–4-word chunks
AntConc Data can be exported	Frequency of individual words given Comparison with a list of lemmas possible Text files only	Produced in comparison to a corpus or word list you must upload Comparison to reference corpus can be measured through log-likelihood	Mutual Information scores produced automatically T-test also available	N-Gram size can be chosen but we can also specify word occurring to the left and right of the target word and how many words away from or near this we wish to search for

There is no suggested answer for this exercise but you should find that the basic features are accessible and get used to using them.

In this book, we have made use of both LexTutor and AntConc tools, as we feel there are useful features in each that you can use to analyse your own corpus data. Table 3.9 gives a summary of the different features available in each piece of software. By trying them, you may find one easier to work with, but bear in mind that the tool you use may need to be supplemented with other types of analysis to reach clearer conclusions about the data.

3.6 Conclusion

In this chapter, we have introduced some key features of the open-access corpora and analysis tools we will use throughout this book. This has included ways to use these tools for analysis of frequency, collocations, chunks and semantic prosody. We will expand on each of these in Part 2 of the book. We have attempted to show how data can be analysed using some simple quantitative, statistical measures and also qualitatively, by examining the data in context. There is not enough space here for a detailed description and discussion of every possible method of statistical analysis so we have tried to keep to those methods that are most commonly used. We suggest that log-likelihood can be used to measure the significance of frequencies in different corpora, T-tests can be used to measure the differences in frequencies of forms in several corpora, and MI the co-occurrence of items in word pairs and larger patterns. For a detailed explanation of a number of statistical measures that can be used to analyse corpus data, see Oakes (2004).

We have also tried to re-emphasise that corpus data (as with any data) is always open to the interpretation of a researcher, and although a corpus can tell us how often a grammatical form occurs, it will not tell us why it is being used or how it functions. Therefore, there is often a need to employ qualitative measures alongside quantitative ones and to train ourselves in searching the data for patterns of meaning.

Further practice

1   Do a basic search for a form in any of the corpora listed above. This could be at the word, clause or sentence level. What does the data tell you? What other data might you need to obtain to develop the analysis?
2   Compare the frequency of a grammatical pattern in two corpora and analyse it using log-likelihood. Is the frequency of occurrence in one corpus statistically significant when compared with the other?

References

Anthony, L. (2013). AntConc (version 3.3.5). [Online], Available: www.antlab.sci. waseda.ac.jp/software.html [1 November 2013].

Bond, T.G and Fox, C.M. (2007). *Applying the RASCJ Model.* Mahwah, NJ: Lawrence Erlbaum.

Cobb, T. (2013) Compleat Lexical Tutor (LexTutor). [Online], Available: www. lextutor.ca [20 October 2013].

Davies, M. (2004). *BYU-BNC* (based on the British National Corpus from Oxford University Press). [Online], Available: http://corpus.byu.edu/bnc [1 July 2014].

Davies, M. (2008). *Corpus of contemporary American English: 450 million words, 1990–present* (COCA). [Online], Available: http://corpus.byu.edu/coca [20 October 2013].

Davies, M. (2012). *Corpus of American soap operas: 100 million words 2001–2012.* [Online], Available: http://corpus2.byu.edu/soap [1 July 2014].

Davies, M. (2013). *Corpus of global web-based English: 1.9 billion words from speakers in 20 countries* (GloWbe). [Online], Available: http://corpus2.byu.edu/GloWbe [20 July 2014].

Dörnyei, Z. (2007). *Research methods in applied linguistics: quantitative, qualitative and mixed methodologies.* Oxford: Oxford University Press.

Cheng, W., Greaves, C. and Warren, M. (2008). *Hong Kong corpus of spoken English* (HKCSE) (Orthographic). [Online], Available: http://rcpce.engl.polyu.edu.hk/HKCSE [20 July 2014].

Chung, T.M and Nation, P. (2004). Identifying technical vocabulary. *System*, 32, 251–263.

McEnery, T. and Wilson, A. (2001). *Corpus linguistics* (2nd edition). Edinburgh: Edinburgh University Press.

Oakes, M.P. (2004). *Statistics for corpus linguistics*. Edinburgh: Edinburgh University Press.

O'Keeffe, A., McCarthy, M. and Carter, R. (2007). *From corpus to classroom*. Cambridge: Cambridge University Press.

Project Gutenberg (2014). *Project Gutenberg*. [Online], Available: www.gutenberg.org/ [10 April 2014].

Rayson, P. and Garside, R. (2000). Comparing corpora using frequency profiling, in *Proceedings of the workshop on Comparing Corpora, held in conjunction with the 38th annual meeting of the Association for Computational Linguistics*. 1–8 October 2000, Hong Kong: Association for Computational Linguistics, 1–6.

Rayson, P. (2014). *Log-likelihood calculator*. [Online], Available: http://ucrel.lancs.ac.uk/llwizard.html [1 July 2014].

Research and Development Unit for English Studies (2014). *WebCorp linguist's search engine* (WebCorp LSE). Birmingham City University. [Online], Available: http://wse1.webcorp.org.uk/home [1 May 2014].

Soar, L. and Soars, J. (1996). *New headway English course intermediate student's book*. Oxford: Oxford University Press.

The University of Michigan English Language Institute (2014). *Michigan corpus of academic spoken English* (MICASE). [Online], Available: http://quod.lib.umich.edu/m/micase [2 June 2014].

VOICE (2013). *The Vienna-Oxford international corpus of English* (version 2.0). [Online], Available: http://voice.univie.ac.a [20 July 2014].

Chapter 4

Frequency

4.1 Introduction

On the face of it, frequency seems to be one of the most straightforward methods of looking at corpus data. In essence, frequency data examines how often the target of a search occurs, whether this is words or structures. Take a very basic example from a website explaining how to operate an oven:

Know your oven. A good cook knows his or her oven through both reading the instructions that accompany the oven and experience through usage. Although recipes may indicate certain temperatures, your own knowledge of how your oven works is vital and it is ultimately up to this knowledge coupled with your cooking experience that will help to determine the most appropriate temperature and cooking length times. Every time that you have to get used to a new oven, always commence with your basic, true stand-by recipes and adjust as needed before branching out into more complicated recipes. And read the manufacturer's instructions if you have access to them; they are full of useful information!

Figure 4.1 Know your oven

Source: www.wikihow.com/Use-an-Oven

As mentioned in Chapter 1, basic analysis of the data for frequency will reveal that of the 115 tokens in the text there are seventy-five types. The most frequent words are 'and', 'oven', 'to' and 'your', all of which occur five times each. This type of analysis is the basis for many studies into corpus data but very quickly questions begin to arise about how frequency counts are made. For example, in the text above, the software used has counted 'temperature' and 'temperatures' as two different items. We may well look at this and say that 'temperatures' is simply a transparent plural form of the word so they should be counted as the same word, which would bring the count for 'temperature' to two. What about 'know' and 'knowledge'? This is clearly a less obvious connection but some corpora, such as the **General Service Lists** (see http://jbauman.com/gsl.html) based on the West Corpus, would bring these words under the same headword as they would also do with 'cook' and 'cooking' and 'read' and 'reading'. So, while frequency may appear to be a very straightforward concept, the way in which words are counted could radically change the results of an analysis.

These issues are even more complex when grammatical patterns are analysed because unlike lexis, grammatical items for analysis have less clearly defined boundaries. Words can be defined by the spaces that separate them (although collocations, multi-word phrases and semi/fixed expressions complicate matters) but grammatical forms can be harder to draw defining lines around or to summon from an online corpus simply by entering a search term. If we take the word 'say', it may be grammaticalised in many ways, including 'He says + object' or 'She said + object' or 'As I was saying', to mention just three possibilities. For these reasons, we feel it is easiest to search for grammatical patterns starting by looking for the basis of a pattern (such as 'He says + object' or even the words 'says' ,'say' or 'saying') and then refining searches before and after the pattern to see how frequent particular grammatical constructions are in particular contexts. We will explore this method in the next sections of this chapter.

4.2 What does frequency look like in corpus data/ how do you find it?

The simplest way to access frequency data is to use a popular search engine (such as Google) and search for the grammatical pattern you wish to access. If we do this with a pattern such as 'I was saying' and compare it with 'I said', two patterns often used to report speech, we get the following results, which appear just under the search bar.

Table 4.1 Search engine frequency results for 'I was saying' and 'I said'

'I was saying'	about 2,220,000,000 results
'I said'	about 5,090,000,000 results

This tells us, quite simply, that 'I said' is more frequent in this search engine because it produces more results, using the internet as a corpus. This is a very crude way to test frequency but it does tell us something and may be useful to a degree. Learners and teachers of English as a second language, for example, may use a facility like this to help them initially prioritise particular grammatical or lexico-grammatical patterns upon which to focus their learning and teaching. This can be helpful, as often our intuitions about frequency do not match the evidence we find in corpora.

Sample exercise

If we consider the example of modal auxiliary verbs (can, may, might, will, shall, must, should, would and could), what would you imagine to be the order of these verbs (1–9) from most to least frequent if we consult a general corpus, such as the BYU-BNC containing samples of both spoken and written language?

The answer is as follows:

1 Would
2 Will
3 Can
4 Could
5 May
6 Should
7 Must
8 Might
9 Shall

This data is taken from the BNC frequency lists, available here: http://ucrel.lancs.ac.uk/bncfreq/lists/1_2_all_freq.txt, where you can also access the exact number of occurrences of each modal auxiliary verb. Naturally, the frequency of a verb alone reveals very little, though it may suggest a possible order in which to learn each of the above, by focusing on the most frequent first and the least frequent last. This may seem very obvious but surprisingly, such basic aspects of frequency are not always reflected in syllabuses within EFL/ESL textbooks, even though there have been attempts to address this (for example, Willis, 1990). However, as we know, modal verbs do not occur alone but cluster into grammatical patterns so analysis at the word level is limited. Intuition suggests that as the words 'I' and 'go' are highly frequent in most corpora, one common pattern is likely to be 'I + modal + go' or 'Pronoun + modal auxiliary + bare infinitive' e.g. 'I must go'. The choice of pronoun will of course affect the function of the pattern in context.

Sample exercise

Which of the following patterns do you instinctively feel are more frequent? Think for yourself and then check by using an internet search engine.

Which pattern has higher frequency?

1 'I've got to go' vs. 'I have to go'
2 'I must go' vs. 'I have to go'
3 'I may go' vs. 'I might go'

You should have found something similar to the following:

1   About 3,600,000,000 results/About 6,420,000,000 results
2   About 2,360,000,000 results/About 6,420,000,000 results
3   About 4,190,000,000 results/About 3,500,000,000 results

As mentioned, this type of frequency search is somewhat crude. Although it can show us that, for instance, 'I have to go' is more frequent than 'I must go' when we use the internet as a corpus, there is still a great deal of information missing. We cannot see if anything frequently follows 'I have to go' such as adverbials 'I have to go now' or 'I have to go soon'. In addition, we do not learn anything about the frequency of a pattern in relation to a particular context of use. This can be very important. As we have mentioned previously, some forms can be far more frequent in one context than another. Biber et al. (1999) show, for instance, that certain modal verbs display a far higher frequency in certain texts than in others. 'May', for instance, is known to have a higher frequency in corpora of academic texts than in spoken language because it serves a particular hedging function in academic writing. Arguments are 'hedged' to make them sound less assertive and more nuanced, something that is generally respected in academic fields of writing. Carter and McCarthy (2006: 280) give examples of this such as the following: 'The change may have been in progress in other countries'. The choice of the pronoun 'you' or 'I' will also affect the function of the pattern in context so that 'I must go' is likely to be a form of obligation to yourself, rather than the imposition of obligation implied by 'you must go'.

One way to improve then on a basic internet search is to compare frequency across several contexts. This can be achieved if we look at several different types of corpora at once. As we have seen in the first part of the book, this is possible using a corpus such as the BYU-BNC interface (http://corpus.byu.edu/bnc). If we look at the pattern 'I have to go' in spoken, fiction, magazine, newspaper and academic corpora, we get the results displayed in Table 4.2 below.

Table 4.2 Frequencies of 'I have to go' in written and spoken corpora

Corpus type	Spoken (9,963,663 words)	Fiction (15,909,312 words)	Magazine (7,261,990 words)	Newspaper (10,466,422 words)	Academic (15,331,668 words)
Total number of occurrences	59	158	9	12	4
Occurrences per million words	5.92	9.93	1.24	1.15	0.26

This suggests that the pattern is most frequent in fiction as it has both the highest number of occurrences and the most per million words. The frequency per million words is an important measure as a pattern may clearly have a greater number of occurrences in a corpus, simply because the corpus itself contains more words. This will generally skew searches in favour of written corpora because by their nature, they are easier to compile than spoken ones and thus generally contain more words. There is no absolute measure to say how many occurrences per million words would in themselves be considered frequent, as corpora themselves vary in size. However, around ten occurrences per million words, or the equivalent in a smaller corpus, is often quoted as a reasonable figure (Carter and McCarthy, 2006). A log-likelihood test comparing the spoken and fiction corpora results in a highly significant score of 12.33 ($p<0.0001$). We will come back to how we can establish more about this frequency in a moment. Before this, it is worth trying a similar search for yourself.

Try it yourself 4.1

Checking the frequency of 'I must go'

First, consider the frequency of 'I must go'. Would you imagine it occurs more frequently in spoken, fiction, magazine, newspaper or academic contexts?

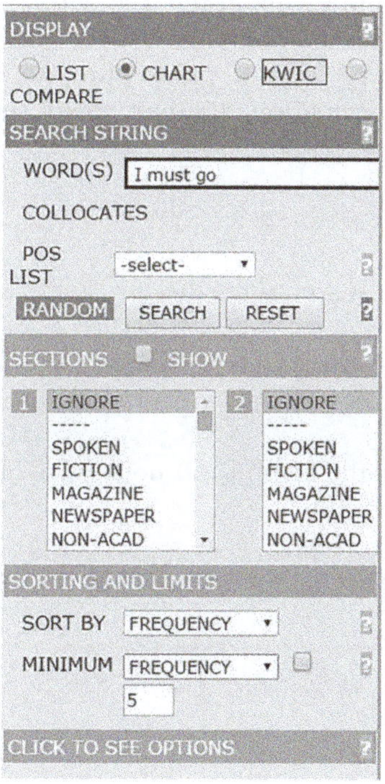

Figure 4.2 Checking the frequency of 'I must go'

Access the website http://corpus.byu.edu/bnc. Under 'display', click on the tab that says 'chart' and in the 'search string' section type in 'I must go'. You can find these results in a table in the suggested answers section.

This style of frequency search is helpful because it does give us information about which context a grammatical pattern is more or less frequent within. However, it is also useful to find out more about the contexts of use and more about the grammatical pattern itself. If we return to 'I must go', we can see that this occurs most often in the fiction corpus. This then poses more questions: what types of fiction is it most frequent within?

The question can be answered to an extent by looking back at the BYU-BNC corpus. When the results are given, the corpus produces a bar chart. If we click on the bar marked 'fiction', we can see that all of the occurrences come from prose. This is not entirely surprising, as the majority of the BYU-BNC fiction corpus consists of prose (219,409 words from poetry, 44,975 words from plays and 15,644,928 words from prose), but as there are no occurrences in even the limited amount of poetry and plays here, we can suggest this is reliable. If we again click the bar chart under fictional 'prose', the corpus produces a number of concordance lines, which allows us to investigate the contexts of use of each occurrence. Clicking on the left of the pattern gives us the expanded context of each occurrence.

It is desirable, however, to understand more about the frequency of this pattern. Does it occur, for example, most commonly on its own in fiction or is it followed more often by another type of noun phrase, prepositional phrase or adverb phrase? To find this information, another type of search is needed as set out in the sample exercise below.

Sample exercise

To find this information, another type of search is needed.

- In the corpus, click the button below 'list' and type 'I must go *' in the search string box. The * simply shows what pattern or patterns most often follow 'I must go'.
- In the areas named 'sections' highlight 'fiction' on both sides of the box.
- Then click 'search' as shown in Figure 4.3.
- Your results should reveal that the patterns shown in Table 4.3 are the most frequent:

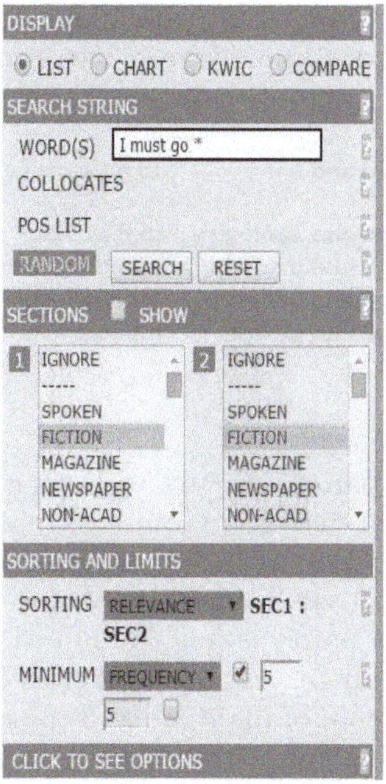

Figure 4.3 Screenshot of search for 'I must go *' in the BYU-BNC fiction corpus

Table 4.3 Frequent patterns of 'I must go' in a fiction corpus

		Number of occurrences	Occurrences per million words
1	I MUST GO	44	2.77
2	I MUST GO AND	34	2.14
3	I MUST GO TO	26	1.63

This tells us that 'I must go' most frequently stands alone as a phrase in the fiction corpus, as the following (edited) examples show:

1	I love you.' 'I know you do. And	**I must go**	.' Just that and she was gone. Jay hurled the
2	I see it's late, I'd forgotten the time.	**I must go**	. I – I won't say any more now, but you
3	Now – my darling –	**I must go**	.' Jack had been sitting in the chair while
4	Excuse me,' she said,' but you,' he said briefly.' Now	**I must go**	. And you will remember, won't you, that Thank

Figure 4.4 Concordance lines for 'I must go'

If we wish to find out which patterns come after 'I must go and', we can simply examine the occurrences (as it only occurs thirty-four times) and quickly see that that the pattern is 'I must go + infinitive verb base form' as in the following (edited) examples:

I	She drained her coffee cup and put it down.'	**I must go and try**	to get some sleep.
2	I'm used to it, you see.	**I must go and apologise**	to the other
3	What a terrible affair.	**I must go and break**	it to dear Dimity,
4	before I go home	**I must go and inform**	Mr Felton's people
5	'Forgive me,	**I must go and powder**	my nose. And

Figure 4.5 Concordance lines for 'I must go and'

Finally, if we wish to know why this pattern occurs with such frequency, we have to interpret the data using qualitative analysis. Frequency data does not tell us why, it tells us 'how many' or 'how often'. Looking at these examples, we can say 'I must go', occurs with more frequency than other possible S + V patterns (e.g. 'You must go,/ He must go,/They must go') and generally serves as a marker to indicate movement between one scene or stretch of dialogue and the next. In other words, 'I must go' has a different function to other possible patterns with different pronouns. Expanded examples (in the BYU-BNC corpus, click on the left of concordances to see these) such as the following indicate this usage:

> a solved, one just needs the will and the courage. Franca, sweetheart, I bless you, I worship you, you have a great soul, I feel I could serve you as if you were God –" Jack, don't worry –" I love you –" Yes, good, but hadn't you better go now? Alison will be waiting for you, and you must be anxious to relieve her mind." Of course. I see it's late, I'd forgotten the time. **I must go**. I – I won't say any more now, but you know –" Yes?" Oh, and – just one other thing." Yes?" About the others." What others? Are there others?" I mean Gildas and Ludens. I know they wish us well, and they're both wise and reasonable people, they're tactful – but naturally they're inquisitive, they want to know what's happening, and make judgments.

A final aspect of frequency that can help us to analyse language is a keyword analysis as mentioned in Chapter 3. The numbers on the left show the order of frequency and the number after that shows the 'keyness'; that is, the frequency with which this occurs in the data examined in relation to a reference corpus. This kind of search can be undertaken in LexTutor (www.lextutor.ca), where the reference corpus is the spoken section of the BNC. For an example, go to the website, click on 'keywords' and choose the sample text 'Dracula' and submit.

The top five keywords for this novel are as follows:

(1) 2481.11 vampire
(2) 1313.58 tomb
(3) 405.24 coffin
(4) 127.13 churchyard
(5) 127.13 shiver

To find out how these words operate once grammaticalised, copy and paste the Dracula text into the 'concordances' section of LexTutor and choose 'text concordances'. Scroll down to find 'vampire' and you will find there are concordance lines given for that word. Examining these words allows us to see how the word is patterned within the book. Here is a sample of the concordances such a search produces.

1	t over to him. And now you may kiss her,' he said. See! The	**vampire**	is dead, and the
2	ng that poor Lucy was killed by a vampire, and that now the	**vampire**	is taking blood
3	Van Helsing said, we have only just begun. We must Find the	**vampire**	that killed Miss
4	to understand so many things! This Count Dracula he was the You haven't understood. The	**vampire**	that killed poor too?' No,' Van Helsing replied.
5	You haven't understood my love' she said softly The	**vampire**	which is taking
6	We found the tombs of the three	**vampire**	women. They cannot hurt us now, and Dracula is dead

Figure 4.6 Concordance lines for 'Vampire'

These concordances show us that the word vampire is preceded most commonly by the determiner 'the', which occurs more often than 'a'. The verb that collates or clusters around the word most commonly is 'kill' and the adjective 'dead'. In terms of tense and aspect, present and past simple forms occur most often. Although this does not tell us everything we may wish to know about this novel, it does give us a 'window' into the style of the writing, which can then tell us a lot about the intentions and themes within this or other novels. This may reveal new ideas about a text or just confirm assumptions we have already made (Stubbs, 2008). One way the novel achieves its dark gothic theme is through the higher frequency of words such as 'vampire' and the way they cluster around verbs such as 'kill' and adjectives such as 'dead'. The use of the definite article 'the' helps to signal that the vampire being referred to is known to the characters and of course the readers. The question that is always in the reader's mind and the minds of the characters is 'when will the vampire appear next?'

This then is the kind of information a corpus can tell us about frequency. We can understand the grammatical patterns a word occupies and how frequent these are in different corpora in relation to each other. What this can then tell us about language use will be explored in the next section.

4.3 What can frequency tell us about language use?

Investigations of frequent grammatical patterns can tell us a number of things about a text and about how the text fulfils its purpose. First of all, as set out in Chapter 2, language is concerned with form and function. The use of particular grammar structures can tell us a lot about how a particular speaker or writer views a particular event. By way of example, Table 4.4 shows the number of occurrences of the present perfect form ('have + past participle' e.g. 'We *have found* that' as mentioned in Chapter 3) in the BYU-BNC. You can carry out the search on the BYU-BNC website by entering have + [v?*]. The [v?*] can be found by clicking in the 'pos' (part of speech) tab below the search bar.

Table 4.4 Frequency data for 'have + past participle'

Corpus type	Spoken (9,963,663 words)	Fiction (15,909,312 words)	Magazine (7,261,990 words)	Newspaper (10,466,422 words)	Academic (15,331,668 words)
Total number of occurrences	16430	32700	15545	30414	37308
Occurrences per million words	1,648.99	2,055.40	2,140.60	2,905.86	2,433.39

What is immediately apparent is that the present perfect (at least in its simple form) occurs with the most frequency in newspapers. It occurs with less regularity in spoken and non-academic texts. Look at the examples below and consider briefly why this might be the case.

1	the fast-breeder reactors which used the reprocessed fuel	**have been**	abandoned as a failure.'
2	They admit they are baffled by their findings because they	**have been**	unable to discover a 35 devastated by Ecstasy,
3	WHOLE families	**have been**	
4	longest-lasting leading ladies, said to	**have been**	paid more than three
5	Dozens of the rhesus macaque monkeys	**have been**	sold to a firm which
6	direction in which Radio One has been going for a couple of years. We	**have been**	doing

Figure 4.7 Concordance lines for 'have been + past participle' in a newspaper corpus

The answer can partly be explained by the fact that newspapers carry information about current events so there is a strong emphasis on the 'recentness' of what is being reported. The time frame in such stories is the recent past. What is also interesting from the examples above, taken from the same results, is the extensive use of passive structures (have + been + past participle). These sentences tend to emphasise the importance of the action rather than the agents (i.e. those carrying out the action).

One further point of comparison could be with frequency in other corpora. The same search carried out in the COCA suggests that while American newspapers also use the form quite extensively compared with other texts (1.6 per million words in American newspapers versus 2.9 million in British newspapers), the overall instances of use in American texts are lower (1.7 per million versus 2.2 per million). However, according to the corpus data, there are more instances of the form in American spoken texts than in British ones (1.6 per million in the BNC vs. 2 million in the COCA).

4.4 Language use in specific texts

It is also possible to look at frequency in single texts as a starting point before going on to construct a larger corpus of similar texts. Keep in mind that you may need to get permission if you are using texts that are copyrighted. In this section we will look at the British Prevention of Terrorism Act 2005. This is an Act of Parliament which like all legislation is available on the internet. The following search was carried out using the search tools available in Adobe document viewer.

Sample exercise

Put the following modal verbs into the order of frequency that they occur in the Prevention of Terrorism Act 2005, from the one that occurs the most to the one you think occurs the least:

can, could, may, might, must, should, will, would

A simple search of the document reveals the following results:

Table 4.5 Modals in the Prevention of Terrorism Act 2005

	can	could	**may**	might	must	should	will	would
Number of occurrences	I	2	**96**	I	40	5	2	I5

What is particularly interesting is the very high frequency of 'may' in this document with over twice as many occurrences than its nearest rival 'must'. Of the uses of 'may' in the text, forty-five (51%) are 'may + be'. The chart below shows the collocations by percentage.

A search within the results for 'may be' shows that around thirty instances (approximately 31%) are examples of the passive structure ('may be brought', 'may be imposed'). This is unsurprising when the purpose of the text is considered. This is a document that is concerned with clearly setting

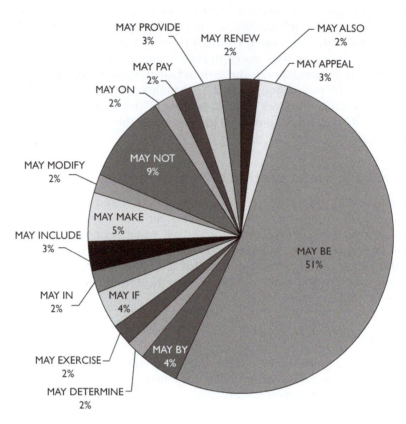

Figure 4.8 The use of 'may' in the Prevention of Terrorism Act

out what the law says on the prevention of terrorism and what processes may occur where there are breaches. The identity of those carrying out the provisions of the Act is either irrelevant because it is the process that matters, or obvious from the context.

4.5 The impact of text type on frequency

The analysis of the Prevention of Terrorism Act illustrates the importance of context and discourse type on frequency within a text (or within a particular text type). As was discussed earlier in this volume, text type is closely identified with the notion of a text purpose. It also involves the consideration of the different metafunctions of a text, as discussed in Chapter 2. In the case of the Act, this is a piece of legislation that sets out the will of parliament to serve as a framework for those involved in the justice system. The document has been produced by parliament's drafters for a professional

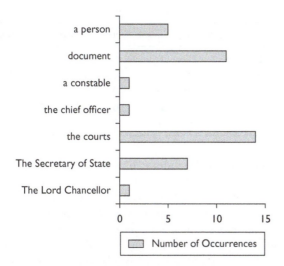

Figure 4.9 Agents identified by use of 'must' in the Prevention of Terrorism Act

and specialised audience and there is a need for terminology to be clear and unambiguous.

When one returns to the figures for modal verbs, one can begin to see why the modals 'may' and 'must' have such prominent roles. 'Must' sets out actions that are essential and non-negotiable and is used to place responsibility upon specific individuals. Figure 4.9 shows that in each case of the use of 'must' in the document an agent, most often someone in a named role is identified or else the modal relates to a function a document must carry out (and in all instances this will be a named document such as a statement, a declaration, an application, a notice etc.). It is also interesting that the use of the article supports this role of specifying closely who is to carry out a task, in that there are comparatively few instances of 'a person' or 'a constable' and even these will be further identified in the document ('a specified person', 'a controlled person', 'a person appointed'). So we can see that the genre heavily influences the type of language found in a text and likely the results of corpus analysis.

This issue can be examined by looking at the presence of modal verbs in another form of official documentation. In this case we are looking at information taken from the UK government's Foreign Office website and advice on travelling to specific countries (www.gov.uk/foreign-travel-advice). We have chosen this example because this is also official information, as in the case of the Prevention of Terrorism Act, but unlike the Act of Parliament, this information has been written for a wider public audience and is concerned with conveying advice rather than laying down the law.

An initial concordance search reveals the following modals in use.

Table 4.6 Modals used in UK government Foreign Office travel advice

	can	could	may	might	must	should	will	would
Country A	0	2	0	0	0	4	0	0
Country B	2	0	0	0	0	1	0	0
Country C	0	0	0	0	0	3	0	0
Country D	1	0	1	0	0	3	0	0
Prevention of Terrorism Act	1	2	96	1	40	5	2	15

Obviously the Act is a far longer document, but the figures still make for interesting comparison. However, this comparison is only meaningful when one considers the type of text and purposes of the different texts under analysis. While the Act is preoccupied with exactly specifying who or what must happen, or what may result from a particular action, the web-pages here centre around giving advice, so it is unsurprising that the most frequent modal is *should* with only *could, can* and *may* being used to discuss potential issues or state that something is possible:

1	further disturbances	**can't**	be ruled out and
2	business, you	**can**	now get an e-visa
3	[country D]	**can**	be affected by severe
4	demonstrations are likely and	**could**	take place in any
5	attacks which	**could**	be indiscriminate
6	There	**may**	be high levels of travel disruption

Figure 4.10 Concordance lines for modal verbs

As has been stated above, it is the modal 'should' that is most used in these texts and as can be seen below, the modal is used directly to relay strong advice to the reader.

1	You	**should**	be especially vigilant
2	You	**should**	stay at or close to home
3	You	**should**	avoid crowds
4	You	**should**	follow the regulations
5	You	**should**	be especially vigilant
6	You	**should**	avoid large public demonstrations
7	You	**should**	avoid the cordoned
8	You	**should**	exercise caution in
9	You	**should**	obey orders from
10	You	**should**	avoid any political gatherings
11	You	**should**	be aware

Figure 4.11 Concordance lines for 'should'

However, the texts also use other methods to relay advice. Consider the following examples, all of which come from the Foreign Office advice webpages and all of which are relaying advice to travellers.

Try it yourself 4.2

Identify the form used to relay advice in each example below:

1   The Foreign and Commonwealth Office (FCO) advise against all travel to
2   The FCO do not advise against the use of
3   If you are already in a part of [country] where the FCO advise against all but essential travel
4   Make sure you keep valid photographic identification with you at all times.
5   You are strongly advised to avoid all demonstrations
6   If you become aware of any nearby protests, leave the area immediately.
7   Don't attempt to cross road blocks erected by the security forces
8   Take out comprehensive travel and medical insurance before you travel.

So, as we can see, the type of text along with its intended audience can influence the use of language very heavily and we can use a single text as a starting point in our investigations. To develop the examples we have given, we would need to extend the corpus to include examples of travel advice and legislation. It is not hard to see therefore how corpora made up of different text types can produce very different results.

4.6 Bringing the analysis together

To illustrate how frequency can be used in a research project to analyse particular text types, we will now revisit reported speech from Chapter 1 by looking at examples of *say (said)* and *tell (told)* in spoken texts. We will start from the word level and move upwards to the sentence and text levels. Such investigations are often driven by particular research questions so in this case we will look at a number of propositions before examining the data further.

Assumptions to be tested:

(i) Since spoken texts often use past forms, *said* and *told* will be more frequent than *says* and *tell*.
(ii) Reported speech using '*said*' will not necessarily backshift a tense to report (e.g. where 'I'm going' would become 'He told me he was going') in spoken contexts.
(iii) Backshift after 'said' is more likely to occur in other (written) corpora.

Assumption 1: 'said' and 'told' are more frequent than 'say' and 'tell'.

For this investigation we will be using the BYU-BNC spoken corpus and the Hong Kong Corpus of Spoken English (HKCSE) corpus (http://rcpce.engl. polyu.edu.hk/HKCSE), comprising almost a million words of conversations, recorded and prepared speeches used in Hong Kong. We have chosen to look at these two corpora partly to give an intercultural dimension to the analysis, as some samples in the HKCSE are examples of English being used as a Lingua Franca. As we have done previously, we started with a simple search to find the total frequency of each word in both corpora. These results show that 'said' has greater frequency in both corpora both in total and per million words.

Table 4.7 Frequencies of 'says', 'said', 'tell' and 'told' in the BYU-BNC spoken corpus and HKCSE

BNC spoken	Says	Said	Tell	Told
Total number of occurrences	7,663	27,814	6,909	3,746
Occurrences per million words	769.09	2,791.54	693.42	375.97
Hong Kong Corpus of Spoken English (HKCSE)* 158		712	427	200

*The HKCSE is a corpus of only about one million words so the number of instances reported here would also be the same count if we presented the occurrences per million words.

Assumption 2: Reported speech using 'said' will not necessarily backshift a tense to report (e.g. where 'I'm going' would become 'He said he was going') in spoken contexts

This assumption was first checked using the BYU-BNC search string 'She said she + [V*]' and using 'She said she' as a search in the HKCSE, which does not allow part of speech searches. We've chosen to use the stem 'She said she' because the phrase 'She said' is most often followed by 'he' or 'she' in the BYU-BNC. The results are shown in Table 4.8.

Table 4.8 The three most frequently occurring patterns with 'She said she + VP'

BYU-BNC spoken corpus	She said she + [V*]	HKCSE	She said she + [V*]
Total occurrences = 235	She said she's (50)	Total occurrences = 11	She said she was [3]
	She said she'd (44)		She said she could [3]
	She said she was (32)		She said she will [2]

These answers seem to suggest that tense backshift is not automatic when reporting speech in spoken language. Speakers in fact report what people have said using present forms very often, particularly in the larger BYU-BNC corpus where 'she said she's . . .' is the most common pattern. We can see this in the following examples, all taken from the BYU-BNC corpus.

I	Well I phoned Shirley (pause) and	**she said she's**	fine.
2	not all that good is she in health? No. So	**she said she's**	no car to
3	so I gave Catherine the number and	**she said she's**	got to ring her
4	she's vegetarian still and	**she said she's**	not coming

Figure 4.12 Concordance lines for 'she said she's'

This may be because the idea of tense 'backshift' being 'automatic' in reported speech is fundamentally flawed. As Willis (1990) observes, there is no reason why speakers automatically switch to past form when reporting what another person has said, if they still feel the focus of what has been said is present, perhaps because it is still true or still of current interest. When speakers do backshift, it is because they wish to locate the speech in the past, in relation to the present, as these examples show:

I	cos	**she said she'd**	bring up the money but she
2	I phoned her and she's going and	**she said she'd**	come for me way, we went
3	And er I think	**she said she'd**	seen a badger as
4	she said no she'd been to pay her poll tax over there,	**she said she'd**	had a rest in one of the

Figure 4.13 Concordance lines for 'she said she'd'

Assumption 3: Backshift after 'said' is more likely to occur in other (written) corpora

To investigate this, we carried out a search using the BYU-BNC for the phrase 'he said he + verb' and 'he said that + verb'.

Table 4.9 'He said he + verb' vs. 'He said **that** he + verb' in the BYU-BNC corpus

	He said he + verb	He said that he + verb
Total occurrences	1,233	209
Occurrences per million words	12.81	2.17
Text type in order of highest frequency (occurrences per million words)	Newspapers (35.26)	Non-academic (3.70)
	Spoken (29.21)	Spoken (2.71)
	Fiction (22.13)	Fiction (2.51)

According to the results, 'he said he + verb' was more common in newspaper texts than in spoken texts. This gives a log-likelihood score of 5.8 which is a significance level of $p < 0.05$. A search of the actual examples found that in the newspaper texts the majority of examples of the verb were far and away a past form, while the lines of data from the spoken corpora showed a much more varied mix with roughly one in four of the examples being a present form of the verb (e.g. 'he said he knows the market's low', 'he said he's telling him point blank that'). These findings seem to confirm our overall assumption that backshifts are more likely to occur in written corpus data and in particular newspaper texts.

By way of extension, we decided to have a look at 'he said that he + verb' as it was felt that this might well make a difference to the pattern. As one might expect with a longer search stem, the number of examples we found was reduced but spoken samples remained the second most frequent category. What was particularly interesting was that examples from newspapers, which had been the highest represented category in the previous search, dropped to fourth position with only 1.91 instances per million words of the string. This led us to ask why this would be the case. The answer may lie in the use of 'that' as an effect employed by writers to achieve either a more objective tone as it suggests a distance from the thing being discussed or reported; as Carter and McCarthy suggest, '"that" is also frequently used to refer to events and entities remote in time and space or to ideas and propositions associated with another person or another participant in the discourse' (2006: 246–7). Newspapers, as we have seen earlier in this chapter, are keen to present their information as being current and often direct from the source, and as a result they are less likely to want to give the impression of being remote from the events they are describing either in time, space or relation.

In summary, what we seem to have found is that it is far too simplistic to present the tense backshift as a mandatory element of reported speech, even in written forms, as many English textbooks and prescriptive grammars assert. What appears to be closer to the actual reality is that the way in which the writer or speaker chooses to represent an event in time is more likely to influence the choice of form that reported speech takes.

4.7 Limitations of frequency

We have noted above that there are some limitations in regard to the use of frequency. The most obvious issue is that while a corpus can tell us how often a grammatical pattern occurs and compare frequency across different types of texts, it cannot tell us why a pattern occurs. This is the job of us as researchers. Frequency data can be used to build an argument about language use, but there is a degree of interpretation involved from the researcher's viewpoint each time we look at data of this kind. This can lead to accusations of bias when looking from the outside, so as researchers we need to use the data to build an evidence base, using frequency as a way into texts.

Frequency is not always the best form of analysis to rely upon in various contexts. In EFL/ESL teaching, for instance, while we can look at a corpus to tell us the most frequent grammatical patterns, these will not always necessarily be the most useful for our learners or the ones we should teach to the exclusion of others (Cook, 1998; Willis, 2001). To take a simple example at the word level, 'pencil' may occur less often than 'the' in any corpus you wish to analyse, but it seems fairly obvious that most EFL/ESL learners will need to know the names of classroom objects such as 'pencil' at a fairly early stage of learning. To give another example, it is intuitive that in terms of **tense** and **aspect**, present simple, used most often to describe habitual actions and facts ('I go shopping every Monday', 'Cats don't like water'), is the most frequent form in English. A search of the BYU-BNC corpus and the GloWbe corpus of internet English across the world (http://corpus2.byu.edu/GloWbe) comparing 'go shopping', 'am/is/are going shopping' and 'went shopping' seems to prove this, as we can see in Table 4.10.

Table 4.10 Frequency of 'go shopping', 'am/is/are going shopping' and 'went shopping' in two corpora

	Pronoun + go shopping		Pronoun + am/is/are going shopping		Pronoun + went shopping	
Corpus	BYU-BNC 100 million words	GloWbe 1.9 billion words	BYU-BNC	GloWbe	BYU-BNC	GloWbe
Total number of occurrences	42	677	12	90	33	478
Occurrences per million words	0.44	0.36	0.12	0.05	0.34	0.25

Although there are more occurrences for all forms in the GloWbe corpus, this is largely because it has a higher total number of words (1.9 billion words, compared with 100 million words) but as the number of occurrences per million words is remarkably similar, we can suggest that this intuition is reliable and 'go shopping', a (present simple) form, is more frequent than 'went shopping', a past simple form, and much more frequent than 'is going shopping', a present progressive form. While it is obvious that learners will need to be taught present simple forms due to their frequency, it does not necessarily follow that this form is the most useful to teach first, or the easiest to acquire in every case. Seminal morpheme order studies in the field of second language acquisition (for example, Brown, 1973; Dulay and Burt, 1974) suggest that the present progressive ('I am working') is acquired much earlier than present simple forms in both L1 and L2 learners. If this is indeed the case, then the higher frequency of present simple forms may not always justify teaching them before present progressive forms.

As we have also noted, frequency is not an absolute concept but must be related to how often patterns occur within particular contexts, texts and corpora. It is, in other words, **register** specific (Biber, 2012). In a general corpus such as the BNC, for example, 'may' is much less frequent than 'would', but in the example Parliamentary Act we have looked at above, 'may' is more frequent than 'would' because it fulfils a specific function in that context. Therefore its frequency is significant in making meaning within that text type. In a literary corpus, 'I must go' may be more frequent than it is in speech because it is used by writers as a demarcation between different points of a text or to mark transition between one piece of the plot and the other. Frequency is also best measured by the number of times a pattern occurs per million words (or the equivalent in a small, focused corpus) rather than a raw frequency score because a higher total number of occurrences may simply be the result of a larger corpus size.

Having acknowledged these limitations, we would still argue that frequency is one very important measure we can use to analyse grammar at the word, sentence and text level. It can be particularly helpful if combined with other types of corpus analysis, which we will describe in Chapters 5 and 6.

Further practice

1   Check the frequency of 'pronoun + need to go' in the BYU-BNC corpus in different contexts of use. What is your intuition about this pattern before you start?
2   Find out the most frequent patterns that come after 'I need to go *' and by using other part of speech tags to investigate the patterns that occur most often after this one.
3   Use LexTutor to check the frequency of keywords in texts and then to investigate the patterns of these keywords. What does this tell you about those particular texts?

References

Bauman, J. (2013). *General service list.* [Online], Available: http://jbauman.com/gsl. html [20 October 2013].

Biber, D., Johansson, S., Leech, G., Conrad, S. and Finegan, E. (1999). *Longman grammar of spoken and written English.* London: Longman.

Biber, D. (2012). Register as a predictor of linguistic variation. *Corpus Linguistics and Linguistic Theory,* 3, 2, 9–37.

Brown, R. (1973). *A first language.* Cambridge, MA: Harvard University Press.

Carter, R. and McCarthy, M. (2006). *Cambridge grammar of English.* Cambridge: Cambridge University Press.

Cobb, T. (2013). *Compleat Lexical Tutor* (LexTutor). [Online], Available: www.lextutor.ca [20 October 2013].

Cook, G. (1998). The uses of reality: a reply to Ronald Carter. *ELT Journal*, 52, 1, 57–63.

Davies, M. (2004). *BYU-BNC* (based on the British National Corpus from Oxford University Press). [Online], Available: http://corpus.byu.edu/bnc [20 October 2013].

Davies, M. (2008). *The corpus of contemporary American English: 450 million words, 1990–present* (COCA). [Online], Available: http://corpus.byu.edu/coca [20 October 2013].

Davies, M. (2013). *Corpus of global web-based English: 1.9 billion words from speakers in 20 countries* (GloWbe). [Online], Available: http://corpus2.byu.edu/GloWbe [20 October 2013].

Dulay, M.C and Burt, M.K. (1974). Natural sequences in child second language acquisition. *Language Learning*, 24, 1, 37–53.

Gov.uk (2015). *Foreign travel advice*. [Online], Available: www.gov.uk/foreign-travel-advice [25 January 2015].

Leech, G., Rayson, P. and Wilson, A. (2001). *Word frequencies in written and spoken English: based on the British National Corpus*. [Online], Available: http://ucrel.lancs.ac.uk/bncfreq/lists/1_2_all_freq.txt [20 October 2013].

The National Archives (2005). *Prevention of Terrorism Act 2005*. [Online], Available: www.legislation.gov.uk/ukpga/2005/2/contents [25 January 2015].

The National Archives (2015). *Under the Open Government License* v2.0. [Online], Available: www.nationalarchives.gov.uk/doc/open-government-licence/version/2 [1 July 2014].

Stubbs, M. (2008). Conrad in the computer: examples of quantitative stylistic analysis, in R. Carter and C. Stockwell (eds.), *The language and literature reader*, London: Routledge, 230–243.

Willis, D. (1990). *The lexical syllabus: a new approach to language teaching*. London: Collins ELT.

Willis, D. (2001). What have the corpus linguists done for us? *International House Journal of Education and Development*, 11, 10–12.

Chapter 5

Chunks and colligation

5.1 Introduction

In Chapter 4, we mentioned how words are often grammaticalised into patterns, which often have particular grammatical features and are of course dictated by context. This chapter will explore these notions further by looking at chunks and colligation.

It is common sense that words do not exist in isolation but cluster together in particular ways to make larger meaningful units of language, and that such clustering is not random but often very formulaic in nature, with each cluster having, in a sense, its own 'in-built' grammar rather than being a simple collection of words. Many learners of second languages experience this when using phrase books, which purport to feature common clusters. Such clusters, it is argued, are retrieved and stored in a speaker's mind as 'wholes' (Wray, 2005), in the same way that we might retrieve single words.

As a concept, this is not new: the notion that language production relies to a great extent on the retrieval of prefabricated chunks was first proposed in the early 1930s (Jackson, 1932; Firth, 1935). These claims were later followed by Hymes (1962) and Fillmore (1979) who proposed terms such as 'collocations' (Firth, 1935) and 'linguistic routines' (Hymes, 1962) to describe such chunks. While it is common to associate terms such as collocation with the analysis of vocabulary, there has also been a long-held notion that we cannot divide language into sections that contain grammar and vocabulary. As we mentioned in Chapters 1 and 2, the notion of lexico-grammar first introduced by Halliday (1961) and Hasan (1987) was further developed by Sinclair (1991, 1996) who proposed that the correlation between syntax and lexis makes it impossible to analyse either of them in isolation, since different words appear to have their own grammar with distinctive collocational, colligational, semantic and pragmatic associations. Sinclair's (1991, 1996) model of language further emphasised the formulaic nature of language production where the majority of spoken and written texts are constructed and can be interpreted using the idiom principle, not the open-choice principle. As we described in Chapter 2, the idiom principle simply means that speakers and writers construct much language

Tad:	Well, <u>hey there</u>, you.
Dixie:	This is Kathy.
Tad:	Oh, yeah, I know. We're old friends. So, you need any quarters from me?
Kathy:	I'm not full of quarters.
Tad:	Are you sure? Are you sure that you wouldn't fib me, huh? (long-narrative) #
Julia:	You spoke with Dr. Martin?
Linda:	<u>Nice guy</u>. He left out the important part. Got it. I don't have much time. I'm going to die. #(long-narrative) #
Tad:	<u>I was wondering</u> if I could get a moment alone with you
Dixie:	Sure. Jamie: You guys smell cupcakes?
Kathy:	Cupcakes!
Jamie:	Oh. Well, hey, <u>let's take a break</u> and <u>go check it out.</u> What do you say?
Tad:	Bring me back one.
Jamie:	Oh. <u>Come here</u>, buddy.
Dixie:	Yeah, well, one for him, a dozen for me.
Jamie:	Oh. Tad: <u>That'd be nice</u>.
Kathy:	One for me. Nothing for him.
Dixie:	Oh, you

Figure 5.1 Sample *All My Children* dialogue

by adding together chunks of language, rather than creating language from the 'open choice' of syntax, each time they speak or write. Therefore, much language production comes 'pre-packaged' as words that cluster together in particular sequences, with their own particular grammatical properties.

If we look at a short section of script from a popular American soap opera, *All My Children*, taken from the Corpus of American Soap Operas (http://corpus2.byu.edu/soap), we can see this in action, with some possible chunks underlined. These are based, at this stage, purely on intuition.

If we accept that some of the samples underlined are likely to be chunks, it is fairly simple to show how such chunks often have their own 'in-built' grammar, by looking at the example 'I was wondering' from the text above. If we explore 'was wondering' through the BYU-BNC corpus as a whole by searching for 'Pronoun + was wondering + *', we can see that it is not simply

Table 5.1 Five most common patterns with 'was wondering' in the BYU-BNC

Patterns	Number of occurrences in total Whole corpus	Mutual Information score
I was wondering + if	59	MI = 5.20
I was wondering + ,	17	MI = 3.52
I was wondering + whether	14	MI = 6.34
I was wondering + about	11	MI = 3.63
I was wondering + how	11	MI = 4.24

a manipulation of a past continuous form but that in fact both 'I' and 'if' are far more likely to co-occur than other possible combinations such as 'she was wondering what', which has only seven occurrences in the whole spoken corpus. When we look at these patterns in the whole corpus, we can also see from the Mutual Information (MI) scores that the strongest collocate with 'I was wondering' is 'whether', despite its lower frequency.

This tendency for language to cluster together in predictable ways has led some researchers to term such examples as 'formulaic sequences' (e.g. Schmitt, 2004), while others have used terms such as 'chunks' and 'lexical bundles' (O'Keeffe et al., 2007; Biber et al., 1999). For the purpose of this chapter, we will use the term 'chunks'. Defining a chunk is not without problems (as we shall discuss later), but for the purposes of this chapter, we will adopt Wray's (2005: 9) definition (she used the term 'formulaic sequence'):

> A formulaic sequence is a sequence, continuous or discontinuous, of words or other elements, which is, or appears to be, prefabricated: that is, stored and retrieved whole from memory at the time of use, rather than being subject to generation or analysis by the language grammar.

If we take the short *All My Children* text above as an example, and look at such a text using the corpus analysis tool LexTutor, we can see a simple example of this. This is purely illustrative, as clearly we would normally wish to look at much larger databases than a single text. The computer searches for 'strings' of words it finds in common co-occurrence and does not have the capacity to decide whether these are what we might normally recognise as meaningful units, as we can see in the five-word clusters found below. To undertake such a search, look at the section of LexTutor (www.lextutor.ca) marked 'NGrams' and click 'submit' on the text pasted within the box.

We can of course intuitively suggest what may come after each chunk, such as 'Are you sure that you mean *that*?', but some chunks such as 'a moment alone with you' seem, at first glance, slightly fragmentary and hard to assign a clear function to. This is of course because a computer programme such as LexTutor simply searches for N-Grams or words that form a sequence in a text.

Table 5.2 Sample five-word chunks identified by LexTutor from *All My Children* dialogue

A BREAK AND GO CHECK
A MOMENT ALONE WITH YOU
ARE YOU SURE THAT YOU
HEY LET'S TAKE A BREAK
I WAS WONDERING IF I

While chunks show us the co-occurrence of words into patterns, colligation can tell us more about the 'in-built' grammar of a cluster. It has been defined by Hoey (2000: 234) as 'the grammatical company a word keeps and the positions it prefers'. Hoey (2005: 43) has also added to this definition as follows:

> The basic idea of colligation is that just as a lexical item may be primed to co-occur with another lexical item, so also it may be primed to occur in or with a particular grammatical function. Alternatively, it may be primed to avoid appearance in or co-occurrence with a particular grammatical function.

In other words, colligation can help to tell us more about a particular pattern by showing us more about its grammar; for example, the word classes it co-occurs with or the tense and aspect it seems to most commonly be used with. It can also tell us about how it may function in clauses and utterances, as for example a subject or object or in mid or final position. Such information can give us a clearer picture of a chunk because we can see the patterns as having distinctive grammatical properties and this can thus be more clearly described as lexico-grammar.

To take a simple example, let us look briefly at the chunk 'at the end of the day'. There is evidence that this is highly frequent in at least native speaker spoken corpora. Adolphs and Carter (2013: 31), for example, show that this is the most frequent six-word cluster (as they term it) in the spoken section of the BNC and in a conversational context. This is likely to be because of its use as a summariser or pause marker, as well as its propositional use as a time adverbial. If we search for this chunk in the BYU-BNC spoken corpus (using the BYU-BNC interface (http://corpus.byu.edu/bnc/), we find 332 occurrences, or 33.1 per million words. If we briefly look at the concordances produced, we can find the following colligation patterns:

1   There is a strong tendency for the chunk to be turn initial or medial, rather than at the end of a turn.
2   In terms of its function in clauses, it acts as an adjunct because it adds additional information to the utterance and it is optional.
3   If we search for the chunk and check which pronouns it is followed by, in terms of pronouns, it is most commonly followed (in order of frequency) by 'you' (23) 'it' (20) and 'I' (18) and there are no occurrences of the chunk followed by 'he' or 'she'.
4   The most common types of verb phrase in the thirty-two examples of 'at the end of the day you' (which includes 'you've' etc, hence the higher number than simply 'you') following this pattern are modal or semi-modal verbs (15), for example 'at the end of the day you've got to/you have to/you'll'.

Figure 5.2 shows some examples of this.

1	to myself what a waste of a day. Cos	**at the end of the day**	you've worked hard and you ain't earned nothing that day
2	I'm not a yes man.	**At the end of the day**	you'll flatly refuse to do a job if you don't
3	When your feet are all swollen	**at the end of the day**	you'll find them too tight.
4	And	**at the end of the day**	you would be into relating what people do in their job descriptions
5	okay, so we have to look on the positive side, if at	**the end of the day**	you're going to get to a situation where,
6	They invest them in various ways and	**at the end of the day**	you can use that erm policy to actually top up your pension

Figure 5.2 'At the end of the day' in the BYU-BNC spoken corpus

It is hoped then that in this chapter, we can illustrate what chunks and colligation can tell us about the grammatical patterning of texts at word, sentence and text level. We will analyse language in this chapter by first looking at chunks and then colligations before bringing both together.

5.2 Finding chunks in corpora

Some open-access corpora provide us with frequency data about chunks of different sizes, with the largest generally agreed to be six words. This in itself can be very helpful, as our intuitions may not always be correct about which chunks are more frequent than others.

To test this, we will look briefly at the HKCSE (http://langbank.engl. polyu.edu.hk/HKCSE). This is a spoken corpus of approximately a million words, gathered from business, academic, public and conversational speech in Hong Kong. As such, it gives us a window into the way English is used in this context by native and non-native speakers, where the chunks used may differ significantly from British native speaker corpora such as the BNC. Looking at chunks used by speakers in this context can help us to see how different varieties of English are used, in this case in a spoken form.

Sample exercise

Based on your intuition, put the following two-word chunks (from the HKCSE) in order of frequency from 1–10. The results are displayed in Table 5.3.

So yeah
Okay so
Hong Kong
Okay yeah
Right yeah

Know so
One two
Know yeah
Don't know
Oh yeah

Table 5.3 Frequency of two-word chunks in HCKSE
(http://rcpce.engl.polyu.edu.hk/HKCSE/CG2_A-Z_EXCL_cutoff10.htm)

1	Hong Kong (2364)
2	Don't know (710)
3	Okay so (321)
4	Oh yeah (180)
5	Right yeah (86)
6	One two (66)
7	Okay yeah (53)
8	Know so (42)
9	Know yeah (42)
10	So yeah (24)

It is worth noting that these results are based upon the 'concgrams' given here (http://rcpce.engl.polyu.edu.hk/HKCSE/CG2_A-Z_EXCL_cutoff10. htm) but differ slightly because they are based purely on the number of occurrences of the chunk, rather than the co-occurring words, as listed in HCKSE data. Once we have this type of data, it is worth making a comparison between the HCKSE and another spoken corpus, to look for possible differences and similarities of use. In this case, we will look again at the spoken section of the BNC, using the BYU-BNC. While this is a much larger corpus, it contains both scripted and unscripted data, as the HCKSE does, so it is reasonably comparable.

Try it yourself 5.1

Predict the frequency of the chunks given given in Table 5.3 (from the HKCSE) in the BNC spoken corpus. Which do you think will be more frequent, less frequent or of similar frequency?

You can check your intuition by using the 'search' tool in the BYU-BNC (http://corpus.byu.edu/bnc) and looking for each chunk in turn, within the spoken section of the corpus. The corpus will give you the number of occurrences of each chunk in total and per million words and these are displayed in Table 5.3. HCKSE contains just short of a million words so the raw frequencies show the occurrences per million words. Note that contracted forms such as 'don't know' need to be typed in to the BNC corpus as follows 'do n't', 'ca n't' etc.

If we wish to find out why differences in the use of chunks in these different corpora may occur, we need to look at the chunk in context. We can do this simply by typing it into the search window and looking at concordances of the word. Let us first consider 'okay so'. Examine the concordances from the HCKSE in Figure 5.3 and try to decide why this chunk is being used.

1	for example three A you have Mary likes that nice dog	**okay so**	a dog we're looking not (.) at itself but (.) where (.)
2	only say that adjective can occur in this position (.)	**okay so**	a lot of things can occur here but things occurring here
3	* started already yeah A: ** started already A: *	**okay so**	a: ** yes a: yes er (.) in fact er th this colleague
4	there's a few of us having a meeting (.) so yeah it's	**okay so**	a1: pick a number B: yeah er (.) H__'s doing the
5	y bye bye W__ b: ** bye bye B: ((laugh)) C025 B:	**okay so**	a1: so B: we're on again a1: yes running again now i
6	B: ** yes mhm in the morning (pause) a1:	**okay so**	actually do you have any idea which hotel would you like
7	three M will award those who are very innovative (.)	**okay so**	again these are the stories (.) okay then the next thing
8	with the virus infections that are spread by droplets	**okay so**	all the evidence we that we have points to the fact that
9	a1: so you're talking about meaning b1: yeah a1:	**okay so**	all the while I tried to you know discourage you to use
10	ermine the bearing from A to point P ((pause)) b1:	**okay so**	and also we've got (.) er angle B here and bearing BA

Figure 5.3 'Okay so' in the HCKSE

Some observations you may have made are that this chunk has a primarily discourse-marking function in these extracts. It seems to serve a purpose of organising talk by, for example, summarising or reiterating a point being made. It can also be used to launch a new topic or section of the conversation. Clicking on a concordance line above gives us the chunk in a wider context, as the following examples show:

Topic launching

> **okay so** a dog we're looking not (.) at itself but (.) where (.) or what kind of neighbours can dog take (.) okay so in this sentence which is a good sentence you have Mary likes that nice dog (.) so you have nice and dog together (.) and for example in three B (.) that dog is my pet

Summarising

> you first no not question er your answer remember what you said because house is an action it indicates action b1: it indicate actions that a1: so

you're talking about meaning b1: yeah a1: **okay so** all the while I tried to you know discourage you to use meaning to identify word class (.) um for example um typical example is the word hug (.) kick okay it's action but give me a hug (.) so is that a verb b1: no a1: why not it's an action ((laugh)) according to your definition b1: but give is the only action

While these uses also occur in native speaker corpora (for example, O'Keeffe et al., 2007), it is worth considering why this chunk is more frequent in the Hong Kong data. There are a number of possibilities:

1   Non-native speakers may have a greater need to organise their talk 'online' as they process and formulate language.
2   The make-up of the HCKSE has a number of spoken texts from contexts that may encourage more discourse marking such as classroom talk and speeches, where there may be a greater need to explicitly mark the boundaries of talk than in casual conversation.
3   Because of the high frequency of both 'okay' and 'so', users of English as a second language may quickly pick up on 'okay so' and use it in preference to alternatives such as 'right' to summarise.

As discussed in Chapter 2, it is also possible to make our own corpora and search them for common chunks using the freeware 'AntConc' (Anthony, 2013) (www.antlab.sci.waseda.ac.jp/software.html). AntConc allows us to upload texts of our own and then analyse them for word frequency, collocations and chunks, amongst other things. We will focus here on using the tool to identify chunks, which as we noted are termed 'N-Grams'. The way we can do this is to open up AntConc and then upload a file of our chosen text(s), as a plain text file. This can simply be done by clicking on 'file' and then importing a file you choose. There are screenshots of these procedures given on the website for the software. Once you have the file available, click on the 'clusters/NGrams' tab and then the 'NGrams' box. Once you have done this, you then have a choice of setting a cutoff point for the minimum frequency and range of each chunk. Although there is no absolute consensus on what this should be, it is generally considered that five occurrences per million words is a reasonable figure and we can adjust this for corpora of fewer words. We can also set a minimum and maximum N-Gram size. The literature suggests that the minimum size should obviously be two and the maximum six (O'Keeffe et al., 2007), after which point there seem to be very few recognisable chunks.

Let us look at an example. Jones and Horak (2014) explored a small corpus of scripts from the popular UK soap opera 'EastEnders'. This was close to 60,000 words of data, from a number of years and episodes of the TV show.

Try it yourself 5.2

What would you predict are the most common three and four-word chunks in the corpus, which occurred a minimum of five times? Contracted forms ('don't', 'can't' etc) were counted as one word. The answers can be found in the back of the book.

Try the same process yourself on a series of texts you have collected. The easiest way to gather a collection of texts is by using written internet files, made into plain text. Predict what you think the most common three and four-word chunks will be and then use AntConc to check. What does this tell you about the language used in the texts?

A criticism of N-Grams, which we have mentioned, is of course that they do not always produce syntactically or semantically 'whole' phrases. This is certainly true, at least at first glance, if we look at the data from the EastEnders corpus. 'You want me to', for example, does not seem to be a 'whole' chunk, and neither does 'a bit of a'. This may of course be because they act as frames for other items to fill e.g. 'do you want me to go' or 'it's a bit of a problem'. This means that the researcher is faced with a choice about whether to discount certain chunks that seem fragmentary, even though there is no evidence that a chunk such as 'a bit of a' is processed any differently than 'at the end of the day'. If we are to do this, then it is perhaps worth producing two lists of chunks: those that have been 'tidied up' and those that have not. It is also then important to explain the methods behind discounting chunks as fragmentary. If we search a corpus for N-Grams, we then have to apply a set of subjective criteria to those extracted. We might ask teachers of EFL/ESL to rate an initial sample of N-Grams. Simpson-Vlatch and Ellis (2010: 12) undertook such a process when compiling a list of academic chunks (the academic formulas list). They asked teachers to evaluate N-Grams by considering the following questions:

1   Do you think the phrase constitutes 'a formulaic expression, or fixed phrase, or chunk'?
2   Do you think the phrase has 'a cohesive meaning or functions, as a phrase'?
3   Do you think the phrase was 'worth teaching, as a bona fide phrase or expression'?

Simpson-Vlatch and Ellis used the results from these questions as part of the process they undertook when deciding which chunks to use on their final list. This resulted in a set of chunks aimed at being of most help to English for academic purposes (EAP) teachers, which were partly based on frequency and partly upon MI scores. Martinez and Schmitt (2012) give a range of other criteria that could be applied to such a process but admit that there is a fair degree of subjectivity involved. Therefore, if a researcher decides to undertake such a process, the principles must be made clear and we need to accept that it is not easy to exclude chunks that at first may seem fragmentary.

Another criticism of N-Grams is perhaps that only looking at how words cluster together does not tell us much about their in-built grammar. To do this, as we have mentioned, we also need to examine chunks in terms of their colligational patterns because by looking at both together we can show how language is often formulated in particular grammatical patterns. It is this we move on to in section 5.3.

5.3 Finding colligation patterns in corpora

As we noted in section 5.2, the chunk 'don't know' has been shown to be highly frequent in native speaker usage (for example, O'Keeffe et al., 2007). This is because it can answer a proposition but also act as a hedged answer. A speaker may be deliberately vague to sound less assertive, reduce an imposition on others or protect the face of others. It is also the case that 'don't know' is not just a random chunk but in spoken language at least has its own 'in-built' grammar. We can discover how it is patterned by looking at the chunk within the BYU-BNC.

Sample exercise

Using the BYU-BNC spoken corpus, conduct a search for 'don't know'. Using the part of speech tags, click on all pronouns before 'don't know' and * following 'don't know'.

You should find (in list view) the following results:

1   'Don't know' is most commonly preceded by 'I', which occurs with by far the highest frequency.
2   The most common words that follow 'I don't know' are 'what' 'whether' and 'if'.
3   The fact that it is also (most frequently) followed by a full stop suggests that it is most commonly used at the end of a turn or as a complete turn in itself.

These results are displayed in Tables 5.4 and 5.5.

Table 5.4 Results from the BYU-BNC spoken corpus for 'pronoun + don't know'

Rank	Pronoun + don't know	Number of occurrences	Number of occurrences per million words
I	I DON'T KNOW	6998	702.35
2	YOU DON'T KNOW	518	51.99
3	WE DON'T KNOW	303	30.41
4	THEY DON'T KNOW	175	17.56
5	HE DON'T KNOW	31	3.11

Table 5.5 Patterns following 'I don't know' in the BYU-BNC

Rank	Pattern	Number of occurrences	Number of occurrences per million words
1	I DON'T KNOW	1292	129.67
2	I DON'T KNOW WHAT	890	89.32
3	I DON'T KNOW,	838	84.11
4	I DON'T KNOW WHETHER	595	59.72
5	I DON'T KNOW IF	448	44.96

This provides us with clear information about colligational patterns in this spoken corpus. The next step is to find more information about this chunk.

Use the search function in the BYU-BNC spoken corpus to find whether 'I don't know' is more common than 'I didn't know' in the spoken corpus. This will give us some information about the most likely tense for this pattern. Then conduct a search for 'I don't know what' and what most often comes after the word 'what'. This will tell us how we may expect it to be patterned. Finally, search for 'I don't know' followed by a full stop and comma, and find examples of where it seems to come at the end of a turn and the start of a turn. Click on the concordance lines to find these examples. Once you have done this, look at some of the results summarised in Table 5.6.

5.4 What can chunks and colligation tell us about language use?

Chunks and colligation can give us vital information about how a text is patterned. We can use quantitative measures to understand the most frequent patterning of texts and this will give us vital information about how they make meaning. Let us look at the example of a political speech because the common chunks and colligations can give us an interesting view of how politicians wish to shape their message.

Try it yourself 5.3

Locate the following conference speech by Ed Miliband in 2013 at www.britishpoliticalspeech.org/speech-archive.htm.

Read through it and try to notice what chunks seem to occur often and what colligation pattern they occur in. Use the example of 'don't know' in section 5.3 as an example. Then paste the text into a Word document and convert to plain text, and use the AntConc software to generate a frequency

Table 5.6 Colligation patterns with 'I don't know' in the BYU-BNC spoken corpus

Results	Data	Conclusion
'I don't know' is more frequent than 'I didn't know'	There are 647 occurrences of 'I didn't know' in comparison to 7004 occurrences of 'I don't know'	This pattern is far more likely to occur in a present form than a past form in this spoken corpus
'I don't know what' is most often followed by 'it' and 'is' Other patterns following 'I don't what it' include 'was' and 's' There are no discernible patterns in this data beyond 'I don't know what it is'	There are 112 occurrences of 'it' following 'I don't know what' and 37 occurrences of 'is' following 'I don't know what it'	The most common discernible pattern in this spoken corpus is 'I don't what it is'. 'I don't what it' also acts as a frame, which can also be filled with other words such as 'was'
'I don't know' occurs more often followed by a full stop than a comma. These uses are predominantly at the end of a turn or as one complete turn in themselves when answering a question. 'I don't know what it is' occurs more often followed by a comma than a full stop	'I don't know' followed by a full stop occurs 1293 times, and followed by a comma 838 times There are 12 occurrences of 'I don't know what it is' followed by a comma and 6 followed by a full stop	It is more likely that 'I don't know' occurs at the end of a turn or as a turn in itself, than at the start of one in this spoken corpus. It seems more likely that 'I don't what it is' will occur in the middle of a turn than at the start of one

list of three and four-word N-Grams that occur at least ten times. After this, search the BYU-BNC corpus for a comparison of the frequency of the most common chunks in each data set. You should find the results given in the answer key.

It is also worth investigating further how the most common chunks in this speech are patterned to discover what this can tell us about the intentions behind it. The first way we can do this is by examining how these two chunks are patterned. To do this, simply click on the concordance line for each and look to the left and right of each chunk to uncover what type of word or words occur before and after each. You should find the following predominant patterns:

Table 5.7 Predominant colligation patterns with 'do better than this' and 'race to the top'

Better than this	Race to the top
Britain + Modal (can) + do + better than this + full stop	(to) Win + determiner (the/a/) + race to the top + main clause
Functions:	Functions:
Subject + Predicator + Complement	Predicator + Object

This suggests that 'do better than this' is used in this speech predominantly as part of an intact clause and in terms of its function acts as a complement to the verb phrase within the clause. Its time reference is both 'all time' and also to the future as it refers to a possibility that Britain can indeed improve. 'Race to the top' is used predominantly in a subordinate clause, which is understood in its relation to the main clause which follows it, as in the example 'to win the race to the top, we've got to call a halt to the race to the bottom'. The chunk acts as the object of the verb phrase 'win' and its time reference again is the general present and future so that winning the race to the top is universally important and also something that needs to happen in the future.

Finally, we may wish to understand the extent to which in Hoey's (2000, 2005) terms these chunks are 'primed' to occur in texts of this sort. Hoey's argument is that certain chunks are far more likely to occur in certain texts and fulfil certain functions than others. He gives a simple example that 'in winter' is primed to occur in travel texts while 'during the winter months' is primed to occur in gardening texts.

To do this, it is worth looking at several political speeches and comparing their use with that of other corpora. To undertake this, combine the Ed Miliband speech with those of Nick Clegg and David Cameron from the same year. These are available here: www.britishpoliticalspeech.org/speech-archive.htm.

Once you have combined these into one plain text file, you have a small corpus of 19,857 words. This does not, of course, provide us with information about all political speeches or indeed all the speeches made by these politicians, but it does give us a way to analyse their concerns while addressing their parties at this point in time.

Once the file is uploaded, click on the wordlist tool. You should see that the first 'content' word that appears is 'people', which has 165 occurrences or 0.83% of the corpus. In the BNC as a whole, there are 119,936 occurrences of the word and 21,289 of these come from the spoken corpus, making up 0.21% of the corpus. It is therefore worth investigating how this word may be primed into certain patterns in these speeches and comparing this with the BNC spoken corpus. We can first look for collocates of 'people' by clicking on the 'collocates' tool in AntConc and setting the minimum number of collocates to '5' and narrowing the search to '1L'; that is, only the words that come immediately before 'people'. We can look in the BYU-BNC spoken and newspaper corpora in the same way by searching for adj + people. The results show, not surprisingly, that there are a number of adjectives used before the term but that these do differ between the two corpora. The results of the most frequent items can be seen in Table 5.8.

Table 5.8 Adjective collocates for 'people' in political speeches and a general spoken corpus

BNC spoken corpus (9,963,693 words) adjectives before 'people'	BNC newspaper corpus (10,466,422 words) adjectives before 'people'	Political speeches corpus (19,857 words) adjectives used before 'people'
Other (837)	Young (544)	Young (16)
Young (277)	Other (305)	British (11)
Old (113)	Local (271)	Hardworking (7)

These results suggest that 'people' is primed to co-occur with 'young' in all sets of data, but more strongly primed to co-occur in the political speeches and the newspaper data as it makes up 0.085% of the political data, 0.005% of the newspaper data and only 0.0027% of the BNC spoken corpus data. A log-likelihood comparison of the occurrences in the political speech corpus in comparison with the newspaper data gives a score of (+) 57.37, showing that this usage is statistically highly significant ($p<0.0001$).

By examining concordances, we can also explore how 'young people' may be primed differently in the different corpora, according to how it functions in the clause. As a noun phrase, it is possible for 'young people' to act as subject, object or complement and if there is a particular preference for it to function in a particular way, this tells us about its colligation. To undertake this analysis, examine the concordance lines from the political speech data and compare with the first thirty from each BNC corpus. This is not intended to be a comprehensive analysis but it will give an indication of how 'young people' is primed in each corpus and similarities between them. Table 5.9 shows the results from each corpus.

Table 5.9 'Young people' as subject, object or complement in three corpora

'Young people'	BNC spoken corpus (9,963,693 words) adjectives before 'people'	BNC newspaper corpus (10,466,422 words) adjectives before 'people'	Political speeches corpus (19,857 words) adjectives used before 'people'
Subject	11	10	7
Object	8	12	7
Complement	11	7	2
Adjunct	0	1	0

This analysis allows us to suggest the following:

1   'Young people' is primed in each corpus not to appear as part of an adjunct.
2   In the political speeches and newspaper data, it is more likely to be primed to occur as a subject or object (young people doing something or having something done to them).
3   In the spoken corpus, 'young people' is more strongly primed to occur as a subject or a complement to modify or add something to the ongoing discourse.

Corpus analysis alone in this case does not tell us why a particular chunk operates in a certain way within a text, but it does give us a starting point for a more qualitative analysis. Naturally, if we wished to make more definitive statements about the speeches of this or other politicians, we would need to gather a number of texts, perhaps from the same year, and use these to illustrate how chunks and colligation are used to build arguments in speeches.

5.5 Bringing the analysis together

To illustrate how chunks and colligation can be used in a research project to analyse particular genres, we will now look at examples of 'was wondering' again. We will again start from the word level and move upwards to the sentence and text levels. Such investigations are often driven by particular research questions so in this case we will look at the number of propositions before examining the data further.

Assumptions to be tested:

(i)   'Wondering' will form into common chunks such as 'I was wondering' and 'I was wondering if'
(ii) These chunks will occur more often in spoken texts than they do in web texts
(iii) 'I was wondering' will more commonly be used in English in first language contexts than in contexts where English may be used as a second language.

To carry out this investigation, we will work with the BYU-BNC spoken corpus and also the GloWbe web corpus (http://corpus2.byu.edu/GloWbe).

Assumption 1: 'Wondering' will form into common chunks such as 'I was wondering' and 'I was wondering if'

The first search is to simply type 'wondering' into the search bar with * before and after the word for both corpora. In list view, we then get an idea of the most common words that proceed and come after this word. The results should be as follows:

Table 5.10 Common chunks with 'wondering' in spoken and web corpora

BNC spoken corpus (9,963,693 words)	GloWbe web corpus (1.9 billion words)
just wondering (85)	was wondering (9458)
was wondering (79)	just wondering (5439)
'm wondering (40)	'm wondering (4199)
're wondering (14)	, wondering (3848)
be wondering (18)	and wondering (3113)
I was wondering (76)	I was wondering (7567)
I'm just wondering (43)	I was wondering if (3435)
I was just wondering (29)	I was just wondering (1339)
I was wondering if (23)	I'm just wondering (843)

This data seems to suggest that wondering does indeed cluster around 'I' and 'was' but it is also interesting to note the frequency of just, and its use as a 'softener' in both contexts, to mitigate against the imposition of a request. The following examples show this usage:

1	Might the (pause) Mr Chairman	**I was just wondering if**	it's worth just mentioning that the, since the Redhill Airport proposal which
2	Right I	**I was just wondering if**	they would i-- if they would like us to suggest a tie break
3		**I was just wondering if**	I could change the timetable of my visit but it isn't important . . .
4	Right on about Leif.	**I was just wondering if**	I can get college credit.

Figure 5.4 Samples of 'I was just wondering'

It is also interesting to note that it is more frequent in a present form in the spoken corpus than the web corpus. This may reflect the immediacy of speech and the need to comment upon ongoing thoughts and experiences.

Assumption 2: These chunks will occur more often in spoken texts than they do in web texts

As noted in Chapter 4, the best measure of frequency is to assess occurrences per million words, rather than the raw number of occurrences. These are shown in bold after the raw frequencies in brackets below. Where the chunks are identical, the log-likelihood scores are also shown, with a plus or minus indicating whether there is overuse in the BNC corpus or the GloWbe corpus, for ease of reference.

Table 5.11 Frequency of chunks in spoken and web corpora

BNC spoken corpus (9,963,693 words)	GloWbe web corpus (1.9 billion words)	Log-likelihood
I was wondering (76) **7.63**	I was wondering (7567) **4.02**	(+)249.27
I'm just wondering (43) **4.32**	I was wondering if (3435) **1.82**	
I was just wondering (29) **2.91**	I was just wondering (1339) **0.71**	(+) 37.95
I was wondering if (23) **2.31**	I'm just wondering (843) **0.45**	

These frequency counts suggest that overall, Assumption 2 is correct. Chunks around 'was wondering' do occur with greater frequency in a spoken corpus, suggesting that the form is more likely to occur in spoken contexts and as we have discovered, the most important colligating patterns are that it will co-occur with 'I' and with 'if'.

Assumption 3. It will more commonly be used in English in first language contexts than in contexts where English may be used as a second language

To check this assumption, simply type 'I was wondering' into the search in the GloWbe corpus and click on the 'chart' view. You will then see results from a number of English-speaking countries, which are compared in Table 5.12.

Table 5.12 'I was wondering' in web-based corpora across the world

Corpus	Number of occurrences and occurrences per million words
British National Corpus (spoken section) **(9,963,693 words)**	(76) **7.63**
GloWbe (Singapore) **(42,974,705 words)**	(347) **8.07**
GloWbe (Malaysia) **(41,643,730 words)**	(211) **5.07**
GloWbe (Philippines) **(43,248,407 words)**	(248) **5.73**
GloWbe (UK) **(387,615,074 words)**	(1674) **4.32**
	Log-likelihood comparison
Singapore and the UK	(+) 97.84
Malaysia and the UK	(+) 4.59
Philippines and the UK	(+) 16.18

This suggests that, contrary to expectations, on the web at least, this form is slightly more frequent in web-based corpora where English is used as a second language, if we take the number of occurrences per million words as the key measurement. The log-likelihood comparisons show that when we compare the overall occurrences in relation to the size of each corpus, these differences are significant. It is worth considering why this may be the case. Perhaps web users in English as a first language context find less need to use this form and are more direct on the web? Perhaps it has been over-taught as a form to those using English as a second language? A detailed look at the concordances would need to be undertaken to uncover the reason for this, but nevertheless it is an interesting initial finding and can point the way forward to other research.

5.6 Limitations

We have noted above that there are some limitations when we extract chunks and colligations from corpora. The biggest issue is that a corpus does not always extract chunks that are syntactically whole. We are there-fore faced with a decision about whether we wish to edit lists down to only those chunks that seem to be formulaic and have some propositional or pragmatic meaning. This is not a simple task and does require a certain degree of subjectivity because it is not entirely clear whether a chunk such as 'I mean I' is processed any differently in the mind to 'I mean'. It can also be difficult, in some cases, to say what the boundaries of any one chunk are. Although it is generally acknowledged that chunks are not normally longer than six words (O'Keeffe et al., 2007), it can at times be difficult to decide what constitutes a chunk. To take the example of 'I know what you mean', if we look at the BYU-BNC spoken corpus and search for this chunk we can see that 'yeah' occurs before it in a lot of cases. Does this then suggest that 'yeah, I know what you mean' is one chunk or that it is better described as '____ I know what you mean' with 'yeah', 'yes' and 'oh' often filling the slot? Again, this is largely a subjective decision we need to make.

When we are looking at colligations, there is also a certain degree of qualitative and subjective analysis involved. A tagged corpus can give us all the patterns around chunks such as 'don't know', but it is the researcher who needs to look closely at the data and see how the chunk operates within and across turns. And as with any frequency count across different types of texts, it cannot tell us why a pattern occurs so often. This is the job of us as researchers. As we have noted, data can be used to build an argument about language use but there is a degree of interpretation involved from the researcher's viewpoint each time we look at data of this kind.

Further practice

1   Download and build a small corpus of texts of conference speeches by a political leader or different political leaders. Analyse the chunks used with the AntConc freeware tool. How do the chunks colligate? How do

they function in each context and what do they tell us about the political speaker?

2   Find out the most frequent patterns centred on a common word such as 'think' in spoken and written texts, using the BYU-BNC corpus. What grammatical patterns can you find for this word? How do they differ according to the text type?

References

Adolphs, S. and Carter, R. (2013). *Spoken corpus linguistics: from monomodal to multimodal.* London: Routledge.

Anthony, L. (2013). *AntConc* (version 3.3.5). [Online], Available: www.antlab.sci. waseda.ac.jp/software.html [1 November 2013].

Biber, D., Johansson, S., Leech, G., Conrad, S. and Finegan, E. (1999). *Longman grammar of spoken and written English.* London: Longman.

British Political Speech (2014). *Speech archive.* [Online], Available: www.britishpoliticalspeech.org/speech-archive.htm [6 July 2014].

Cobb, T. (2013). *Compleat Lexical Tutor* (LexTutor). [Online], Available: www.lextutor.ca [20 October 2013].

Davies, M. (2004). *BYU-BNC* (based on the British National Corpus from Oxford University Press). [Online], Available: http://corpus.byu.edu/bnc [20 October 2013].

Davies, M. (2012). *Corpus of American Soap Operas: 100 million words 2001–2012.* [Online], Available: http://corpus2.byu.edu/soap [1 July 2014].

Davies, M. (2013). *Corpus of global web-based English: 1.9 billion words from speakers in 20 countries* (GloWbe). [Online], Available: http://corpus2.byu.edu/GloWbe [20 July 2013].

Fillmore, C.J. (1979). On fluency, in C.J. Fillmore, D. Kempler and W.S.Y. Wang (eds.) *Individual differences in language ability and language behaviour.* New York: Academic Press, 85–101.

Firth, J.R. (1935). The technique of semantics: transactions of the Philological Society, in J.R Firth (ed.) *Papers in linguistics.* London: Oxford University Press, 7–33.

Halliday, M.A.K. (1961). Categories of the theory of grammar. *Word,* 17, 3, 241–292.

Hasan, R. (1987). The grammarian's dream: lexis as most delicate grammar, in M.A.K. Halliday and R.P. Fawcett (eds.) *New developments in system linguistics.* Amsterdam: Frances Pinter Publishers, 184–211.

Hoey, M. (2000). *Textual interaction: an introduction to written discourse analysis.* London: Routledge.

Hoey, M. (2005). *Lexical priming: a new theory of words and language.* London: Routledge.

Hymes, D. (1962). The ethnography of speaking, in T. Gladwin and W.C. Sturtevant (eds.) *Anthropology and human behaviour.* Washington, DC: Anthropological Society of Washington, 5, 13–53.

Jackson, J.H. (1932). *Selected writings, vol. II.* New York: Basic Books.

Jones, C. and Horak, T. (2014). Leave it out! The use of soap operas as models of spoken discourse in the ELT classroom. *The Journal of Language Teaching and Learning,* 4, 3, 1–14.

Leech, G., Rayson, P. and Wilson, A. (2001). *Word frequencies in written and spoken English: based on the British National Corpus.* [Online], Available: http://ucrel. lancs.ac.uk/bncfreq/lists/1_2_all_freq.txt [20 October 2013].

Martinez, R. and Schmitt, N. (2012). A phrasal expressions list. *Applied Linguistics,* 3, 3, 299–320.

O'Keeffe, A., McCarthy, M. and Carter, R. (2007). *From corpus to classroom.* Cambridge: Cambridge University Press.

Schmitt, N. (ed.) (2004). *Formulaic sequences: acquisition, processing, and use.* Amsterdam: John Benjamins Press.

Simpson-Vlatch, R. and Ellis, N.C. (2010). An academic formulas list: new methods in phraseology research. *Applied Linguistics,* 21, 4, 487–512.

Sinclair, J. (1991). *Corpus, concordance, collocation: describing English language.* Oxford: Oxford University Press.

Sinclair, J. (1996). The search for units of meaning. *Textus: English Studies in Italy,* 9, 75–106.

Wray, A. (2005). *Formulaic language and the lexicon.* Cambridge: Cambridge University Press.

Chapter 6

Semantic prosody

6.1 Introduction

Semantic prosody (sometimes termed 'discourse prosody') is the concept that certain forms carry with them positive, negative or neutral shadings. The notion that language carries connotations is well established in relation to lexis. If you consider the word 'skinny' when it is applied to someone ('he looks really skinny!'), it clearly has a negative shading when contrasted with the word 'slim'. Those working with lexis have long argued that the concept of synonyms is a tricky one for precisely this kind of reason; we could argue that 'slim' and 'skinny' are synonyms in that they mean the same thing, but clearly the words carry different meanings when they are actually used. The same principle, that language carries connotations, applies to grammatical structures. Consider the two examples below.

1   I added the potassium to the water.
2   The potassium was added to the water.

When learning how to write up experiments at school, children are often taught to use the language found in the second example, rather than the first one. The removal of the subject or agent from the description often strikes children as being strange, as they were the one who carried out the action, but as we get older we recognise it as a particular form of discourse and that the use of the passive form (object + verb 'to be' + past participle) has a more objective tone to it than the active form in example 1. To return to our discussion of the problems of synonyms (as typified by 'skinny' and 'slim' above), it could be argued that 1 and 2 above are synonymous on a literal meaning level but, just as in the case of lexis, on a connotative level they are not parallel. In short, the grammatical pattern we choose to express an idea can be as significant as the actual choice of lexis.

Sample exercise

Look at the following lines, all taken from the BYU-BNC (www.corpus.byu. edu/bnc), and describe what you can about the structure, the probable origin of the discourse and whether you feel the underlined structure carries positive, negative or neutral connotations.

1	The Purchaser	**shall be deemed**	to have accepted all goods upon their delivery
2	The funny thing is,	**he's not very**	chatty or friendly
3		**I know what you mean**	yeah the rivet's come out there would be a
4		**I would say**	a similar, but a different er definition
5	If you got into trouble	**you were made to**	sit on a chair

Figure 6.1 Concordance lines from the BYU-BNC

This exercise probably did not take very long to carry out and that is part of the point; semantic prosody is so engrained in the meaning it conveys that sometimes it is almost invisible. Here is a short commentary on the sentences:

1   Neutral. The text is probably best described as being legal in terms of field and thus the language used is objective – it doesn't matter who the purchaser is and the act of 'deeming' is objective.
2   Negative. This is probably a piece of spoken language (gossip?) within which a criticism is being made of the individual.
3   Positive. This is certainly spoken language and the speaker is offering agreement or acceptance of another's view or observation.
4   Neutral. Spoken language. An opinion is being offered but the speaker has modified their comment with the use of 'would', effectively hedging their view perhaps to soften the message (which might otherwise be taken as criticism) or else to give themselves room to back-track if they need to later.
5   Negative. It's not clear from the context whether this is written or spoken but the connotation of 'being made to do something' is often seen as an imposition upon someone, effectively a direct threat to their freedom to act.

One of the strange things about grammar is that it is often viewed as if it were simply the structure on top of which meaning is placed. In Chapter 3 we made it clear that this is not how we view grammar and that we align ourselves with Widdowson's (1998) view that this dichotomy between meaning and grammar is flawed in that, as illustrated above, grammar often carries **semantic** meaning. Added to this is the issue of grammatical choice, as outlined in Chapter 3, that a speaker not only has the freedom to decide which lexis to use but also to select the structure and the colligation with which to convey their intended meaning. The use of the modal 'would' as a hedge is a good example of what is considered to be a grammatical word which

1	I'd got er a daughter, nineteen twenty nine,	**I would say**	,nineteen twenty eight.
2	Just a few hours,	**I would say**	before, less than twenty four hours before they went.
3	All else being equal,	**I would say**	October with the lithium level
4		**I would say**	that's an eight so you'll need definitely a seven.
5	Oddly enough I mean it's so far away from the yellow	**I would say**	it isn't wrong.

Figure 6.2 Concordance lines for 'I would say' from the BYU-BNC

actually carries semantic meaning and contributes a particular 'colour' to an utterance. Consider the concordance lines taken from the BYU-BNC in Figure 6.2.

Each of these sentences could have been said in another way or without the use of 'would', but the choice of form in these examples is linked to the intention of the speaker to include an element of uncertainty or vagueness in what they say, presumably to allow them to change their minds later on if necessary.

6.2 Finding semantic prosody in corpora

The decision to search a corpora for examples of semantic prosody is usually instigated by the researcher noticing a particular pattern in a text. For example, let's consider that we have noticed that the structure 'subject + to be + made' frequently carries the suggestion of compulsion and our research hypothesis is that most instances of the use of this pattern are for this usage. Our intention now is to search a corpus to find examples to support or reject this hypothesis.

Using the BYU-BNC, such a search can be carried out by instructing the computer to search for 'pronoun + verb to be + made to' (this is entered into the search field as the formula [p*] [vb*] made to). This results in 153 matches which divide as set out in Table 6.1. We can also identify that the full form is more frequent than the contracted form and that the majority of uses appear to be focused on 'they', 'he' and 'it'. Looking at Table 6.1 and using the per million word calculation, we can also see that the structure is most common as a percentage in newspapers (2.29 instances per million words) followed by fiction (1.95) and then non-academic texts (1.76). Overall the phrase occurs 1.59 times per million words.

Table 6.1 Instances of 'pronoun + verb to be + made' in the BYU-BNC

	Counts in the BNC	Used in the sense of 'compulsion'
They were made to	23	19
He was made to	23	23
It is made to	14	0
I was made to	12	12
They are made to	9	6
It was made to	7	7
They're made to	6	6
She was made to	6	6
You were made to	6	6
We are made to	6	6
Who is made to	5	5
You're made to	4	4
We were made to	4	4
He is made to	3	3
Others	25	18

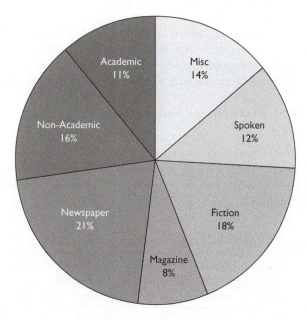

Figure 6.3 Use of 'pronoun + verb to be + made to' according to category (part per million) in the BYU-BNC

At this point we must look at the actual corpus lines to identify qualitatively how many of the lines generated fit our hypothesis. This is basically a question of counting how many times the specific meaning is being used in the concordance. However, once we begin the count, the researcher quickly comes up against a further issue as illustrated in the following exercise.

Sample exercise

Consider the examples below. How many of them would you count as being examples of '[p*] [vb*] made to' being used to mean 'compelled'?

I		**They were made to**	wash their hands and faces in a rain barrel outside
2	peace of mind each time you use it.	**It is made to**	BS1363 and 4293
3	is not always as easy as	**it is made to**	sound.
4	very irritating for them if	**they are made to**	feel that they are regarded
5	he, too, was murdered, though	**it was made to**	look like suicide.

Figure 6.4 Concordance lines for 'pronoun + verb to be + made to'

A quick examination of the corpus lines shows that sentences 1 and 4 can be counted as meaning 'compelled' while the others mean something else. However, when one looks at the other examples one might wish to consider why they do not carry this semantic meaning and it is also possible that a line like 3 might appear to some to fit the meaning we are looking for. For this reason, any qualitative investigation requires measures that will, as far as possible, ensure reliability or consistency in the categorisation process.

6.3 Finding further patterns of semantic prosody in corpora

We will now use a different example to explore patterns of semantic prosody in corpora, in this case the BYU-BNC corpus where we have conducted a search for the string 'pronoun + to be + not very'. The search produces the results shown in Table 6.2.

Table 6.2 Results by category of 'pronoun + to be + not very' in the BYU-BNC

Corpus type	Spoken (9,963,663 words)	Fiction (15,909,312 words)	Magazine (7,261,990 words)	Newspaper (10,466,422 words)	Academic (15,331,668 words)
Total number of occurrences	343	165	31	28	22
Occurrences per million words	34.43	10.37	4.27	2.68	1.43

What is immediately striking is the prevalence of this particular form in spoken language rather than in other areas of use; it is very clearly a piece of spoken language. This is borne out by the log-likelihood score of 174.57 when the spoken corpus is compared with the fiction corpus. If one considers the form intuitively, the following sorts of expressions come to mind:

- I'm not very well.
- It's not very easy to find.
- She's not very easy to work with.

Intuition tells us that the form is usually employed to express something negatively but the construction is interesting: why say you're not very well, when you could just say that you are ill? Table 6.3 shows us the different patterns for 'pronoun + verb to be + not very' in the BYU-BNC spoken corpus using the search parameters shown in Figure 6.5.

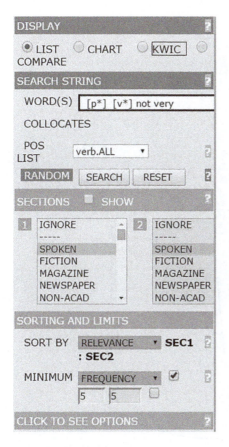

Figure 6.5 Search for 'pronoun + verb to be + not very' in the BYU-BNC

Table 6.3 Results for 'any pronoun + verb to be + not very' in the BYU-BNC

	WORD/PHRASE	Number of occurrences	Number of occurrences per million words
1	IT'S NOT VERY	158	15.86
2	I'M NOT VERY	72	7.23
3	THEY'RE NOT VERY	40	4.01
4	SHE'S NOT VERY	22	2.21
5	HE'S NOT VERY	19	1.91
6	YOU'RE NOT VERY	15	1.51
7	WE'RE NOT VERY	5	0.50

The results tell us that the most common use is to talk about objects or situations ('it's not very') while the second most frequent usage is for talking about one's self. Let us consider the use of 'it's not very'. A search in the same corpus for the string 'it [vb*] not very [j*]' produces the results in Figure 6.6 below.

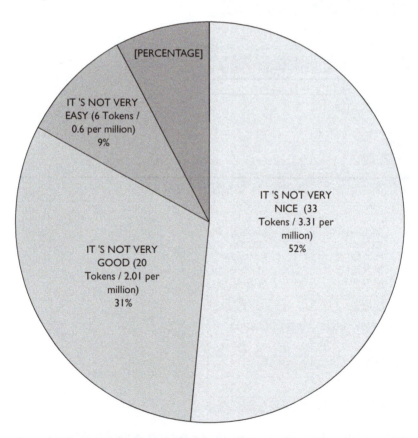

Figure 6.6 Search results for 'it [vb*] not very [j*]' in the BYU-BNC spoken corpus

The results show that 'it's not very nice' is by far the most frequent combination, but as we discussed in Chapter 3, perhaps we might want to consider the functions that this statement has.

Try it yourself 6.1

Look at the lines taken from the BYU-BNC in Figure 6.1 and try to label each utterance's function. What do these functions suggest about the way this particular structure is used in English?

1	It's not,	**it's not very nice**	darling, to do that.
2	well don't do that,	**it's not very nice**	, go get an apple
3		**It's not very nice**	weather is it?
4	I know it frightened the kid-dies. I mean	**it's not very nice**	, is it.
5	Oh Angie,	**it's not very nice**	that you're not very well. I hope you feel better.
6	Mum,	**it's not very nice**	when the wind hits it is it mum?

Figure 6.7 Concordance lines for 'it's not very nice' from the BYU-BNC spoken corpus

The second most frequent use of the form is 'I'm not very good at' with twenty-four instances in the corpus, followed by 'I'm not very happy (about/with)' with eleven instances. There appears to be a preference among speakers to use this particular structure to carry out a number of functions such as identifying a weakness in their abilities, display modesty or to indicate displeasure at a situation or state. The point is that these functions could have been carried out in a different way but they were not.

So, when we consider the use of the form 'pronoun + to be + not very', we find that while it is used for a variety of functions it seems to convey a 'softening' role to the message, especially when considered against how it might be rephrased without the 'not very'. This message is often softened to make the message more palatable or acceptable to the recipient, or to avoid making an overly strong statement that might invite contradiction or opposition.

6.4 Further applications

Thus far we have looked at examples of searches across broad corpora, but researchers have also carried out studies on more specific text types to look at how particular grammatical patterns are used in English. One such investigation was by Saracini (2008) who was interested in looking at how transitivity and non-transitivity – that is, the active and the passive voice – were used to bring about different meanings and to colour the language. To illustrate this he presented two newspaper texts reporting on the same event and showed how the use of the passive or active form was used to implicitly assign motivation or blame in what he calls 'the rhetoric of conflict'. Take for an example this line from the BNC:

> Official data suggests that 80 per cent of Milanese houses **were struck by** bombs or incendiaries.

The sentence comes from a guidebook to Milan explaining the miraculous survival of Leonardo da Vinci's painting of The Last Supper during the allied attacks of the Second World War. Consider the change in implication if the sentence is re-written.

> Allied bombs **struck** 80 per cent of Milanese houses according to official data.

By choosing an active form, the text becomes inherently more critical of the actions of those launching the bombs. Transitivity in particular has a number of very interesting uses from this perspective, in the way that it is used to either conceal identities, focus attention or cover for identities the speaker or writer does not know.

Try it yourself 6.2

Consider the following statements in Figure 6.8 taken from the BYU-BNC newspaper corpus. For what reason do you think the speaker or writer might have chosen the underlined form in each?

1	The Queen flew into Lanacka Airport	**and was met by**	the Greek Cypriot President, Mr Clarides.
2	It's obvious that the execution of these policies was flawed, and	**mistakes were made**	.
3	It was also the year in which the train robbers	**were sentenced**	and France and England agreed to the principle of a Channel Tunnel.
4	An acid house party attended by children as young as 12	**was broken**	up by police yesterday.
5	Recently my own son	**was attacked**	a few yards from Princes Street.
6	For the first time ever in Britain, CS gas	**was fired**	at rioters by the police.

Figure 6.8 Concordance lines for passives from BYU-BNC newspaper corpus

6.5 What can semantic prosody tell us about language use?

We have seen in the previous examples that investigation of corpus data can show us that context is an essential feature in grammatical choice. In the opening part of this chapter we provided the illustration of the use of the passive voice in providing an 'objective' tone in writing, and therefore that children are often taught to write in this manner when describing science experiments despite it seeming counter-intuitive to them. Another area where learners (both native and non-native) often feel that they are being made to say things in a forced or artificial way is in academic writing, and in particular in the avoidance of the first-person pronoun (I). The point at which this often becomes a major difficulty for some writers is when they have to give an opinion in their piece of writing. Table 6.4 shows the frequency according to the BYU-BNC lists of four phrases with the function of giving an opinion. What the table illustrates is that while structures like 'I think' and 'I believe' have a higher frequency in written language than the other forms, they are in no way as prevalent as they are in spoken language. The log-likelihood score for the spoken versus the academic corpus is 41470.45, which is highly significant (p<0.001). The phrases 'in my opinion' and 'in my view' are more common in written language than in spoken language, but interestingly both are often presented to learners of English as being ways of giving one's opinion in spoken language. Even this cursory examination of the data suggests that this is not entirely the case.

Table 6.4 Comparison of written and spoken forms for giving an opinion from BYU-BNC

	Academic written and spoken corpus (15,331,668 words) (per million words)	Spoken corpus (9,963,663 words) (per million words)
I think	55.11	2,591.92
I believe	19.37	85.81
In my opinion	12.91	7.83
In my view	11.22	10.34

When writing an academic essay, students are often encouraged to avoid any use of 'I' or 'my' which leads them to seek out alternatives that will fit better with the expectations of the genre. These alternatives are often the type of phrase illustrated in Table 6.5 where either a passive structure or

Table 6.5 Comparison of written and spoken forms for explaining an opinion from BYU-BNC

	Academic written and spoken corpus (15,331,668 words) (per million words)	Spoken corpus (9,963,663 words) (per million words)
It will be shown	0.59	0.10
It is believed	6.06	0.10
It is clear	53.61	1.81
It can be argued	7.76	0.0
This demonstrates	0.52	0.0
This shows	6.46	1.20

an impersonal subject is used. It is interesting that many of these constructions are extremely infrequent in spoken language, for example 'it is clear', and that these structures are perhaps seen to carry a more 'objective' tone. When a log-likelihood is carried out on 'it is clear', it results in a significant difference of 682.73 (p<0.0001).

The role of 'objective' language in academic writing is clearly vital in the context of education and university study, with failure to conform to the demands of the context likely to result in academic failure. Hyland (2003: 24) observed that 'without the resources to understand these genres, students in universities . . . will find their own writing practices regarded mainly as failed attempts to approximate prestigious forms'.

However, there is a risk of oversimplifying the issues in academic writing. Hyland (2004) explores the way that the interpersonal is represented in academic textbooks and makes the point that such conventions are also determined by the discipline within which an author is writing. Based on a corpus of textbooks he observes that personalised judgements such as 'I think' or 'I am convinced' do occur in fields such as Philosophy or Applied Linguistics where the writer can be confident of their own judgement and opinion, but are much more rare in the 'hard' sciences. While Hyland also points out that textbooks are not the same as academic articles and are intended for a different audience and purpose, he also argues that the context – that is, the academic discipline within which an author is writing – is an essential area to consider as what may be acceptable practice in one discipline may not be in another.

6.6 Bringing the analysis together

All of the examples above, from the use of passives to impersonal pronouns, to structures like 'it's not very' and the use of transitivity and agents, illustrate that grammar is far more than simply a skeleton upon which we hang meaning via lexis. The choice of how we structure something influences the message and can also determine whether the message is acceptable or more palatable in the context. It is through the linguistic choices both lexical *and* grammatical that writers represent themselves and construct their voices. In some cases, such as in academic writing, the way in which the author does this can be as important as the actual propositional content of the text.

Sample exercise

Look at the following short texts and for each identify how the use of different grammatical patterns contributes to the creation of the message. Think of aspects you would investigate using a corpus.

Text 1

Pensions Minister says the Budget means rich retirees are now 'free to blow their savings on Lamborghinis'

(Source: *Daily Mirror* headline 21 March 2014,
www.mirror.co.uk/news/uk-news/pensions-minister-
says-budget-means-3266197#ixzz2wab8VtSY)

Text 2

Schools, after all, are not the only places in which children learn. They acquire a vast amount of information about their world without direct intervention from their parents or their teachers. No structured programme is necessary to teach a baby its mother tongue, to enable the child to master the complexities of sentence construction or grasp the subtle nuances and meanings conveyed in phrase and tone. No blackboards, desks or text books are required, no special buildings: yet even the least able learn. Notwithstanding such examples, children growing up in a rapidly changing technological society cannot be expected to master all that they require to know if their learning is totally haphazard and unstructured. There must be a framework within which their learning (incidental and guided) is supported and directed. The issue raised by Hadow and developed by Plowden was simply this – is it possible to construct an educational programme which will meet in broad terms the needs of young children and adequately prepare them for secondary schooling,

(Source: BYU-BNC. http://corpus.byu.edu/bnc)

Text 3

Hi Matt,

Hope your feeling better, and that Rory and Maria are fully recovered. Can you ring Suze On Tuesday as dad and I will be out that evening. I need to know as soon as possible if you are all able to come for all the week march 3rd or even for just part of the time, as getting accommodation for 8 is quite difficult and one we liked as just been booked. Hope all your work is going OK.

Love mum.

(Personal correspondence)

Text 1 is a newspaper headline which is marked by the use of the present tense. Newspaper headlines almost always use present tense to stress the immediacy of the news but also because it seems more dramatic (and therefore more attention-grabbing), plus these forms are often shorter than pasts and so fit better. An active form is also used ('Pensions Minister says') for the dramatic impact and presumably also because this text comes from a left-wing newspaper which is critical in its stance towards the story and the individual and so makes no bones about identifying who made the comment. It would be relatively straightforward to build your own corpus of newspaper headlines and then analyse them using AntConc to find out just how prevalent this pattern is.

Text 2 is an academic text taken from the BYU-BNC. This is marked by the use of depersonalised language (parents, children and teachers are referred to in general). There is considerable use of linkers ('yet', 'notwithstanding') and these are relatively low-frequency ones more typical of written language ('yet' in the contrastive use as opposed to its more frequent use as a time marker). Issues are highlighted over the writers cited (Hadow and Plowden) because it is the argument that is the focus rather than the action of writing by these individuals. Modals such as 'cannot' are used in full form without contraction and complex sentences, extended noun clauses and relative clauses are employed alongside lexis to give the text the authority of academic writing. Looking at a corpus such as the BYU-BNC academic sub-corpus would allow us to investigate these types of patterns in greater detail.

Text 3 is a personal e-mail, a genre that mirrors spoken language much more closely and within which a lower level of formality allows for errors and typos to be more overlooked than in other more formalised written forms. The request function ('can you') is asked directly because of the close relationship between writer and intended reader. Sentences can be quite extended but remain relatively simple in structure, and are constructed through addition rather than through complex forms and relations as used in Text 2. Individuals are referred to directly (I, you, we). You could collect your own corpus of e-mails (with the appropriate ethical considerations) and then analyse features of register depending on relationships.

The three texts above, representing different genres, show how semantic prosody employs grammatical forms alongside lexis to carry out the intended purpose of the text.

6.7 Limitations

In this chapter we have considered how grammatical semantic prosody can be central to the way in which a message is formulated, and made the argument that a view of grammar that relegates it to merely the skeleton upon which lexis hangs shows a lack of awareness of how central grammatical choice is to communication. However, while using corpora to investigate instances of grammatical use can be interesting and rewarding, this is a feature that requires the researcher to observe language in context and then formulate a hypothesis about how the language is used. As we have mentioned before, frequency data alone will not be enough; we also need to examine the data subjectively, making use of carefully defined criteria for the selection of relevant examples.

Further practice

1   Look at the samples below taken from the BYU-BNC:

- Do you not think that our women readers will be interested in what I have written?
- Do you not think so?
- Do you not remember that two hundred head teachers gathered and protested

2   Search the BYU-BNC for structures using 'do/are/have + pronoun + not'. What meanings do these structures seem to present? Think about why speakers/writers might choose to phrase something in this way (and what they might use as an alternative).

References

Beattie, J. (2014). Pensions minister says budget means rich retirees are now 'free to blow their savings on Lamborghinis'. *Daily Mirror,* 20 May 2014. [Online], Available: www.mirror.co.uk/news/uk-news/pensions-minister-says-budget-means-3266197#ixzz3BDlqVHm4 [25 January 2015].

Davies, M. (2004). *BYU-BNC* (based on the British National Corpus from Oxford University Press). [Online], Available: http://corpus.byu.edu/bnc [2 February 2014].

Hyland, K. (2003). Genre-based pedagogies: a social response to process. *Journal of Second Language Writing*, 12, 17–29.

Hyland, K. (2004). *Disciplinary discourses: social interactions in academic writing.* Ann Arbor, MI: The University of Michigan Press.

Saracini, M. (2008). Meaningful form: transitivity and intentionality. *ELT Journal,* 62, 2, 164–172.

Widdowson, H. (1998). Context, community and authentic language. *TESOL Quarterly*, 32, 4, 705–716.

Chapter 7

Applications to English language teaching

7.1 Introduction

Corpora have had an influence on ELT (particularly in EFL and ESL contexts) for a number of years and have been used to help inform syllabuses, learner dictionaries, reference grammars, self-study grammar practice books and textbooks. While this influence may seem obvious, it is worth pausing for a moment to consider, as we have done up to now, what a corpus might tell us about an aspect of grammar that our own intuitions may not. Imagine you are writing the grammatical syllabus of an English textbook for EFL/ESL learners. What information could a corpus give you that your own intuition cannot? Check with the list below.

Consulting a corpus might tell us:

1   How frequent an area is in a particular context and in contrast with other forms. When teaching past forms, for example, we might wish to know whether past simple ('I went') is more or less frequent than past perfect ('I had just woken up when . . . ') in spoken narratives and which verbs are most commonly used when these forms are produced. We may also wish to know about the frequency of different aspects such as continuous forms vs. simple forms in particular contexts. For example, it may be useful to know whether continuous forms are used more often in a type of text we wish to teach such as business e-mails. It is also helpful to investigate aspects of morphology, such as the use of noun phrases. Written academic research, for instance, tends to make more extensive use of modified noun phrases (e.g. 'the aim of this study' rather than 'this study aims to . . . ') than gossip magazines.

2   How aspects of language colligate and collocate. We might wish to know, for example, whether 'I went' is more likely than 'he went' in certain contexts or where this pattern most often occurs in a turn, sentence or clause. We might also want to know which words commonly make partnerships with 'I went' and how these are also grammatically patterned into chunks, such as 'I went shopping'. In addition, we may wish to discover likely combinations of words such as which pronouns tend to co-occur with which modal verbs.

3   If a feature has a particular semantic prosody in certain contexts. It is helpful to know, as we outlined in Chapter 6, how particular forms can be used to have negative, positive or neutral connotations.

4   Corpora can also provide information about how spoken forms differ from written ones in particular contexts and also about specialised uses of language applicable to English for Specific Purposes, such as Business English or English for Engineering.

This is not an exhaustive list and many more things could be added to it. In addition, we may not wish to use all of this information but it can certainly help us to build up a comprehensive picture of how language works. If we wish to check whether a corpus really can tell us more than our intuitions, it is easy to test this.

Sample exercise

Predict the five most frequent forms that are most likely to follow 'I went' in spoken and written (newspaper) language. Once you have done this, check the BYU-BNC corpus (http://corpus2.byu.edu/bnc) by simply searching for 'I went*' in list view, first choosing the spoken section of the corpus and then the newspaper section.

The results you found should be the same as those displayed in Table 7.1, which give the total number of occurrences and occurrences per million words in brackets after each form.

Table 7.1 Patterns following 'I went' in the BYU-BNC spoken and newspaper corpora

BNC spoken (9,963,663 words)	BNC newspaper (10,466,422 words)
I went to (638, 64.03)	I went to (103, 9.84)
I went in (161, 16.16)	I went out (21, 2.01)
I went down (117, 11.74)	I went into (19, 1.82)
I went out (102, 10.24)	I went for (14, 1.34)
I went and (87, 8.73)	I went back (14, 1.34)

This suggests that prepositions and adverbs are the most frequent items to follow this pattern in both corpora but that these differ. This perhaps goes against an intuitive guess which might lead us to believe that noun phrases in 'ing' form such as 'swimming' and 'shopping' would be the most frequent (and perhaps useful) items to follow this pattern. If we investigate a little further, by searching for 'I went to the' and 'I went to *' in both sections of the corpus, we find the following patterns are the most common. Again, the total occurrences and then the occurrences per million words follow each pattern.

Table 7.2 Noun phrases following 'I went' in the BYU-BNC spoken and newspaper corpora

BNC spoken (9,963,663 words)	BNC newspaper (10,466,422 words)	Log-likelihood
I went to the + NP (119, 11.94)	I went to the + NP (24, 2.29)	73.61
I went to the doctor (9, 0.90)	I went to the toilet (3, 0.29)	
I went to the hospital (5, 0.50)	I went to the front (2, 0.19)	

Such information is useful at the very least to inform decisions we make about what to include in a syllabus and which patterns we may want learners to focus on at the initial stages of learning. It is clear that 'I went to the + NP' is a frequent colligation around the past simple form 'went'. It is far more common in the spoken corpus, something the log-likelihood score shows is significant, and in both corpora the range of nouns that follow it is very wide. This would therefore indicate that teaching this as a frame, 'I went to the + NP', is likely to be most useful for comprehension and production of speech rather than attempting to teach only 'I went to the doctor', for example.

In this chapter, we will examine the influence corpora have had on ELT and the potential further influence they could have in terms of classroom and reference materials, testing and also within mainstream education in terms of first language learning.

7.2 Corpora in ELT

Lexical syllabuses

As mentioned in Chapter 1, during the 1980s applied linguists were able to conduct analysis aiming to incorporate corpus data into ELT. An early and influential development was the COBUILD project founded in 1980 and led by John Sinclair. The work conducted by COBUILD was initially set up to produce the Collins COBUILD English language dictionary (www.collinslanguage.com), the first learner dictionary to be based on corpus data. This meant that a corpus could be used to give learners vital evidence-based information about words, including their frequency, collocations and colligations. The samples used to illustrate the meanings were also drawn from real examples in use, where previously they may have been based on a lexicographer's intuitive examples. Now, all learner dictionaries are based on corpus data and the information about words is extensive. To take an example, if we search the Macmillan Dictionary (www.macmillandictionary.com) for a word such as 'go', the entry shows a learner that 'go' is highly frequent (frequent words are marked in red in the dictionary and starts indicate frequency with *** being the most frequent), and also gives lots of information about the grammatical properties and patterns associated with this word, alongside some restrictions in terms of contexts of use. The meaning senses are also shown in order of frequency. This allows a learner (and teacher) to build up a clear picture of a word and its patterns at word and sentence level, with indications of the type of texts we may find it in. Dictionaries are now also including information that indicates the expected level at which a learner may be expected to (at least) start to use a word. The Cambridge Advanced Learner's Dictionary (http://dictionary.cambridge.org/diction ary/british), for example, now lists the Common European Framework of Reference for Languages (CEFR) (Council of Europe, 2001) levels next to each word it lists. These levels range from A1 (beginner) to C2 (advanced) and the information is based on corpus data from the Cambridge English Profile Corpus (www.englishprofile.org/index.php/corpus), a large collection of student written and spoken exams at various levels. We will return to the CEFR in more detail later in this chapter.

Corpora have also been used to influence syllabus design in ELT. Based upon the COBUILD corpus, Sinclair and Renouf's (1988) notion of a lexical syllabus was developed as an alternative to the grammatical syllabuses popular at the time (and since). Sinclair and Renouf proposed a syllabus based around the most frequent words and word patterns that emerged during text analysis conducted by COBUILD. According to Sinclair and Renouf (1988: 155), analysis of word patterns, rather than explicit instruction on grammar, leads to language acquisition since 'if the analysis of the words and phrases has been done correctly, then all relevant grammar, etc. should appear in a proper proportion since verb tenses are combinations of some of the commonest words in the language'. In other words, the suggestion was that basing a syllabus on frequent words and the way they are patterned in collocations and colligations would provide learners with a useful language syllabus, rather than suggesting we can separate grammar and words. Sinclair and Renouf's work was developed by Willis (1990) who, together with Jane Willis, designed a course based around the 2,500 most frequent words and word patterns found in the COBUILD corpus. Willis' (1990) practical implementation of the lexical syllabus took the form of three course books (for example, Willis and Willis, 1998). Willis (1990: 38) justifies the linguistic focus in the following way:

> The commonest patterns in English occur again and again with the commonest words in English. If we are to provide learners with language experience which offers exposure to the most useful patterns of the language we might as well begin by researching the most useful words in the language.

Therefore, the first course was based on the most frequent 700 words of English found in the COBUILD corpus and the patterns they commonly occurred in. This meant that the frequent words were taken as the starting point and the learners were then provided with a picture of how the words colligated and collocated into larger grammatical and lexico-grammatical patterns.

Willis (1990: 77–80) provides examples of words included in the first course. High-frequency words such as 'visit', 'window', 'would' and 'so' were incorporated, together with words of high importance in the classroom context such as 'teacher', 'student', 'group' and 'share'. All words were presented within their most frequent patterns and their uses were highlighted and illustrated with COBUILD data. Willis (1990: 80) presents an entry from the reference section in the first course which focuses on six uses of 'so':

- **Marking a summary or a change of subject**
  So what do you do at quarter to eight?
- **Expressing amount**
  There are always *so* many tourists.
- **Meaning 'therefore'**
  The suitcase looked exactly like mine, *so* I said 'Excuse me, sir . . . '
- **Pointing back**
  V: Wouldn't you think Cairo was 1500? DL: Yes, out of the ones given, I would've thought *so*.
- **'So that' used to talk about result or purpose**
  Let me know as soon as you have fixed your travel plans, *so that* I can make sure that you are properly looked after
- **Meaning 'also'**
  JV: The woman next to him has orange trousers. DL: *So* has mine.

This corpus-based approach to syllabus design seems logical and helpful for English language learners as it acknowledges the aspects of corpora we can use to analyse grammar we have described so far. However, it is also clear, as Willis shows, that a teacher or course designer has to interpret the data available from a corpus and decide which to include or not include in a syllabus.

Despite the pioneering work in using corpus data to inform syllabus design in ELT, there has only been a somewhat limited impact upon the design of EFL/ESL textbooks since then, possibly because the COBUILD series of textbooks were not a commercial success. Recently, there have been several corpus-informed course books teaching general English and English for Specific Purposes (for example, McCarthy et al., 2014; Koseter et al., 2012). The influence of corpora has also been widely used in self-access grammar and vocabulary practice books (for example, Thornbury, 2004; O'Dell and McCarthy, 2008). Unfortunately, this use of corpus data is not universal and there is some way to go before English language textbooks are credible even if they are not corpus-informed, as is now the case with learner dictionaries. Instead, many textbooks appear to pay scant regard to corpus data when analysing language and do not give learners information about context, frequency and so on (Waller and Jones, 2012). We will look at an example of this below.

Sample exercise

Look at the classroom material in Figure 7.1. Search for the language areas in the BYU-BNC corpus and think what could be added to this language description to create a fuller picture of the language for learners. This piece of material is focused upon the past forms used in narratives and is taken from an online resource produced by Warsaw (2014) (http://random-idea-english. blogspot.co.uk/2011/05/narrative-tenses-practice.html), where lesson ideas and exercises are added for free. While this is not a textbook, it is the kind of open-access resource that many teachers may turn to when looking for resources. The intention here is not to criticise the materials but rather to understand what a corpus-informed description could add to them.

Random stories – Narrative tenses
Narrative tenses – a quick reminder

Past simple
Describes the main events of the story
Describes sequences of events
It is the 'standard' narrative tense. If in doubt, go for past simple

Past continuous
Describes unfinished actions, especially around a certain time
Describes longer actions interrupted by shorter ones
Is often used for describing background actions
Is sometimes used to make the actions in a story seem more immediate, especially with the word 'now'

Past perfect
Describes actions that took place before the main actions in the story

Past perfect continuous
Describes longer continuous actions that took place before the main actions in the story
Is sometimes used to explain the condition of people or things at the time of the main events in the story
Now practise them with this little story

Exercise – Fill the gaps with suitable forms of the verbs given in brackets

The Tragic Tale of Ruddy Wee Hoody

Part I

There was this young girl called . . ., actually I don't know what she _____ (1) (be called)
really, because I only ever _____ (2) (hear) her being called by her nickname – 'Ruddy Wee
Hoody', at least I think it was her nickname. It was how they usually _____ (3) (refer) to her in
the village, anyway. I always _____ (4) (assume) that it _____ (5) (come) from the red hooded
top that she _____ (6) (wear), day in day out, wherever she went. But I might have been wrong.

Anyway, one day her mother _____ (7) (tell) her to take a basket filled with goodies to
her granny, who _____ (8) (happen) to live on the other side of the forest. Sorry, I forgot to
tell you that this girl _____ (9) (live) in a small cottage on the edge of a big forest, and that she
_____ (10) (spend) all her life there, up until that fateful day.

She _____ (11) (set) off in a happy mood. The sun _____ (12) (shine) through the trees, the
birds _____ (13) (sing). It was just as though everyone _____ (14) (wait) for Walt Disney to
come and draw the scene. What _____ (15) (can) possibly spoil such a perfect day?

What indeed? While she _____ (16) (walk) through the forest, she _____ (17) (see) a wolf
_____ (18) (stroll) slowly towards her, humming something to himself. A minute or so earlier,
the wolf _____ (19) (watch) her from behind a tree, and _____ (20) (think) to himself, 'She'd
make a nice juicy meal'. But as he _____ (21) (not want) to frighten her off he _____ (22)
(decide) to play it nice and cool, and so the nonchalant walk.

Figure 7.1 Sample exercise on past forms used in written narratives

A quick search in the BYU-BNC fiction corpus (http://corpus2.byu.
edu/bnc, 15,909,312 words) for samples of these past forms ('I went', 'I
had gone', 'I was going', 'I had been going') reveals the following about
frequency, to take one aspect of the language area we can investigate. In
terms of frequency, the order is past simple ('I went' = 1539 occurrences,
96.74 per million words), past continuous ('I was going' = 61 occurrences,
28.98 per million words), past perfect simple ('I had gone' = 30 occurrences, 1.89 per million words), and 'I had been going' (2 occurrences,
0.13 per million words). This is implicitly signalled in the material by the
number of examples of each form and in the instruction that past simple
is the 'go to' form. However, it would be simple to alert students to the
differing frequencies and suggest that past perfect continuous is probably
only needed for receptive purposes. We can also check frequencies of the
verbs in the story used in past simple to discover which occurs most and
least often.

1   A search for past simple (* went *) shows that in the fiction corpus, the
     most common patterns around this form are 'He went on' (543, 33.57),
     'I went to' (454, 28.54) and 'And went to' (432, 27.15). Again, such pat-
     terns (and others contained in the story) could easily be highlighted
     for students.

2   'He went on' is most frequently followed by a comma in the fiction cor-
     pus because it functions, in mid-clause position, to report speech in fic-
     tion, as in the following example from the corpus: 'We decided to have
     a rota for the beds as well,' **he went on**, still inspecting the mushrooms,
     'Otherwise the same two people have to . . . '.
3   It is fairly simple to search for information on common chunks from the
     story and fiction corpus and investigate their usage. A search around
     the chunk 'her mother told her' (* told *), for example, reveals that in
     the fiction corpus 'I told you' is the most frequent pattern around this
     verb (795 occurrences in total, 49.97 per million words) and is used to
     report speech, as in this example: 'Did you hit something, did a tyre
     burst?' '**I told you**, I didn't look. I was knitting', in a similar way to 'he
     went on'. While nobody would argue that learners need this informa-
     tion for every single pattern in the exercise, an in-depth look at some
     patterns could be very useful.

Methodology

Using a corpus to inform a syllabus or textbook does not of course give
us any indication about how we might use corpus data in the classroom.
One methodology that has tried to address this is data-driven learning
(DDL) (Johns, 1986, 1991), which suggests clear ways in which teachers
could bring corpus data into the ELT classroom, particularly in the form
of concordance lines and tasks using them. Johns (1991) argues that
DDL forms part of an inductive approach to grammar learning, whereby
learners look for patterns in data, rather than the teacher choosing data
to fit a pre-conceived rule or pattern. This necessarily changes the role
of the teacher from one of explainer to one of helper and guide in
student-initiated language research, which at the same time fosters student autonomy. Finally, he suggests that DDL may open up many areas
of grammar that have been under-described in simplified pedagogic
grammars.

Johns argues for the use of concordance lines i.e. giving learners real
samples of language in use to find patterns related to areas they enquire
about. He suggests that a useful framework for learning from concordances is 'identify-classify-generalise' (Johns, 1991: 5). Learners look at some
data and identify something about the pattern or patterns, related to form,
meaning or both; they then classify these findings into groups and see if
the patterns they have found can be further generalised. The process can
be assisted by the teacher finding and editing the corpus samples so that
they are manageable, as the following exercise shows. This is taken from an
English for Academic Purposes website and explores some patterns around
the word 'area', from www.nottingham.ac.uk/alzsh3/acvocab/index.htm
developed by Sandra Haywood.

VOCABULARY STUDY: AREA

TASK ONE: Study the concordance lines.

Which preposition is fairly common after *area*(s)?

1	with other supporters in your	area	and plan work together.
2	respectable, lived in a nice	area,	and I'd grown up wanting for nothing
3	aid agencies who work in these	areas	are increasingly recognising the
4	The Black Country is not an	area	defined on any map. It became famous
5	erupted in the Johannesburg	area	in August. Two months ago, again on
6	education as a highly important	area	of social behaviour to modern
7	space surveys show that the	area	of deforestation has doubled approximately
8	into the most inhospitable	areas	of Africa by other more technologically
9	continued to read and explore the	area	of new knowledge that my profession
10	is jeopardising food supplies in	areas	of Angola, the Sudan and Rwanda and
11	They would come into an	area	that had been sprayed days or weeks
12	the delicate and sensitive eye	area.	This light, non-greasy gel is

Area **has two main meanings:**

A: physical part of a town, country, region etc

B: part of a more general situation or activity

Study the concordance lines below and mark each one A or B according to the meaning of *area*(s).

1	whilst also venturing into new	areas	of study. In addition to this,
2	engaging in research work or other	areas	of professional activity. It
3	Balsall Heath and Moseley	areas	of south Birmingham, which
4	it is difficult to watch every	area	of the port, and yachtsmen would
5	One of the most interesting	areas	of research has demonstrated that
6	Driving around different	areas	of Abidjan, there was no immediate
7	the Afro-Caribbean community in	areas	of welfare benefits, child care
8	what is going on in such a vital	area	of our national life.
9	3-bedroomed home in an upmarket	area	of Basingstoke.
10	US state early yesterday. Huge	areas	of southern California were turned
11	returned to a hilltop residential	area	of the same city two days later.
12	addictions affect many different	areas	of a person's life, including:

Figure 7.2 Sample material – data-driven learning

While DDL is a very useful and practical methodology, it is probably fair to say, at least from anecdotal evidence, that it is not used very commonly in many ELT classrooms. This is a shame as it potentially offers us a useful bridge between the corpus and the classroom and a way for learners to investigate grammatical and lexico-grammatical patterns in language. The key, it seems, at least for the teacher, is to help learners by making the data manageable but not editing so that only pre-conceived patterns occur.

Try it yourself 7.1

Look at the concordance lines in Figure 7.3, taken from the BYU-BNC spoken corpus, contrasting the modal verbs 'should' and 'must', which many learners have difficulty distinguishing between. The examples taken below are all from association or trade union meetings so they share a common context. The lines have been edited to make them easier to read and comprehend for second language learners. Try to devise a similar

1	said, anybody who is interested in becoming a (unclear) in nineteen ninety three,	**must**	register an interest on sixteenth this year, which is really
2	He should know about them shouldn't he? (unclear). Well we	**must**	(pause) that's why, certainly have to, before (unclear)
3	A B C whenever they are put in these cardboard boxes they have to be sorted so somebody	**must**	sort them.
4	A B C're not asking (unclear) sorting, oh I see. Erm (pause) so there	**must**	be somebody responsible and I think if, if we write swimming pool and people
5	A B C collecting cost. Because the (pause) money they can get for this (pause) mixed paper	**must**	be a pittance. Mm. Almost hardly worth their while but (unclear)
6	A B C Charity shops. (Ah pause) er the other item that we	**must**	mention is any extra plastic bags Yeah, I'll ask about plastic bags
7	what see says any rate on Monday. But I don't think we	**should**	give her too long, cos she's got herself into (unclear)2. Mm.
8	A B C at Kathy (-----) says, she's afraid of being left out, if there	**should**	be a, another Tory Government, so a lot of people are in the
9	A B C it and to say how, how they tackled it, so I think it	**should**	be an interesting meeting, hopefully we'll get a few, you know interesting people
10	A B C women's committee and they assure me that they, the hospital says these tests	**should**	come through in a week, at the most three week'
11	A B C if we established a, a demand, and I don't see why we	**shouldn't**	have a bash at. Well then I have the inspector (unclear)
12	A B C S A branch, you know, I don't see why, why we	**shouldn't**	give it a try. There is one at the (unclear)

Figure 7.3 Concordance lines for 'should' and 'must' from the BYU-BNC spoken corpus

exercise to the one above, which may help learners to identify, classify and generalise from the data.

Language testing

The use of corpora has also been of particular interest to those engaged in the world of language assessment for a number of reasons. Assessing organisations have always collected examples of candidate work in the form of scripts or recordings for the purpose of standardisation and moderation. To put it simply, even the best marking scheme in the world is largely subjective until one is able to see samples of work. For example, marking criteria for an essay may say that a candidate 'is able to successfully link sentences into a cohesive paragraph using appropriate linkers'. But without illustrations of what 'successful' means or what 'appropriate linkers' are, the statement remains open to wide interpretation. So organisations would often hold large banks of candidate samples but perhaps not in the form of an electronically searchable corpus.

The issue above, of determining what comprises successful performance at different levels of language proficiency, became more important with the release of the CEFR. This document (which is freely downloadable from the Council of Europe website: www.coe.int/t/dg4/linguistic/source/framework_en.pdf) provides a model of language and language levels (see Table 7.3).

Table 7.3 Common European Framework of Reference for Languages (CEFR) levels

Proficient User	C2*
	CI
Independent User	B2+
	B2
	BI+
	BI
Basic User	A2+
	A2
	AI+
	AI
	(A0)[1]

[1] The existence of the A0 level is implied by the CEFR, because to be level AI it is necessary to be able to carry out some simple operations in the target language. One of the creators of the CEFR, John Trim, is reported to have said that the AI level requires not just that a learner can parrot phrases but also that they are able to demonstrate some creativity in their use. It is also important that the C2 level is not taken to be a level of native speaker-like ability. One of the best descriptions of this level was provided by Dr Nick Saville of Cambridge ESOL Examinations at an English Profile meeting, who identified C2 as the last level at which it is worth explicitly focusing on language skills.

The way in which the CEFR defines levels of proficiency is through the use of 'Can do' descriptors at each level. For example, at level B2, a learner is said to be able to 'explain a viewpoint on a topical issue giving the advantages and disadvantages of various options' (Council of Europe, 2001: 35). The CEFR then provides illustrative tables of how different activities may be broken down at each level, so for example on page 62 of the CEFR (Council of Europe, 2001) there is an illustrative table on 'writing reports and essays' which states that at the B2 level the learner 'can write an essay or report which develops an argument systematically with appropriate highlighting of significant points and relevant supporting detail'. Rather crucially from the point of view of those designing language courses and assessments, the CEFR does not tell us what linguistic structures should be used to carry out this activity successfully at each level (Weir, 2005). The decision not to state the grammatical or lexical exponents for the competences was a purposeful one on the part of the designers of the CEFR; the framework extends across all European languages and obviously grammatical and lexical forms may not have exactly corresponding equivalences in other languages. However, the CEFR has been heavily criticised by writers such as Fulcher (2010) for being a performance model and not one that was built upon empirical data. The English Profile project, with its use of learner corpora (the Cambridge English Profile Corpus, as mentioned above) based on candidate scripts from English language tests and frequency data from other corpora, can be seen as an attempt to rectify this. The grammar profile and functions profile projects explicitly explore the grammatical features and structures used at each level (Green, 2012). We can therefore see that language testing has not only produced extensive learner corpora but is a field that has actively engaged with corpora. One criticism that might be made is that due to the commercial nature of many language testing organisations, many of these highly interesting corpora are not accessible for free to teachers or learners.

There are also practical applications of corpora data in language assessment that are available to designers and teachers for the production of assessments. For example, when producing a multiple-choice question to test a language point such as the past continuous, rather than inventing an example sentence, the designer can go onto a corpus such as the BYU-BNC and carry out a search for 'was + verb-ing'. This search reveals that 'was going' is the most frequent combination of these words (which could include the 'future in the past' 'I was going to'). However, we can also extract the following from the examples given:

> today he phoned me just as I **was going** out and I didn't really sort of stop and talk to him

This gives us a ready-made sentence which could then be gapped and turned into an item on a test with the benefit that it is a genuine example of the form in use.

This use of corpora is also extremely helpful in the development of answer keys to open-cloze sections on tests. A common problem when marking cloze-style questions is the range of answers that candidates generate. Frequently markers will come up against an answer that 'sounds right' but with which other assessors disagree. The ability to search a corpus can effectively allow for data-informed decisions to be made, thereby ensuring that candidates are treated fairly and not simply on the subjective judgement of an examiner.

Try it yourself 7.2

Below you will find an item extracted from an open-cloze (gap-fill) test along with the responses that learners have given in the gap. Which answers do you think you would accept? Then, use the BYU-BNC to look at the words to see whether you can find any evidence to support your decisions.

Extract from test

During the French Revolution and in the **(01)** _____ chaos, there was a marked growth in political graffiti, which has continued to this day.

Candidate responses

complete, continuous, ensuing, huge, general, political, resulting, widespread
   Suggested answers are at the end of the book.

7.3 Other uses of corpora: first language learning

So far we have discussed the use of corpora in ESL and EFL contexts, in terms of how they have informed syllabus design and methodology. The uses of corpora could also easily be extended into other areas, as a means of developing learner and teacher language awareness; that is, awareness of grammar, vocabulary and phonology.

There is a reasonably long history of debate regarding explicit language teaching to English as L1 learners in primary and secondary schools in the UK. In the late 1980s and early 1990s, this was characterised as the knowledge about language (KAL) movement, which culminated in the Language in the National Curriculum (LINC) Project, an attempt to introduce a context-sensitive development of language awareness into the national curriculum, as a result of the Report of the Committee of Inquiry into English Language Teaching (Department of Education and Science, 1988). The intention of this project was to produce a descriptive version of language aspects such as grammar, drawing upon an L1 learner's intuitive understanding of language and looking at real texts to assist with this process. This took the form of an extensive pack of teacher training materials. The proposals (as described in Carter, 1990) seem very sensible and although this was at a time where corpora were not widely used, there is much attention in the LINC materials to language used in real contexts. Sadly, the ideas suggested in the LINC Project did not meet with favour from the government of the day and publication was banned (Carter, 1997: 39). Since that point, developing language awareness in schools has fallen in and out of favour until the present day where 'Spelling, punctuation and grammar' (SPAG) were introduced in 2013 as discrete lessons in the primary curriculum (www.gov.uk/government/uploads/system/uploads/attachment_data/file/182674/2013_keystage2_grammarpunctationandspelling_test_framework.pdf), and are to be the subject of a test for learners in their final year of primary education. Teachers are now expected to explicitly teach areas of language that may not have been previously taught or tested. Although the emphasis (sadly) appears to be upon language used at the level of the sentence and often out of context, it also seems clear that teachers (and learners) could easily benefit from supplementing such material with corpus data.

Sample exercise

Consider how the invented exercise below could be developed with the use of corpus data. The intention here again is not to criticise this type of exercise but merely to consider how we may enhance it.

Underline the main clause and the subordinate clause in the following sentences:

1 When the rain fell, everybody put up their umbrellas.
2 While the sun shone, everybody relaxed.
3 After the wind died down, everybody went outside.

Here are some ways we could develop such an exercise:

1 Pupils are asked to read and briefly summarise a series of extracts from written materials they will be familiar with e.g. short stories.
2 Pupils identify which ones have complex sentences and which do not. They can also discuss why there are more or fewer complex sentences in any given text.
3 A teacher can use edited concordance lines from the BYU-BNC corpus (spoken and fiction) and ask learners to classify these into spoken and written examples.
4 Pupils should be guided towards the idea that main and subordinate clauses are more likely to occur in fiction than speech and that in spoken grammar, subordinate clauses often stand as a turn in themselves, unattached to a main clause. This would not normally be accepted in most written forms.

7.4 Further applications

Corpora are also being used to inform the content of mobile applications, in a world where Mobile-Assisted Language Use (MALU) (Jarvis, 2012) is becoming increasingly prevalent. Learner dictionaries, for example, are now available as applications for use with mobiles and tablets, allowing learners to access the common colligation patterns, frequency, semantic prosody and chunks of words almost instantly, wherever they may be. This suggests that a mobile device will replace a learner's phrasebook because it offers learners immediate access to corpus data in the form of the information listed above. If a learner wishes to focus on grammar, or aspects of grammar, the British Council (2014) has produced a series of applications such as LearnEnglish Grammar (UK), which allow learners to work on aspects of language such as tense and aspect. The extent to which this particular application has used corpus data to inform its content is unclear, but there is a lot of potential for developing applications such as this based on corpus data. We might also envisage an application that uses the internet as a corpus, as WebCorpLSE (http://wse1.webcorp.org.uk/home) currently does for researchers and learners. This is a free resource, which uses the internet as a searchable corpus and subdivides the data into subject areas. It allows the researcher to search for words and patterns, part of speech tags and the position in a sentence you wish to find your search. A search examining the grammatical patterning of the word 'well' shows a clear contrast between the 'health' and 'shopping' subject domains.

This short sample of data shows us that 'well' occurs in medial position in both corpora but that in the health data it is often found as part of the subordinating conjunction 'as well as', whereas in the shopping data it operates most often as an adverb of manner modifying the verb, for example 'run well', 'stir well'. We can envisage such data being used in applications where a learner might be able to ask (through voice activation) 'how can I use

Health

1	Work for men as	**well**	.The new drug eases
2	Reduce stress levels as	**well**	as taking other medication.
3	non-genetic socio-economic circumstances as	**well**	as maternal and foetal
4	recommendations. Physicians should be	**well**	informed about the medical
5	in overall health and	**well**	being. The Notice to

Shopping

1	your personal finances very	**well**	. 8. Posting names of
2	This versatile pad works	**well**	with swirl removers and
3	the race, and run	**well**	, get laps, and gain
4	percentage of carbohydrates as	**well**	as protein back to
5	a large skillet; stir	**well**	. Cool over medium heat

Figure 7.4 'Well' in health and shopping subject domains

"well" when talking about shopping?' or a similar command, and the applications searching a corpus and providing simple (modified) examples.

7.5 Limitations

As we noted in Chapter 4, it would be unreasonable to suggest that corpora can provide all the answers in ELT textbooks, syllabus designs and methodologies. Frequency, as we have also mentioned, is not the only measure of an item's usefulness (Cook, 1998) and we would very much suggest that a textbook or methodology should be corpus-informed rather than led by a corpus. It may be the case, for example, that although past perfect continuous forms are fairly infrequent, learners in a particular context may have a pressing need to learn or use them and it would be unreasonable to suggest we should not teach them if this is the case. Using corpora in the classroom also places a burden on the teacher in terms of the time and effort required to locate, edit and construct exercises for particular areas of grammar (or vocabulary). This requires a certain amount of 'buy in' from a teacher and without training and encouragement, this area may pass teachers by.

Despite these issues, we would still argue in favour of corpus-informed syllabuses, methodologies and textbooks in ELT. This is on the basis that it is far more desirable to have the information a corpus can provide us than not have it.

Further practice

1 Examine an EFL or ESL textbook and look at the lexical, functional or grammatical syllabus. What information can be found on frequency, colligation and semantic prosody? How is this conveyed to learners? Is it helpful?
2 Compare two textbooks teaching the same area of grammar. Do they differ in the information they provide?
3 Take a piece of textbook material that teaches an aspect of grammar you feel reasonably familiar with. How could this be enhanced through the use of corpus data?

References

British Council (2014). *LearnEnglish*. [Online], Available: https://learnenglish.brit ishcouncil.org [12 February 2014].
Davies, M. (2004). *BYU-BNC* (based on the British National Corpus from Oxford University Press). [Online], Available: http://corpus.byu.edu/bnc [2 February 2014].
Cambridge Dictionaries Online (2014). *Cambridge advanced learner's dictionary*. [Online], Available: http://dictionary.cambridge.org/dictionary/british [7 February 2014].
Carter, R. (ed.) (1990). *Knowledge about language and the curriculum: The LINC reader*. London: Hodder.

Carter, R. (1997). *Investigating English discourse: language, literacy and literature.* London: Routledge.

Collins (2014). *Collins COBUILD English language dictionary.* [Online], Available: www.collinslanguage.com [2 February 2014].

Common European Framework of Reference for Languages (2014). *Cambridge English Profile Corpus.* [Online], Available: www.englishprofile.org/index.php/ corpus [7 February 2014].

Cook, G. (1998). The uses of reality: a reply to Ronald Carter. *ELT Journal,* 52, 1, 57–63.

Council of Europe (2001). *Common European Framework of Reference for Languages: learning, teaching and assessment.* Cambridge: Cambridge University Press. [Online], Available: www.coe.int/t/dg4/linguistic/source/framework_en.pdf [25 January 2015].

Department of Education and Science (1988). *Report of the Committee of Inquiry into the teaching of English language* (The Kingman Report). London: HMSO.

Fulcher, G. (2010). *Practical language testing.* London: Hodder.

Green, A. (2012). *Language functions revisited: theoretical and empirical bases for language construct definition across the ability range.* Cambridge: Cambridge University Press.

Haywood, S. (2014). *Academic vocabulary.* [Online], Available: www.nottingham. ac.uk/alzsh3/acvocab/index.htm [12 February 2014].

Jarvis, H. (2012). *Computers and learner autonomy: trends and issues.* [Online], Available: http://englishagenda.britishcouncil.org/sites/ec/files/B208_ELTRP%20 Jarvis%20Report_AW.pdf [13 February 2014].

Johns, T. (1986). Micro-concord: a language learner's research tool. *System,* 14, 2, 151–162.

Johns, T. (1991). Should you be persuaded: two examples of data-driven learning, in T. Johns and P. King (eds.) Classroom concordancing. *English Language Research,* 4, 1–16.

Kingman, J. (1988). *The Kingman Report: report of the Committee of Inquiry into the teaching of English language.* London: HMSO.

Koseter, A., Pitt, A., Handiford, M. and Lisboa, M. (2012). *Business advantage intermediate student's book.* Cambridge: Cambridge University Press.

Macmillan Publishers (2014). *Macmillan Dictionary.* [Online], Available: www.mac millandictionary.com [5 February 2014].

McCarthy, M., McCarten, J. and Sandiford, H. (2014). *Viewpoint student's book 2.* Cambridge: Cambridge University Press.

O'Dell, F. and McCarthy, M. (2008). *English collocations in use: advanced.* Cambridge: Cambridge University Press.

Research and Development Unit for English Studies, Birmingham City University (2014). *WebCorpLSE.* [Online], Available: www.webcorp.org.uk/live/wlse.jsp [12 February 2014].

Sinclair, J.M. and Renouf, A. (1988). A lexical syllabus for language learning, in R. Carter and M. McCarthy (eds.) *Vocabulary and language teaching.* Harlow: Longman, 140–158.

Standards and Testing Agency (2013). *English grammar punctuation and spelling test framework.* [Online], Available: www.gov.uk/government/uploads/system/ uploads/attachment_data/file/182674/2013_keystage2_grammarpunctation- andspelling_test_framework.pdf [8 February 2014].

Thornbury, S. (2004). *Natural grammar: the key words of English and how they work.* Oxford: Oxford University Press.

Waller, D. and Jones, C. (2012). Equipping TESOL trainees to teach through discourse. *UCLan Journal of Pedagogic Research*, 3, 5–11.

Warsaw, W. (2014). *Random idea English.* [Online], Available: http://random-idea-english.blogspot.co.uk [7 January 2014].

Weir, C. (2005). *Language testing and validation: an evidence-based approach.* London: Palgrave Macmillan.

Willis, D. (1990). *The lexical syllabus: a new approach to language teaching.* London: Collins ELT.

Willis, D. and Willis, J. (1988). *Collins COBUILD English course: part 1.* London: Collins COBUILD.

Chapter 8

Wider applications

Data-driven journalism and discourse analysis

8.1 Introduction

A frequently heard complaint these days is that people do not read enough anymore. Usually it is suggested that this is down to the internet and the multitude of electronic distractions around us. However, the complaint seems paradoxical when one considers that there is certainly more to read readily available to us now than at any point in history. The internet could be viewed as one giant corpus that draws its texts globally from just about every genre imaginable (and quite a few that are beyond that!). It is also multi-modal in that it contains countless videos and recordings. People have begun to find ways of harnessing some of this information. Friedman (2008), for example, reports on getting his Japanese learners of English to use the internet as a lexical database, allowing them to find examples of target language in context. The other way of looking at this is that anyone who has learnt how to negotiate the internet to find the information they want has in effect gained skills in negotiating what might be the largest corpus of them all.

Teachers are not alone, though, in finding ways to harness the information on the internet. Journalists and discourse analysts have also set about using the internet as a giant repository or corpus. The Data Journalism Handbook (Gray et al., 2012) describes data-driven journalism as combining the traditional 'nose for news' that a journalist has with the digital resources that are now available. Data-driven journalism has also made use of documents that are not so readily available to the public; for example, the MP expenses scandal in the UK where a national newspaper obtained and released details of the less than faithful claims made on public funds by members of the UK parliament, or the Wikileaks website to which whistle-blowers have released huge amounts of confidential data. Both of these examples, like the internet, involve the examination of huge numbers of documents, and effectively treating them like a corpus is one way of making sense of them. Journalists increasingly make use of corpus analysis tools to illustrate a story with data. An example of this can be found on the BBC

website (www.bbc.co.uk/news/uk-politics-24363746) where the same political speeches we looked at in Chapter 5 are analysed for their most frequent
content words.

This chapter will explore the use of corpora to investigate the world
around us, whether as journalists looking at political speeches or discourse
analysts looking at intercultural communication. As in previous chapters,
we will show how such investigations can start by looking at frequency at the
level of individual words and then extending this to grammatical patterns
at sentence and text levels.

8.2 Beginning an investigation

Sample exercise

Based on what we have discussed so far in this book, consider the following
situation. Imagine that you have been released a set of 10,000 documents
related to a high-profile organisation, effectively providing you with a corpus. Putting aside the ethical dimension and considering it from a grammatical perspective, how would you begin to interrogate this corpus?

Given the previous chapters, you have probably come up with the following:

- Identify a set of research questions – what would you like to know about
  the patterns of language used by the organisation? Maybe this would be
  based on insights you have about the kind of specialised lexis they use
  or the level of formality of their documents. All organisations, whether
  governmental, business or even hobbyists, have their own specialised
  language (what we often call jargon). In the UK, the magazine *Private
  Eye* has a regular feature where the government is parodied as being
  a school with a school newsletter. What is interesting about this from
  our perspective is that the style of the text and the use of language are
  instantly recognisable as being so ('There will be an end-of-term school
  auction of desirable items, including all the playing fields'). In short, by
  using our insights into the language we would expect we can formulate
  the research questions that will give us a focus for analysing the data.
- By way of example, the phrase 'hard-working families' has long been a
  staple expression of members of the British political establishment. Back
  in 2005, the BBC included it in a list of words on its 'cliché watch' (http://
  news.bbc.co.uk/1/hi/uk_politics/4393925.stm). However, in 2013, the
  Daily Mirror (www.mirror.co.uk/news/uk-news/pensions-minister-says-
  budget-means-3266197#ixzz2wab8VtSY), presumably using MPs' written answers and Hansard (the official record of parliament), calculated
  that the phrase had been used a total of 134 times with the Conservative
  Party using it on seventy-three occasions, Labour using it fifty-three
  times and the Liberal Democrats using it four times (Plaid Cymru and
  the Scottish Nationalist Party used the phrase a total of three times).

When the figures were broken down further, David Cameron, the Prime Minister at the time, was the highest scorer with seven uses of the phrase.

- Once we begin interrogating the data through our research questions, we can decide how we want to analyse it and then use a range of other measures to compare what we have found against other corpora. We can establish how frequent a particular expression is in our corpus vs. a more general or another specialised corpus using tools such as log-likelihood. These tests can give us some insights into how atypical a particular piece of language is when considered against other fields.

- In the case of 'hard-working families', we can't calculate log-likelihood as we do not have an indication of the size of the corpus the *Daily Mirror* used. However, a search of the BYU-BNC corpus reveals the following.

  o There are no instances of the phrase 'hard-working families'. The phrase 'hard working' has fifty-five counts.
  o The most frequent noun collocations with 'hard working' are horses, people, man, team and women, each with two counts.
  o The phrase appears twelve times in newspapers, ten times in spoken language, six times in non-academic texts and sixteen times in miscellaneous texts.

- Once we have our data, we can start to think about what our results mean and what they tell us about a particular type of text and context. Is it significant that the phrase 'hard-working families' does not appear in the BNC corpus which was produced in the early 1990s? Why has the phrase become more frequent in recent political discourse?

8.3 Data-driven journalism and political speeches

We've seen in the example of 'hard-working families' above that political discourse can be a vivid and fascinating source of material for analysis, so the example of data-driven investigation we will consider now will focus on the conference speeches of political leaders. In Chapter 6 we used the 2013 conference speeches from leaders of the three main political parties in the UK to investigate colligation and chunks. In this chapter, we will use the same speeches but extend the corpus from around 19,857 words to 53,103 words.

Conference speeches have been chosen because they are often perceived by the media as 'make-or-break' events. It is not uncommon to read the view in a newspaper that one leader or another has to give 'the speech of his/ her life'. These speeches are also interesting because of the intended audience. The speaker is addressing his/her own party but they are also aware that these speeches are some of the most public ones they can make and will probably help to form the public perception of him or her. They know that these speeches will be pored over by pundits and that the all-important sound-bites (the key phrases used) will be replayed over and over on the news channels, perhaps for years. One only has to consider the following phrases, all taken from UK politicians' addresses, to see that some of them at least have stuck in the psyche.

Sample exercise

See if you can match the words with the speaker. If you are not reading this in the UK context, then you'll have to take my word on this, but I'm sure you could come up with examples from your own context!

1 Do not underestimate the determination of a quiet man
2 You turn if you want to. The lady's not for turning
3 Ask me my main three priorities for government and I will tell you: education, education and education
4 Tough on crime, tough on the causes of crime
5 Prison works
6 I grew up in the 30s with an unemployed father. He didn't riot; he got on his bike and looked for work

a. Tony Blair

b. Iain Duncan Smith

c. Margaret Thatcher

d. Norman Tebbit

e. Michael Howard

(Answers: 1-b; 2-c; 3-a; 4-a; 5-e; 6-d)

The corpus was assembled from the website www.britishpoliticalspeech. org/speech-archive.htm which archives major speeches by politicians and a search facility which allows you to look for speeches by date, by party or by speaker.

Speeches were taken for three years (2011, 2012 and 2013) from each of the three main party leaders. The information was then saved as a text-only file and analysed using the concordance tool in LexTutor (www.lextutor. ca).

At this point we need the hypotheses for examination, and as discussed above these can based on what we know about the type of text in question. We know that these speeches are made with two distinct audiences in mind: the party faithful at the conference and the wider British public. We also know the speaker is attempting to appeal to and connect with both audiences, so perhaps we could look at how this interaction takes place.

With this in mind, one way of exploring the data is through metadiscourse. Hyland (2005) explains that metadiscourse is the language used either to guide a reader/listener through a text or to involve a reader/listener in a text. The concept of metadiscourse has links to Halliday's division of language into different functions: ideational, interactional and textual (see Chapter 3 for more on this). Hyland argues that all metadiscourse is interactional because it is ultimately concerned with the relationship between the producer of the text and the intended audience. For example, the text is structured according to the conventions the reader will expect and bearing in mind the level of support required by the anticipated audience. Hyland also states that to investigate metadiscourse, it is the function of the linguistic exponents that must be examined.

Two categories of metadiscourse are 'self-mention' and 'engagement markers'. Hyland (2005: 53) defines self-mention as 'the degree of explicit author presence in the text measured by the frequency of first-person pronouns and possessive adjectives' while engagement markers are language directed explicitly at the audience to gain and/or hold their attention. Based on what we know about the context of political conference speeches, we can construct our initial hypotheses.

1　There will be heavy use of 'we' alongside other forms such as 'us/our/ ours' as an engagement marker.
2　Use of 'we' will encompass both audiences: those at the live speech (i.e. the political party) as well as those watching on TV (i.e. the country at large).

After uploading the data, the following results were obtained for 'we'.

Table 8.1 Instances of 'we and related forms' in the conference speech corpus

We	1169
Our	577
We're	121
We've	149
We'll	32
Ourselves	15
Ours	7
We'd	6
TOTAL	2,076

If we compare the results from the conference corpus with a comparable spoken corpus, we can get an indication of what the number of occurrences of 'we' means. In this case we have taken only the results for 'we' (and not the other permutations) and compared them to the use of 'we' in the BYU-BNC spoken sub-corpus of parliamentary speeches. This has been chosen because it represents the same field (i.e. political) but with a different intended audience. A log-likelihood check was run and can be seen in Table 8.2:

Table 8.2 Log-likelihood scores – 'we' in the BYU-BNC spoken and conference speech corpora

	BNC spoken (Parliament) (95,025 words)	Conference corpus (53,103 words)	Log-likelihood
Frequency of word (we)	801	1169	447.76

We can see that despite the BNC corpus being almost twice the size of the conference corpus, there is a larger number of uses of 'we' in the conference corpus. With a log-likelihood of 447.76, this is highly significant (p<0.0001) and indicates overuse in the conference corpus.

At this stage we might want to consider why 'we' is so prominent in the conference corpus, and we would go back to the notion of the dual audience as well as Hyland's concept of the engagement marker. We know that those speaking to public audiences seek to keep the attention of those listening and we should expect this to be particularly essential in the case of a leader of a political party addressing his conference and the country. We could also keep in mind that speeches delivered within parliament are intended for a much more restricted audience. Although there are TV cameras in the Houses of Parliament (and a public gallery), those making speeches are often addressing their peers and fellow MPs and there is not the same need to be inclusive in their speech.

Use of the N-Gram function in LexTutor can provide us with more information about how 'we' is used in our corpus of conference speeches as shown in Figure 8.1. Note that the results below were re-checked using AntConc and the 'find' feature in Word, as the LexTutor N-Gram tool can sometimes produce anomalies. If we bring up the list of chunks with three words (with contracted forms counting as one word), we find that 'we' is present in two of these in the top ten. Numbers of occurrences are in brackets before each chunk.

Returning to the corpus, we can see how 'we' is used in these examples to examine our second hypothesis: i.e. that 'we' is used as an engagement marker to refer to both the live audience of the party faithful and the extended television audience. If we bring up the thirty-five examples of 'we've got to' from the concordance, we can try and classify them into one of two groups:

a)   Instances where 'we' refers to the speaker and their political party
b)   Instances where 'we' refers to the speaker and the people of the country as a whole

We may also have a third category:

c)   Instances where it is unclear whether 'we' refers to the political party or the country.

001.**[40]**   I want to
002.**[36]**   **WE'VE GOT TO**
003.**[27]**   in the world
004.**[26]**   The British people
005.**[25]**   better than this
006.**[25]**   **WE NEED TO**
007.**[23]**   let me tell you
008.**[23]**   race to the
009.**[22]**   one of the
010.**[22]**   the Liberal Democrats
011.**[21]**   the party of
012.**[20]**   the next Labour
013.**[19]**   me tell you
014.**[19]**   the right thing
015.**[18]**   a one nation

Figure 8.1 Three-word chunks in the conference speech corpus

1	Baccalaureate. A qualification to be proud of. You know,	**we**	've got to change the culture of this country friends. We
2	wages. No those countries are becoming our customers. and	**we**	've got to compete with California on innovation; Germany
3	truly the People's Party once again. To change our politics	**we**	've got to do more than that, we've got to hear the voices
4	that's the equivalent of five cities the size of Birmingham.	**We**	've got to do something about it and the next Labour government
5	age at the right level, and we've got to do the same again.	**We**	've got to do something about it. There are some sectors –
6	together to set the minimum wage at the right level, and	**we**	've got to do the same again.
7	ith them. If we're going to be a win-ner in this global race	**we**	've got to beat off this suffocating bureaucracy once and
8	don't talk about it because somehow it doesn't seem right.	**We**	've got to change that. It's an after-thought in our Nation

Figure 8.2 Concordance lines for 'we've got to' from the political speech corpus

Try it yourself 8.1

Look at the concordance lines in Figure 8.2 and decide which category you would count each instance as being.

What exercise 8.1 demonstrates is the need not only for quantitative results but also for careful inspection of the context and the function of the words or chunks under review. In terms of results, of the thirty-five instances of 'we've got to', around twenty-five can be classified as 'we' relating to speaker and political party, while four are related to the country as a whole and six seem to be addressing both. This last category may seem to be overly ambiguous but it also includes some fascinating uses. Consider the following stretch of text from which concordance line 8 above comes:

Nowhere do we need to put the values of the British people back at the heart of our country than in the National Health Service, the greatest institution of our country. I had a letter from a 17 year old girl suffering from depression and anxiety. She told me a heart-breaking story of how she ended up in hospital for 10 weeks: mental health is a truly One Nation problem, it affects rich and poor, north and south, young and old alike. And let's be frank: in the privacy of this room; we've swept it under the carpet for too long. It's a very British thing, we don't like to talk about it: if you've got a bad back or you're suffering from cancer you talk about it, but if you've got a depression or anxiety you don't talk about it because somehow it doesn't seem right. We've got to change that. It's an afterthought in our National Health Service.

The question of who the speaker is addressing is extremely complex here. The speaker says 'let's be frank: in the privacy of this room'. Given that the speech is being made in a conference room with representatives from just about every British newspaper, TV station and possibly the international press, the notion of 'privacy' is obviously a conceit. He is talking to the party, but in doing so he is also addressing the nation. Surely it is not only the party delegates who have 'swept it under the carpet for too long' and this tendency is apparently 'a very British thing'. The identity of 'we' has been conflated here; ostensibly he is talking to his party and lecturing them on what they need to do (signalled by the conceit of it being a 'private' discussion), but in actual fact he is saying something quite critical of the British people. I would suggest that in this example the speaker is deliberately manipulating the use of 'we' to get his message across.

Another interesting point about the use of 'we've got to' in the corpus examples is that the phrase appears to be overwhelmingly used to refer to the political party delegates rather than the country as a whole. Again, given the context, perhaps this is not so surprising. The purpose of the leader's speech is to motivate, enthuse and impress the need for action. Party leaders want to be seen as directing, guiding and leading from the front; galvanising their followers into action. 'We've got to' with its modal meaning of obligation and necessity is used to emphasise the importance of the action and to illustrate just how serious the speaker is about what he says while on the podium. We can compare it to another modal of obligation, 'we have to', which has eleven instances in the corpus.

Try it yourself 8.2

Look at all eleven examples of 'we have to' and carry out the same classification as you did above so that the examples are divided into:

a) Instances where 'we' refers to the speaker and their political party
b) Instances where 'we' refers to the speaker and the people of the country as a whole
c) Instances where it is unclear whether 'we' refers to the political party or the country.

1	to tighten their belts the most? Our position is clear. If	**we**	have to ask people to take less out or pay more in, we'll
2	The fact is this. The West Coast mainline is almost full.	**We**	have to build a new railway. and the choice is between an
3	we can see off that most short sighted of arguments: that	**we**	have to choose between going green and going for growth.
4	, our police and our courts all rose to the challenge. But	**we**	have to ensure that the offenders become ex offenders for
5	we should feel about every child. That's the responsibility	**we**	have to every parent. To support them at every stage: from
6	. ast Labour government's proudest achievements, friends. But	**we**	have to face facts: there are millions of people in this
7	Iain Duncan Smith and David Cameron. But at the same time	**we**	have to face the truth. Even after reforms of recent year
8	with the next Labour government. To be a One Nation economy	**we**	have to make life just that bit easier for the producers,
9	ers for good. hree out of four had previous convictions. So	**we**	have to push ahead with the Government's rehabilitation
10	I'm not satisfied, we're Britain, we're better than this. And	**we**	have to rebuild anew. One Nation. An economy built on you
11	believe rewards should be for hard work. But you've been told	**we**	have to tolerate the wealthiest taking what they can. And

Figure 8.3 Concordance lines for 'we have to' from the political speech corpus

With concordance lines examined, we find that just as in our investigation of 'we've got to', category A is highest, making up around 63% of the instances (compared to 71% in the 'we've got to' lines), category C is next with 27% (and 18% in the 'we've got to' lines) and category B is lowest with around 9% (11% in the 'we've got to' lines). A similar pattern appears if we examine 'we need to' (category A = 45%, B = 20% and C = 33%). All of this suggests that we can propose that when 'we' and a modal or semi-modal denoting obligation is used in these conference speeches, they are usually addressed to the live audience for the purpose of communicating importance and accuracy. We can also see that in their speeches leaders may choose to be unclear as to whom 'we' refers to and that this may be done for purposes such as to share criticisms. We could analyse the examples where the reference is unclear in more detail and develop a range of uses, which we could then use to analyse future speeches and continue to test the hypotheses.

Having considered the use of 'we' as an engagement marker, let us now look at instances of self-mention, in this case by examining use of the high-frequency chunk 'I want to'. There are forty instances of this chunk in the data. Given the context of the speeches, we might construct a hypothesis for the use of this chunk which is related to the idea of the speaker presenting himself as being dynamic and forceful. When we look at the concordance lines we do find a number of verbs used that demonstrate action (Table 8.3 gives some examples of this).

Table 8.3 Examples of 'I want to + verb phrase' showing actions

	change	the values
		the way
	make	this the most family friendly
	mend	that link
I want to	see	a new cross party approach
		a payback to every citizen
	win	it for Britain
	work	with you

These instances, while clearly present in the concordance lines, only account for eleven out of forty instances (around 27.5%). What quickly emerges is a different grammatical pattern and a different function, that of announcing goals or explicit signalling within the text (Hyland, 2005: 51). Look at the instances in Table 8.4.

Table 8.4 Examples of 'I want to + verb phrase' announcing goals or signalling

	do	something different today.
	explain	why
	make	a serious point today [the argument]
	pay	Tribute
	say	something to you to them today
I want to	start	by thanking someone
	Talk	about our . . . mission to all the people to you about today very directly
	tell	you about one business you my story
	thank	everyone here one colleague in particular the people who have

Overall, there are twenty-eight (around 70%) uses of 'I want to' that fall into this function of what might be termed announcing goals. If we consider the reason for the use of this piece of language, we can identify a number of reasons for it. First of all, the explicit use of the first person 'I' is a direct intervention in the text by the speaker. By choosing to use 'I', the speaker is directly associating himself with the message and showing a personal stake in it. At the same time the phrases are being used to flag up what the speaker is doing in the speech as well as to structure the message. As in our examination of previous texts, it is important to consider that what the speaker has said could have been said in a different way, but the speaker chose to do it in this particular way. We can probably relate the reason for this choice back to the desire to create a personal connection with the audience (both the live and the television ones) as well as to come across as a forceful individual.

There are two other high-frequency chunks in our list of N-Grams that we can consider at this stage: 'the British people' and 'the party of', which also seem (upon first inspection) to contribute to the positioning of the speakers in relation to their audiences. The aim here is to investigate whether our instincts about the way these phrases are used in the corpus are correct.

Try it yourself 8.3

Keeping in mind the context within which these speeches have been made, come up with a hypothesis about how you think the two phrases 'the British people' and 'the party of' are used before you look at the concordance lines which are also in the answer section for 8.2.

Examining the concordance lines (see the answers for 8.3 if you have skipped the exercise above to see the lines) for 'the British people' reveals a rather interesting finding. Most instances of 'the British people', twenty-four out of twenty-six in fact (approximately 92%), have the speaker referring to 'the British people' as a separate entity. In only two of the lines (13 and 18) does the speaker overtly identify himself as being part of 'the British people' through the use of 'us'. While we might be surprised by the level of this apparent distance between the speaker and the wider audience, we can look again at the context to consider why this may be the case. Perhaps this gap is a product of the need to address the 'immediate' live audience. The speaker is addressing his or her own party and perhaps is attempting to appear as if a private conversation has been 'overheard' by the wider public. When a speaker says 'The patients said no. And the British people said no. And what did he do?', he is giving the impression that he is conveying the views of a notionally unified British public to his party. By being apart from the British people, the speaker actually tries to demonstrate unity with this wider audience by speaking about their beliefs or values to a 'private' audience.

If we consider the concordance lines for 'the party of', we find that it is always followed by an abstract noun phrase (aspiration, education, government, small business) and that just about every example (excepting two examples, 6 and 7) is a positive statement. It is unsurprising that a leader should choose to 'brand' his party as 'the party of aspiration'. Interestingly enough, the two negative connotations in this corpus are when a speaker is talking about a different political party and tarring them as being 'the party of' an undesirable noun phrase.

All of the examples above taken from our corpus illustrate how grammatical corpus data can be examined to investigate real-world contexts. With the internet and the growing number of websites that act as repositories for official documents, speeches, interviews and the like, it is easier than ever to interrogate data and carry out forensic investigations of different types of text. Journalists may choose to go through texts looking at how particular nouns have been used (e.g. hard-working families) or to consider how a leader might use patterns such as 'I want to + verb' to bolster their authority and perhaps create a stronger public image. They might also want to consider how leaders play two audiences simultaneously; what is the message to the room, what is the message to the wider world? The examination of lexico-grammar and, crucially, the functional use of language offers many different ways of examining such corpus data.

8.4 Intercultural discourse analysis

For anyone working in business, culture is not simply an abstract notion but often a very real consideration which can mean the difference between successful business ventures or commercial failure. The ever-increasing number of books and websites on doing business in other countries attests to this phenomenon, and often these sources include lurid tales of misfortune which have occurred as a result of intercultural misunderstandings.

The following are some tips intended for visitors to the UK who wish to do business in the country taken from the website www.worldbusinessculture.com. You might want to take a moment to consider these, and if you are from the UK or have experience of doing business with British nationals, consider the relative usefulness of these tips.

Tip 4
Job descriptions in the UK are often very unclear and imprecise leaving a potential vacuum in ownership of task and decision.

Tip 5
Managers try to develop a close, friendly relationship with staff and like to be seen as part of the team rather than removed from the team.

Tip 6
The value of pure academic education is viewed with some suspicion. Respect is earned through experience rather than qualification. It is rare to see a professor or doctor on the senior management committee of a large UK company.

Tip 7
Managers find it difficult to articulate direct instructions and will often couch instructions in very diplomatic language.

Tip 8
There are a lot of meetings in the UK and they often fail to produce the desired decision.

The initial reaction to these sort of tips is often a form of wry amusement. While we may certainly recognise some of the elements described, our response is often to say 'yes, but . . . '. Most of these lists have a grain of truth in them – most people who regularly attend meetings would agree with Tip 8. The issue here is that these forms of guides have to generalise to make their point and they are often constructed from anecdotal evidence. The use of corpora, specifically business-related corpora, can offer us a way of examining the artefacts of cultures and allow us to investigate how differences manifest themselves through language.

A key point here is the definition of culture. Even a brief consideration will lead you to conclude that it is not monolithic; there are many different cultures within nations. The same is true of the business world. It no longer follows that a company's corporate culture will be that of the host-country simply because they work in a particular region of the world, so corpus studies of business culture are not limited to national boundaries. Documents from two organisations in the same country could be considered to examine how the members of one organisation compose e-mails, for example, compared to another.

An example of intercultural discourse analysis is an article produced by Vergaro (2005) which looked at two corpora of For Your Information (FYI) letters produced by English and Italian writers. Vergaro (2005: 116) defined FYI letters as being part of a wider 'business letter' group and as 'informing the addressee about something (change of address, management, prices, etc.) that will affect the way in which the business transaction will be carried out in the future'. The letter makes no demand on the receiver other than to take note of the change. This can be an interesting type of text to look at because it is quite ubiquitous, if one considers the letters or e-mails from banks and businesses that many of us receive informing us of offers or adjustments to interest rates. Another element Vergaro identifies is that these letters come either in the middle of an established relationship because contact has already been made, or towards the end (e.g. written confirmation of an account being closed). These two points, the availability of a particular text type and the social function of it, are excellent reminders of some of the factors around creating one's own corpus. As mentioned earlier in the book, you need to ensure that you have access to sufficient quantities of examples to be able to construct a principled corpus, and you need to think carefully about the social role the text type plays. One suspects that Vergaro chose this type of letter because it would provide insights into how two groups (English and Italian writers in this case) used correspondence to manage an ongoing relationship and therefore had the potential to provide interesting insights into cultural behaviour.

Vergaro's corpus consisted of forty-three Italian FYI letters and thirty English ones (eighteen British, twelve American), representing thirty-five Italian business organisations and twenty English ones respectively. Vergaro does not inform us of the number of words in the corpus but we would imagine that it is fairly small since FYI letters tend to be quite brief. Vergaro's analysis of the corpus is qualitative in nature (which one can do with a relatively small corpus). She examines the 'moves' the writers go through (that is, the 'steps' that the letters go through to achieve their communicative purpose) and uses a range of cultural theories to analyse and account for the results. She does, however, carry out a metadiscourse analysis of the texts and reports the following (Vergaro, 2005: 129–30):

- There was very little metadiscourse in the letters overall.
- 72% of the Italian letters made use of an illocution marker to begin the letter (what Hyland would term 'announcing goals', e.g. 'I am writing to inform you . . . '). These markers were rare in the English letters but provided more background to the announcement being made, so Vergaro suggests that this negates the need for the illocution markers.
- There were some markers for sequencing the text (e.g. finally) and connecting bits of text (besides, in addition). The English letters used a wider variety of metadiscourse for these functions. The Italian letters used *pertanto* ('so', 'thus', 'therefore') only in the part of the letter where a request was being made of the reader.

Vergaro concludes from her overall analysis that Italian writers are more inclined to see the letters as part of an ongoing business relationship and that the wider context can be assumed, whereas the English writers make more effort to provide a background to the information being relayed. It is not hard to see from this how such letters could be regarded as being 'abrupt' to an English reader when in fact there are simply just different assumptions in play. This kind of study is perhaps more useful to those who engage with such cultures on a regular basis, for example if a manager is dealing with an Italian counterpart. Perhaps e-mails from this individual sometimes appear curt while the English manager's correspondence seems to the Italian to be constantly treading over old ground. This is a guess, based on Vergaro's findings, but we could build on her analysis by constructing a corpus of such e-mails and examining them.

8.5 Investigating 'hereby' in GloWbe

The kind of intercultural discourse analysis described above can also be undertaken using larger corpora such as the GloWbe. The corpus can be used to investigate aspects of language use that might indicate particular cultural forms of communication. To demonstrate this, we will look at the use of a particular word in written web texts across different countries using the GloWbe corpus and then use this to consider grammatical patterns.

The word we've chosen to focus on is 'hereby'. This has been chosen because, first, it is a low-frequency word usually reserved for very formal legal documents or speech (or else it is being used in a 'marked' way for comedic effect). Second, it is a performative word, which formally enacts the verb that accompanies it (e.g. 'I hereby pronounce you man and wife'). Thinking about the GloWbe corpus, a 1.9-billion-word collection of web-pages from around the world, we would anticipate that 'hereby' would be relatively infrequent. We could also extrapolate the following hypotheses:

1   Use of hereby will either be with the first person ('I hereby') or the passive ('you are hereby informed . . . ').
2   The use of 'hereby' in passive constructions may show cultural differences in the language used on websites in different English-speaking countries.

A search for 'hereby' on GloWbe finds 7882 instances of use with a part per million occurrence of 4.18. The results for each country are in Table 8.5. Countries with more parts per million than the average have been bolded.

Table 8.5 GloWbe occurrences by country for use of 'hereby'

Country	Number of occurrences	Part per million occurrences
US	1398	3.61
Canada	**563**	**4.18**
UK	644	1.66
Ireland	**607**	**6.01**
Australia	352	2.38
New Zealand	239	2.94
India	**239**	**5.07**
Sri Lanka	164	3.52
Pakistan	166	3.23
Bangladesh	**236**	**5.98**
Singapore	**241**	**5.61**
Malaysia	**240**	**5.76**
Philippines	623	14.41
Hong Kong	**206**	**5.09**
South Africa	**337**	**7.43**
Nigeria	**432**	**10.13**
Ghana	**272**	**7.02**
Kenya	**212**	**5.16**
Tanzania	**243**	**6.91**
Jamaica	**218**	**5.51**

What is immediately of interest from this word-level investigation is how most of those countries sometimes referred to as the 'inner circle' of English-speaking countries (the UK, Ireland, the USA, Canada, Australia and New Zealand) tend to come below the average number of occurrences. The other noticeable feature is the higher scores from the Philippines and Nigeria. The fact that these two countries are considerably above average in terms of frequency suggests that something is going on in their texts which is not as prominent in texts from other countries.

Table 8.6 compares the results of immediate collocates on the left and right of the word 'hereby' from three countries; the Philippines which was the highest-scoring country, Ireland which was the highest scoring of the 'inner circle' of English-speaking countries and the UK which was below the average level of use of the word.

Table 8.6 Collocates (one place left and right) for 'hereby' from GloWbe

	Philippines		Ireland		UK	
	WORD/PHRASE	Number of Occurrences	WORD/PHRASE	Number of Occurrences	WORD/PHRASE	Number of Occurrences
1	IS	297	IS	139	I	131
2	ARE	161	ARE	81	IS	76
3	CREATED	46	YOU	79	YOU	67
4	DECLARED	35	,	51	ARE	61
5	REPEALED	33	I	45	WE	46
6	AUTHORIZED	30	APPLIES	42	DO	35
7	DO	26	AGREE	35	,	29
8	YOU	26	AMENDED	26	DECLARE	28
9	AMENDED	25	DO	20	AGREE	28
10	DIRECTED	23	DECLARED	18	GRANT	22
11	I	22	EXPRESSLY	17	AND	20
12	ORDERED	21	GIVEN	17	PARTIES	15
13	AFFIRMED	15	OF	17	GIVE	14
14	ORDER	14	GRANT	16	GRANTS	14
15	,	13	REPEALED	16	EXCLUDED	14

One thing that is immediately noticeable from the Philippines data is the tendency of verbs to be in the past participle form, thereby signalling that the passive form is the preferred pattern of use. Figure 8.4 shows some examples of this pattern.

The examples from Ireland and the UK use fewer of these past participle forms and more active verbs (apply, agree(s), do). The use of passive verb forms creates a more official-sounding statement of authority. Compare, for example, 'rules are hereby adopted' with 'we have adopted some rules'. The use of 'hereby' is a conscious decision because it adds a level of illocutionary

1	if any (but not those of any Third Party Site), are	**hereby incorporated**	into and made a part of these Terms by reference
2	A B C of the Services are governed by Chill's privacy Policy, which policy is	**hereby incorporated**	into these Terms by reference. 20. JURISDICTIONAL ISSUES The Site
3	Provided, That the Philippine Legislature, herein provided for, is	**hereby authorized**	to provide by law for the acquisition of Philippine citizenship by those natives of
4	All those interested in English online Teaching and learning are	**hereby invited**	to register in our website and send us their article. The articles will
5	conformably to Section 17 thereof, the following Rules are	**hereby adopted**	in order to carry out the provisions of the said Code:

Figure 8.4 Examples of 'hereby' in the Philippines sub-corpus of GloWbe corpus

force by making the statement sound more legalistic. These results give initial indications of the different ways in which quasi-legal notices are realised in these countries on websites. The different grammatical choices may indicate cultural differences – something that could be followed up with a more detailed examination of the corpus data. It is of course important not to overplay the significance of such findings, but they can offer an evidence-base from which intercultural discourse could be examined.

8.6 Limitations

In this chapter we have shown that it is possible to use corpora to investigate the world around us, whether for journalistic purposes or as someone interested in intercultural communication. We can look at the frequency of patterns in the texts we are investigating and think about the semantic prosody of these. However, there are limitations. Corpora cannot tell us everything we want to know about political speeches or culture; they can only provide clues as to what is going on in the form of statistics. As we have already described, we will then have to use qualitative methods to investigate the data we have generated and make decisions about it, for example the use of 'we' in the political conference speeches corpus. We are then left to interpret what we have found. If we were to continue the investigation into the use of 'hereby', we might want to look at different theories of culture and the work of writers in the field to help us account for the differences.

Further practice

1   Pick a number of speeches by a famous figure (e.g. Martin Luther King, Margaret Thatcher, John F. Kennedy) and compile them into a corpus. Use tools such as N-Grams to identify frequent chunks or uses of particular patterns, then bring up those examples in a concordance and

see what they tell you about the way the speaker shapes their message with language. Pronouns and discourse markers are always interesting features to start with.

2   There is much discussion about other varieties of English such as Singaporean English or the way the language is used in Hong Kong. Identify a particular feature you would like to investigate and use the GloWbe corpus to look at that particular feature or a corpus like the HKCSE. What does it tell you about the way this piece of language is used in this culture? Does it provide any cultural insights?

References

BBC News (2005). *Election cliché watch.* [Online], Available: http://news.bbc.co.uk/1/hi/uk_politics/4393925.stm [12 August 2014].

BBC News (2013). *Miliband, Clegg and Cameron: three leaders and their speeches compared.* [Online], Available: www.bbc.co.uk/news/uk-politics-24363746 [12 August 2014].

Belam, M. (2014). Is 'hard-working families' the hardest worked phrase in Parliament? *The Daily Mirror.* [Online], Available: http://ampp3d.mirror.co.uk/2013/12/19/is-hard-working-families-the-hardest-worked-phrase-in-parliament.

CDA Media (2014). *World business culture.* [Online], Available: www.worldbusiness-culture.com/Doing-Business-in-Britain.html [25 January 2015].

Davies, M. (2013). *Corpus of global web-based English: 1.9 billion words from speakers in 20 countries* (GloWbe). [Online], Available: http://corpus2.byu.edu/glowbe [1 July 2013].

Friedman, G.L. (2008). Learner-created lexical databases using web-based source material. *ELT Journal,* 63, 2, 126–136.

Gray, J., Chambers, L. and Bounegru, L. (2012). *The Data Journalism Handbook: how journalists can use data to improve the news.* Sebastopol, CA: O'Reilly Media.

Hyland, K. (2005). *Metadiscourse: exploring interaction in writing.* London: Continuum.

Vergaro, C. (2005). 'Dear Sirs, I hope you will find this information useful': discourse strategies in Italian and English 'For Your Information' (FYI) letters. *Discourse Studies,* 7, 1, 109–135.

Chapter 9

Research projects

9.1 Introduction

In this chapter, we aim to bring together some of the methods of analysis we have described in this book to explore how corpus data can be used in research projects you may become engaged in. To achieve this, we look at three different case studies to demonstrate a possible research approach in the areas of ELT (EFL/ESL), Literature and English Language/Linguistics. Each study examines grammar using one of the techniques we have outlined: the first frequency, the second collocations and colligation, and the third colligation and semantic prosody. As we do so, we will attempt to demonstrate how corpus data may be analysed and interpreted.

To undertake a research project, we need to plan our research in a principled manner. To start you thinking about this, make a brief list for yourself regarding what is needed to undertake principled research. Think about the different aspects you need to consider. One might be 'how am I going to collect the data?', for example.

Figure 9.1 shows the aspects we feel are essential. It also shows how we can view research as a cyclical process, with one element feeding into the other.

To take an example, let us imagine I have an interest in how the 'get passive' ('he got arrested' etc) is used. I may have noticed that it is not really covered in English language textbooks and wonder if it should be. I look at the literature and find that the form has been analysed fairly extensively (for example, Carter and McCarthy, 1999). Therefore, it would not be productive simply to re-analyse this as a form. However, there seem to be few studies that focus on the use of this form by learners of English at different levels. If it is fairly common in the spoken English of native speakers, it seems worth considering the extent to which the use by learners differs or is similar. This may, therefore, be worth investigating and we may wish to set ourselves research questions such as 'how frequent are "get passive" forms in the speech of English language learners in comparison to native speaker usage?'

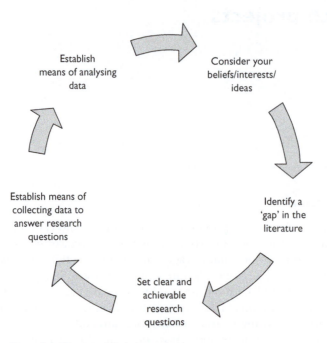

Figure 9.1 The principled research process

Once we have set our questions, we need to consider the kind of corpora we have access to. For such a study, we would need a spoken learner corpus and one based on native speaker data. The corpora need to be comparable–some learner data from spoken tests would not be comparable to a corpus of prepared speeches, for example. Ideally, as the research indicates that this is frequent in unplanned, conversational speech, we need corpora that allow us to compare its use. Finally, we need to consider how we are going to analyse the data. Will we look only at frequency of correct usage or also explore incorrect usage? Will we undertake a keyword analysis to understand if the 'get passive' is used more frequently in certain contexts? These are all considerations we must undertake as we are planning and designing the research project. We will return to this research cycle in the next sections, as we examine three sample studies.

9.2 Sample study 1: Real and unreal conditionals in a general corpus

This study and the sample shown are from a previously published piece of research (Jones and Waller, 2011), which sought to examine the frequency of different patterns of conditional forms or 'if' clauses (e.g. 'If I could choose to live anywhere (condition), it would be in Thailand' (result should the condition be fulfilled) in the BYU-BNC corpus. This study started from a belief that such forms are often inadequately described in English language textbooks, where there is a tendency to identify and teach four conditional patterns only. These are as follows:

1 The zero conditional. If + present simple, present simple, e.g. 'If water reaches a hundred degrees, it boils'. This is said to describe habitual actions or universal truths.
2 The first conditional. If + present simple, will + infinitive, e.g. 'If it rains later, I'll probably get wet'. This is said to describe the possible result if a condition is met in the future.
3 The second conditional. If + past simple, would + infinitive, e.g. 'If I could live anywhere, I would live in Thailand'. This is said to describe an unlikely result in general time or in the future because the condition is hypothetical.
4 The third conditional. If + past perfect, would have + past participle, e.g. 'If I had woken up earlier, I wouldn't have been late'. This is said to describe a hypothetical result in the past because the condition is also hypothetical and the event is finished i.e. I was late and I did not wake up early enough.

Our belief is that such a description is an oversimplification and that many other constructions are possible. We feel that this leads to a poor description of this language area for both learners and teachers and one that did not equip for language in use.

Try it yourself 9.1

It is easy to check this intuition by conducting a very simple search for 'if' patterns. Go to WebCorpLSE (http://wse1.webcorp.org.uk/cgi-bin/SYN/index.cg) and click on the 'synchronic web corpus', consisting of 339,907,995 words taken from webpages in the years 2000–2010. Search for 'If I + verb, I + verb', using the parts of speech tags under the search item. You can check the results in the back of the book.

Reading the literature, we found that these questions about the four conditionals had been raised before within ELT. As far back as 1988 Maule wrote an article questioning the 'traditional' division of conditionals into zero, first, second and third conditional patterns. Inspired by the refusal of one student to accept as correct a conditional form ('If he comes, I go'), which did not fit the patterns she had been taught, Maule recorded 100 samples of conditionals from a random selection of scripted and unscripted television programmes. He suggested that rather than the zero, first, second and third conditionals, it was more accurate to divide the samples into real non-past/past uses and unreal non-past/past, with a variety of forms being used to realise these uses. To give just one example, a real past form may be 'If you felt so strongly about it, why did you agree to do it?', whereby the pattern 'If + past simple, past simple' is used to describe a condition that was fulfilled in the past. In the time following Maule's work there has been a lot of research using corpora. Willis (1990), for example, found that the majority of hypothetical uses of 'would' in the COBUILD corpus were not with an accompanying 'if' clause, so that 'I'd probably say no' is more frequent than 'If he asked me, I'd probably say no'. In a sample of written academic, narrative, magazine and newspaper texts, Fulcher (1991: 166) also found that real non-past uses made up a large percentage of his sample of 299 conditionals, with the 'If + present simple, present simple/continuous/present modal/imperative' accounting for 65.55% of his data. More recently, Carter and McCarthy (2006: 749–50) found many samples of real non-past and real past conditionals in the Cambridge International Corpus, in a variety of forms.

The 'gap' we therefore identified in the literature was that despite this research evidence, the four conditional patterns were still often the only ones presented in ELT textbooks. We therefore felt it was necessary to reconfirm the evidence Maule (1988) discovered and explore it using corpus data. We then wished to explore what it meant for pedagogy and course design. Our research questions were therefore:

1   To what extent do samples of 'if' clauses from the BYU-BNC confirm or add to Maule's (1988) categories of past and non-past, real and past/non-past unreal conditional forms?
2   What are the implications for classroom pedagogy and materials design in ELT?

To answer the first question, we decided to focus on frequency of the forms only, which was combined with a qualitative analysis to determine, from the context, if the usage was describing something 'unreal' or 'real' and the exact time reference. To do this, we decided to extract 250 concordance lines from the BYU-BNC corpus by simply searching for 'if'. This decision was made as we felt there was a need to look at more samples than Maule (1988) was able to, but that looking at all samples in the corpus would simply be too time-consuming and may in any case produce similar results. There is never a clear-cut answer about how many corpus samples we may need to consult to answer a research question as it will depend on what the question is, but the key point is we need to be able to justify the amount of data we analyse.

Once we had identified the 250 samples of 'if' clauses, we had to analyse them. This meant manually going through each sample and then categorising the form according to the construction of the pattern and whether it could be said to be real past, real non-past etc. The decision was made to interpret the data in this way because although a corpus allows us to look for patterns such as If + verb + pronoun etc., it would not be able to categorise these into 'real non-past' etc.

Try it yourself 9.2

Look at some of the edited samples we used in the study. Categorise these into either real past/non-past uses or unreal past/non-past uses. There is one sample of each. Then decide on the construction of each pattern.

1 If they'd done that, they would have won the Championship
2 If you wanted to know the answer. . . you had to keep zapping from channel to channel.
3 If we could get three or four items, that would be very nice
4 If I'm making a film of myself. . . , I can pass or fail. . .

Figure 9.2 Concordance lines for real and unreal patterns

When analysing our results in full, the findings did in general replicate the suggestions of Maule (1988). We found many patterns beyond the traditional four conditionals and could also show that the most frequent category by far was the real non-past usage. These results can be seen in Table 9.1. These frequency figures are supported by MI scores found by a search for 'If I *' and 'If you *' as shown in Table 9.2 below.

These figures show that there are more present forms following these patterns and in particular after 'If you'. The data is supported by higher MI scores for present forms, in particular 'If you're', 'If I'm' and 'If you want'. This last pattern is likely to cluster together because it can function as a chunk to make requests or offers or indicate choices to other speakers. The sample concordance lines in Figure 9.3 give examples of this.

This data allowed us to answer our first research question. We could confirm Maule's findings and examine some of the patterns we found and show that purely based on frequency, real non-past forms are the most common. The data does not allow us to say why this may be and the research question we set was not designed to answer this, therefore any suggestions in this regard are speculative. Further research would also be needed to analyse how real non-past forms function in different modes of discourse, such as conversation or news stories. The data did allow us to make suggestions for our second question. Here we proposed that teachers could at least make students aware of real/unreal non-past and past forms by looking at

Table 9.1 Conditional patterns (Jones and Waller, 2011)

Form	Example line from corpus	Frequency of form
If + present simple, present simple	If an earn out is to be used, it is recommended that it does not form too significant a part of the purchase price. . .	61
If + present simple, may	If a vacancy on the committee exists, then the trustee may appoint some other creditor. . .	10
If + present simple, present perfect	if we get to alimony, I've seen the film!	4
If + can, present simple	if it can be shown that. . . can lead to. . . , it does not logically follow that	2
If + would like, imperative	If you would like to make any suggestions. . . , please contact. . .	1
If + present simple, should	If a vacancy on a committee exists, then. . . a meeting of creditors should be convened. . .	3
If + may, will	Even if Bernard Stasi may be right in describing. . . , it will be a challenge to succeed him. . .	1
If + present simple, can	Of course you can have a boiled egg if that's what you want.	8
If + present continuous, can	if I'm making a film of myself. . . , I can pass or fail. . .	1
If + can't, must	If you cannot find a pulse, you must begin chest compression. . .	1
If + present simple, must	. . . even if the plaintiff overcomes the difficult hurdle of. . . , he must further show that the contravention has caused him loss.	3
If + present simple + should, present simple	if you take. . . the starting point that the new settlement should have good access to primary network, you immediately limit. . .	1
If + present simple, could	If this happens the frescoes could be damaged. . .	3
If + present simple, present continuous	A motoring breakdown scheme. . . is offering members a 20 per cent. . . discount if they do not call out the service during the year.	2
If + present perfect, imperative	If the pose you have selected is a tense one, feel the tension. . .	2
If + present perfect, shall	the proprietor shall not be liable. . . if it has been compiled with. . .	1
If + present simple, will	She'll just become a laughing stock if she's not that already	17
If + present simple, shall	If food and beverages are not so provide, the holder of the licence. . . shall be guilty of an offence.	2
If + present simple, going to	If he don't serve her he's gonna die, she's gonna punch him right!	3
If + can, will	. . . they won't be able to tell us if we can have Ian until tomorrow.	1
If + will, present simple	If the pump still will not run. . . it is probably in need of servicing. . .	1
If + will, can	If the cast will just relax. . . , it can only improve. . .	1
If + going to, should	. . . if you're not going to join us, then. . . you should let us join you.	1
If + as + participle, would	if as educationalists. . . , we would care to make some comment then. . .	1

a) Real Non-Past

Category	Pattern	Example	Count
b) Real Past	If + present simple, past continuous	If it means anything else, Hume was making fun of Adams.	1
	If + present simple, past simple	. . if it's the thing I'm thinking of there was some discrepancy	2
	If + past simple, past simple	if you wanted to know the answer. . . you had to keep zapping from channel to channel.	11
	If + could, could	if anything could send strange signals, the Thing could.	1
	If + could, might	If we could listen to the conversation. . . it might be anything but fascinating.	1
	If + past simple, present simple	even if we did, we have no divers aboard. . .	1
	If + past simple, would ('d)	I'd give it a good hiding if it didn't behave.	21
	If + present simple, would	if two members of staff happen to fall in love and decide to marry it would be churlish to be appointing blame.	4
c) Unreal Non-Past	If + was going to, would	. . if you was gonna do the one at King Arthur's I would of had some rice.	1
	If + past simple, could	An operation could be said to have increased efficiency either if fewer inputs were used. . .	3
	If + could, would	. . if we could get three or four items, that would be very nice.	3
	If + past simple, shall	if she did not do so, ';this pre-eminence wherein ye are placed shall be your dejection to torment and pain everlasting'	1
	If + past simple, might	If they got a few more of those it might help.	2
d) Unreal past	If + past perfect, would + present perfect	If they'd done that, they would have won the Championship	6
	If + past perfect, might + present perfect	it ';might have saved time'; if. . . Hindley and. . . Brady had been shot.	2
	If + past perfect, past simple	If it had been believed in Paris, there was a further complication. . .	1
TOTAL			192

Table 9.2 MI figures for 'If I + *' and 'If you + *'

Form	Frequency of collocates	MI scores
If I *	Had (1096)	3.11
	Can (926)	3.72
	'm (853)	5.50
	Could (806)	4.06
	Do (710)	3.12
If you *	're (4188)	5.67
	Are (4078)	3.11
	Do (3411)	3.63
	Want (2946)	5.71
	Can (2035)	3.10

1	reading this they're not really going to help us a great deal.	**If you want**	to pass it round and read it. It's they
2	pause erm membership form which actually explained what what we did in	**if you want**	to join return this sort of thing. Yeah. I've
3	think it would be wise. Yes. If you wouldn't mind. Well	**if you want**	to just ring and ask someone to bring them.
4	And change! Well you can stay here till twenty five past	**if you want**	that's up to you! Erm am
5	it's easy to hop in a car and get from here to Chelmsford,	**if you want**	to do it by public transport it is a nightmare erm
6	all in this system Fine. because it will be very complex.	**if you want**	to, if you start building a system that's gonna record

Figure 9.3 Sample concordance lines for 'if you want' from the BYU-BNC

samples from textbook recordings and reading texts, which inevitably do contain patterns beyond those often taught.

9.3 Sample study 2: Corpus stylistics and Sherlock Holmes

In recent years, there have been an increasing number of corpus-based studies of literary texts, often under the banner of 'corpus stylistics'. This form of study can be defined as follows:

> Corpus stylistics investigates the relationship between meaning and form. Thus it is similar to both stylistics and corpus linguistics. Whereas stylistics pays more attention to deviations from linguistic norms that

lead to the creation of artistic effects, corpus linguistics mainly focuses on repeated and typical uses, as these are what the computer can identify.
(Mahlberg, 2007: 4)

In other words, stylistics seeks to analyse how the language used in a text contributes to the meaning(s) made by it, and corpora have been used to demonstrate the particular ways in which authors make meaning through their use of language. We can do this by identifying aspects that can be analysed with a corpus, such as keywords and collocations. As we mentioned in Chapter 4, using corpora in this way gives us a 'window' into the language choices of an author. The reason for using corpora is either to uncover what we may be unable to find intuitively or at least to provide further evidence for ideas we already have (Stubbs, 2008). We may, for instance, suspect that the way an author uses particular grammar or lexico-grammar helps to shape the style of her/his writing and to foreground his/her theme or message. A corpus search can demonstrate the extent to which this is correct and potentially reveal new areas of analysis. It does not replace subjective or qualitative analysis but can provide quantitative data to support a researcher's opinions. For reasons of copyright, literary corpora are not found as often as some others but WebCorpLSE does contain an open-access collection of Charles Dickens novels (http://wse1.webcorp.org.uk/home). As we will explain below, small corpora can be built by accessing literature that is out of copyright.

Generally, the researcher will follow the kind of research cycle we have outlined in Figure 9.1 and will often use a corpus of a particular author's works in comparison to a general reference corpus. For example, Spencer (2011) sought to examine semantic prosody in the novels of H.P. Lovecraft and found that some N-Grams had distinctly negative semantic prosody. Mahlberg explored a corpus of Charles Dickens' novels and looked at clusters (which we termed 'chunks' in Chapter 5). She suggests that clusters help to form textual patterns 'that are relevant to the creation of characters in readers' minds' (Mahlberg, 2013: 26). She shows that by analysing key clusters in the work of Dickens (the clusters that occur with significantly greater frequency in his fiction in comparison to a reference corpus), we can illuminate how the writer creates his particular fictional world. She highlights Dickens' use of 'with his back to the fire' and the way this chunk is commonly used to contribute details to the characterisation of male characters in the novels (Mahlberg, 2013: 114). O'Halloran (2007) shows how the exploration of keywords can be used to reveal thematic concerns in a text. He explores the use of keywords such as 'would' in Joyce's *Eveline* and demonstrates, at least in part, the way in which 'would' is used with greater frequency in this story to demonstrate how Eveline is hypothesising about possibilities for her future. A corpus can be used in this type of analysis to help us identify repeated patterns, which can then be interpreted in relation to specific texts and contexts.

Using a form of corpus stylistics to analyse literary works is now relatively simple to undertake using works out of copyright via Project Gutenberg (www.gutenberg.org), whereby the researcher can construct a corpus of a particular author they may wish to study. In this example, as mentioned in Chapter 2, we have chosen to look at Conan Doyle's Sherlock Holmes stories. The sample corpus is based upon the following stories and novels: *The Valley of Fear, The Lost World, The Sign of the Four, The Hound of the Baskervilles, The Adventures of a Dying Detective, The Memoirs of Sherlock Holmes, His Last Bow, The Adventures of Wisteria Lodge, The Adventures of the Cardboard Box, The Adventures of the Red Circle,* and *The Adventures of the Devil's Foot* (372,841 words). While we could not claim this was fully representative of all Conan Doyle's Sherlock Holmes stories, it did at least represent a sizeable sample of his works from Victorian to Georgian eras and thus we could test some of our hypotheses. As we have set out above, all research should follow a cycle whereby we start with a hypothesis, locate a gap in the literature and set realistic and achievable research questions.

Sample exercise

Imagine you wish to use corpus stylistics to conduct research on Sherlock Holmes stories and novels. What assumptions do you start with about these novels? How could you test these?

Some possible examples:

1   A comparison of the use of 'observation' verbs such as 'looked/studied/observed' in the Sherlock Holmes stories in comparison to a general corpus and what this tells us about the characterisation and mood created in the stories.
2   Analysis of the high-frequency keywords in the Sherlock Holmes stories in comparison with Charles Dickens' novels and what these indicate about the themes of the stories. These may support our understanding of thematic concerns or suggest new themes.

In our case, the process we used was as follows:

We started from an assumption that particular keywords and chunks might be used in Sherlock Holmes to help with characterisation. We also felt that certain chunks would colligate in particular grammatical patterns and that these could be analysed to reveal ways in which Conan Doyle used language to develop our idea of a character. We decided that the character of Sherlock Holmes (being the key character in the stories) was the one we would focus on. We looked at the literature and found that there have been a number of studies that have analysed the character of Sherlock Holmes. Kestner (1997), for example, argues that Conan Doyle constructed a particular type of masculinity through the character of Holmes. He suggests that Holmes can be viewed as a hero of the established social order of the time and of a traditional role of masculinity, both of which were seen as being under threat with the fall of the British Empire and increasing women's rights. Discussing the first appearance of Holmes, Kestner (1997: 43) suggests that 'Holmes' use of expressions such as "I perceive" or "Don't you see" aligns him not only with masculinity but with dominance from the first chapter of the novel'.

This literature therefore suggests that one view of Holmes' character is that it illustrates a certain type of masculinity. We can suggest he embodies rationality, intelligence and (perhaps) dominance. Although this has been written about fairly extensively in the literature, at the time of writing it would seem that nobody has attempted to support these assertions from a corpus stylistic view. Therefore, our research questions were:

a) What are the most frequent chunks in our sample of Sherlock Holmes stories when compared to the BYU-BNC fiction corpus?
b) How is the use of these words different or similar to the fiction sub-corpus of the BYU-BNC corpus?
c) To what extent does this contribute to the characterisation of Sherlock Holmes in the stories?

To answer these questions, we first analysed the data using the free-ware AntConc. We looked for the most frequent five-word chunks in the Sherlock Holmes data and then compared this with the BYU-BNC data, and undertook statistical analysis to show that the more frequent chunks in the Sherlock Holmes data were in fact 'key' chunks; that is, they appeared significantly more in this data than in the general fictional data. The statistical analysis used was log-likelihood as mentioned previously (http://ucrel. lancs.ac.uk/llwizard.html). For ease of reference, plus and minus symbols are used before these figures to indicate the greater occurrence in the first corpus (+) or second corpus (−).

In a limited way, this data helps us to answer research question a). It shows which are the most frequent five-word chunks in the Holmes data.

Table 9.3 The most frequent five-word chunks in the Sherlock Holmes data

Sherlock Holmes corpus (378,230 words)	BYU BNC fiction sub-corpus (15,909,312 words)	Log-likelihood
I have no doubt that (19)	I have no doubt that (9)	(+)16.34
What do you make of (15)	What do you make of (37)	(−) 0.08
From one to the other (10)	From one to the other (122)	(−) 42.18
To the edge of the (10)	To the edge of the (126)	(−) 44.49
Do you make of it (8)	Do you make of it (16)	(+) 0.08

The raw data and the log-likelihood calculations suggest that it is only 'I have no doubt that' which we can say with assurance is a key chunk in the Sherlock Holmes novels because only this chunk occurs more frequently in the Holmes samples than in the general literature corpus and can be considered statistically very significant, at the level of p<0.0001.

To answer research question b), we decided to manually examine concordance lines and look for patterns of colligation to investigate whether the chunk 'I have no doubt that' is primed (Hoey, 2005) differently in the Holmes data. To do this, we looked at the position of the chunk in

Table 9.4 Colligation patterns of 'I have no doubt that' in the Holmes data and BYU-BNC corpus

I have no doubt that	Sherlock Holmes mini-corpus	BYU-BNC fiction corpus
Sentence or turn initial	13 Example: not been for my knowledge of what they had done. **I have no doubt that** there were times when my life hung in the balance	3 Example: you will admit it has been a most interesting assignment. **I have no doubt that** you will emerge from it with your reputation enhanced.
Clause initial following a conjunction	3 Example: and the pangs of leave-taking behind me, and **I have no doubt that** I show it in my bearing.	4 Example: are known only to us, here on the island. But **I have no doubt that** all are known to God.
Sentence or turn initial with something preceding the chunk	3 Example: cried Mr. Pinner with a ghastly smile. "Yes, **I have no doubt that** we shall be able to do something for you. What is	2 Example: your future, if you choose to accept it. Otherwise, **I have no doubt that** you can maintain yourself by writing.
Followed by a pronoun + VP	12 inued out loud, 'and you will get food and drink. **I have no doubt that** I shall find you a situation.' 'Thank you, sir,	2 **I have no doubt that** you will emerge from it with your reputation enhanced.'
Followed by determiner + NP	7 **I have no doubt that** the house might have been purchased at the price	6 I want to know exactly what you are doing here. **I have no doubt that** a brilliant article will appear

clauses, sentences and utterances and also what type of patterns tended to co-occur with the chunk. In other words, we wished to see how this chunk was grammaticalised.

This data (Table 9.4) seems to show us the following:

1   In the Sherlock Holmes data 'I have no doubt that' is more strongly primed to be sentence or turn initial than in the general fiction corpus and to work as a 'stand-alone' chunk, i.e. with nothing (such as an adjunct) preceding it.
2   In the Sherlock Holmes data 'I have no doubt that' is primed to be followed by a clause made from a pronoun and a verb phrase (e.g. 'I have no doubt that we shall have all our details filled in') as opposed to a clause made from a determiner and noun phrase (e.g. 'I have no doubt that this woman had plunged him over head and ears').

We can therefore suggest that as well as being more likely to occur in the Holmes data, it is also primed to occur at the start of a turn, not be preceded by an adjunct and be followed by a clause with a pronoun and verb phrase. The other comparisons made do not seem to indicate large differences between the data sets so we cannot argue that 'I have no doubt that' is primed differently in these cases.

For research question c), we considered the data produced so far and also examined the contexts of use of this chunk to make suggestions about what this can tell us about how the chunk helps to establish the characterisation of Holmes. To do this we looked at each example of 'I have no doubt that' in context and checked which character said it most often. The results are shown in Table 9.5.

Table 9.5 Users of 'I have no doubt that' in the Sherlock Holmes data

Other characters	Holmes	Watson
5	9	5

This confirmed to us, alongside the other results described above, that the chunk is most often used in this data to help establish the character of Holmes as rational, intelligent, authoritative and dominant, in the sense that he always seems to have the answer to things. Of course, we may make this judgement by reading the novels and literary criticism, but the corpus data at least offers some support for this view, by way of objective evidence. We can summarise this evidence as follows:

1   'I have no doubt that' is used as a chunk more often in the Holmes data than in a much larger general fiction corpus. This use is statistically highly significant (p<0.0001).

2   It is a chunk used most often by Holmes himself or by Watson, where he frequently uses the chunk about Holmes. As such it helps to establish the character of Holmes as rational, intelligent and authoritative.

3   The colligation patterns in which the chunk occurs add to this picture in the reader's mind. The turn initial placing adds to the 'authority' the chunk imbues, which is reinforced by the fact that it is generally not mitigated by other adjuncts preceding it. It is followed by a clause with a pronoun and verb phrase, and the placing of 'I have no doubt that' in front of this clause adds weight to its conclusions. Compare, for example, 'I have no doubt that you would have had a more lively evening' to an alternative such as 'you would have had a more lively evening, I have no doubt'.

9.4 Sample study 3: Colloquial language: the use of 'bloody' in a blog corpus

The study of taboo language, swearing and colloquial forms has often been done in the context of pragmatics research. This type of work seeks to explore language in use and analyse the pragmatic meaning of sentences and utterances in context. A simple example of this is the use of common expressions such as 'the door's open'. What has been termed the '**entailment**' of this utterance (Grundy, 2008) is simply that the door is not shut. The **implicature** (the pragmatic meaning) could be 'please shut it', 'come in' or simply 'I'm cold' depending on the context in which the utterance is used.

Explorations of words such as 'bloody' have examined them from various angles. Wierzbicka (2002), for example, suggests that the usage of this word in Australian English gives us key insights into Australian attitudes and values. She argues that it is not simply a meaningless filler but is in fact packed with meaning. The word has also been analysed in terms of its politeness/impoliteness. Hong (2008), for example, analysed a corpus and interviewed Australians and non-Australians to explore the use and perceptions of 'bloody' as a result of the controversial use of the phrase 'where the bloody hell are you?' in a tourism advert. The corpus data revealed that the word is used as an adverb to intensify positive and negative adjectives ('bloody good', 'bloody awful'), as an expletive with neutral adjectives ('it's bloody quiet') and as a swearword ('bloody hell'). She also found that different nationalities viewed the use of 'bloody hell' differently in terms of its politeness. Non-Australians could perceive it as impolite, whereas Australians tended to view it as an ordinary part of Australian discourse (Hong, 2008: 33).

How do you think the word 'bloody' is mainly used in the variety of English you are most familiar with? Does it tend to have a negative perception? In British English, our assumption was that 'bloody' is used more as an adverb to intensify adjectives or nouns in general, rather than as an adjective with literal meaning. We also assumed that there would be some differences between its frequency of use in blogs compared to other written forms. While we could predict some of the common adjectives, such as 'good', which 'bloody' would intensify, we were not sure how these would differ between different corpora or what the most collocations and colligations would be. We were also unsure how the use of the word may differ in terms of semantic prosodies but felt that this would differ in each written context. Looking at the research, we found that although 'bloody' had been investigated in pragmatics research, its use in e-contexts such as blogging or commenting seemed relatively under-researched, although blogging itself has been the subject of much research. Dayter (2014), for example, investigates the notion of a new speech act of 'self-praise' in blogging, and Langlotz and Locher (2012) discuss the use of emotional stance in online commenting on newspaper websites. For these reasons, we set ourselves the following research questions:

RQ1. Is 'bloody' more commonly used as an adjective with a literal meaning (e.g. a 'bloody nose') or intensifier (e.g. 'bloody good') in a magazine and blog corpus?

RQ2. What are the most frequent collocations and how do they differ in each corpus?

RQ3. To what extent do the most common patterns in the blog corpus have clear semantic prosodies in each case?

Each research question comes with an assumption and it is perfectly possible to include these in the write-up of any research project. For reference, we have done this below.

Hypothesis 1: Bloody is more common as an intensifier of adjectives or nouns in blogs.

Hypothesis 2: We would assume that adjectives such as 'good' and 'terrible', which are evaluative, would both be more frequently intensified by 'bloody' than neutral adjectives such as 'long'.

Hypothesis 3: The most common collocations with 'bloody' will have a clear semantic prosody in the blog corpus.

To investigate this, we examined the use of 'bloody' in the BYU-BNC magazine corpus and the WebCorpLSE (http://wse1.webcorp.org.uk/cgi-bin/SYN/index.cg) blog corpus.

To answer the questions we first simply searched for 'bloody' in a learner dictionary. We then searched each corpus and compared the frequencies of

Table 9.6 Most frequent collocates to the right of 'bloody' in the blog corpus

Word	RI
Murder	281
Good	142
Hell	142
Nose	106
Violence	92
Thing	89
Brilliant	81
Mess	80
Awful	63
Hard	63

some common collocations. We then manually searched the concordances to confirm the assumption that 'bloody' is more frequent as an adverb that intensifies adjectives or nouns, rather than as an adjective with a literal meaning. Finally, we looked at sample concordance lines to check the typical semantic prosody of the word in these contexts.

The Macmillan Dictionary (www.macmillandictionary.com) and the Longman Dictionary of Contemporary English (www.ldoceonline.com) both list the use of 'bloody' as an adverb intensifier as the most common usage of this word. For example, the Longman Dictionary suggests that it is 'used to emphasize what you are saying in a slightly rude way' and gives examples such as 'It's bloody cold out there!'.

There are 7193 instances of 'bloody' in the corpus as whole. A search for the most frequent collocates occurring to the right of the word is shown in Table 9.6. This suggests, as in the information in the dictionary, that 'bloody' is largely used to intensify NPs or AdjP, rather than as an adjective with a literal meaning. There are some examples of this usage in the concordance lines below.

1	The ark is a	**bloody good**	idea. Get it built
2	I know we're in	**bloody good**	hands with them as
3	their protest. Camilla: Oh,	**bloody hell**	we are running
4	be one, inhaled like	**bloody hell**	object to those photos,
5	an x-ray revealed the	**bloody thing**	was stuck and refusing
6	exorcism performed on the	**bloody thing**	months ago and then

Figure 9.4 Concordances for 'bloody' in the blog corpus

The exception seems to be 'bloody nose' and 'bloody violence' which largely do seem to be used in a literal sense but these are only two examples amongst the ten collocates.

The answer, therefore, to research question one is that 'yes', bloody is predominantly used as a modifier of adjectives and nouns in the blog corpus, rather than an adjective with its literal meaning.

To search for the wider patterns of use, we then searched for the most frequent patterns around 'bloody murder', 'bloody hell' and 'bloody good'. This was undertaken by searching for the term and looking for collocates spanning five spaces to the left and right of each collocation. These results can be seen below.

Table 9.7 'Bloody hell' and collocates by position in the blog corpus

Word	L Total	L5	L4	L3	L2	LI	Total	RI	R2	R3	R4	R5	R Total
----	22	1	4	2	6	9	28	3	1		1	1	6
oh	14					14	15				1		1
said	4	1	1	1		1	7	1	1		1		3
thinking	3			3			7		2	1	1		4
x	3				3		7	1	1	1		1	4
get							5			3	1	1	5
know	2		1	1			5			2		1	3
got	3	2		1			5	1		1			2

Table 9.8 Collocates of 'bloody murder' in the blog corpus

Word	LTotal	L5	L4	L3	L2	LI	Total	RI	R2	R3	R4	R5	RTotal
screaming	130					130	130						
country	61		2		59		61						
scream	61		1			60	61						
see	1		1				60				59		59
business-types	59	59					59						
screamed	33					33	33						
people	13	1	6	2		4	14				1		1
just	3	2				1	13	2		5	1	2	10
quest	12				12		12						
killed							12					12	12
daughter							12			12			12
screams	9					9	9						
cried	8					8	8						
think	1		1				8	1		5		1	7
cry	7					7	8	1					1
tell							8		7	1			8
fans	7		1	1	5		7						
mean	7		1		6		7						
8	6		3	3			6						
overly	6	6					6						
time	2	1		1			6		3		1		4
dramatic	6		6				6						
hang	6	6					6						
swingsets	6			6			6						
now	4			3	1		5	1					1

Table 9.9 Collocates with 'bloody good' in the blog corpus

Word	L Total	L5	L4	L3	L2	L1	Total	R1	R2	R3	R4	R5	R Total
----------	9	2	3	3	1		24	1	9	1	3	1	15
time	2		1	1			12	9				1	10
job	1				1		11	10					10
looks	8			5	3		9	1					1
fun							6	6					6
movie	1				1		6	4				1	5

In terms of frequency, we can then see that 'screaming bloody murder', 'oh bloody hell' and 'bloody good job' are most common. This suggests that in this blog corpus, these words are most strongly primed to co-occur with the target collocations and that of these, the sequence with the strongest priming is 'bloody' with 'murder' and 'screaming' with 'bloody'. When we compare these results to another written corpus (the COCA magazine corpus), the results are quite different. In this corpus (95,558,725 words), there are 1424 instances of 'bloody'. This is not so different (in fact, the log-likelihood score shows us that it is statistically more frequent in the magazine corpus). However, the collocations are also markedly different in the magazine corpus when we check those immediately to the right of the word in Table 9.10.

Table 9.10 Collocates immediately to the right of 'bloody' in the magazine corpus

1	,	75
2	MARY	54
3	KNIFE	52
4	AND	39
5	SUNDAY	31
6	.	30
7	MARYS	23
8	BATTLE	21
9	CIVIL	19
10	NOSE	19
11	GLOVE	17
12	MURDER	17

These show that there is a much stronger tendency in this corpus to use 'bloody' as an adjective with its literal meaning sense than to modify other adjectives or nouns. For example, where 'bloody' is followed by a comma it tends to be used as a descriptive adjective alongside others.

1	Watch out! # N2: The headlights catch sight of a person in	**bloody**	, shredded clothing. # N1: Taylor slams on the brakes just in time
2	The sergeant wore his sword on his belt. His hachimaki was tattered and	**bloody**	, and as he paced back and forth, tears flowed freely down his face
3	wasn't nuts). He had to settle for being popular. NOW:	**Bloody**	, vicious serial killer terrifies Los Angeles. WINNER: O'Hara
4	were small people in a big man's world. The steak was moist,	**bloody**	, and delicious, but far too rich for me. I felt sick
5	We were greeted as liberators and then we saw a massive,	**bloody**	, dangerous insurgency began. And it wasn't frankly until we were able in

Figure 9.5 Samples of 'bloody' in the COCA magazine corpus

Looking for further patterns (by searching for collocates up to five spaces to the left and right of 'bloody + comma', 'bloody + Mary' and 'bloody + knife') confirms this in the different patterns produced. To give an illustrative example, Table 9.11 shows the most frequent of these for 'bloody + comma'.

Table 9.11 Collocates with 'bloody + comma'

		Number of occurrences	Per million words
1	,	127	1.33
2	AND	32	0.33
3	THE	29	0.30
4	.	24	0.25
5	A	22	0.23
6	WAS	12	0.13
7	TO	11	0.12
8	IT	10	0.10
9	IN	9	0.09
10	OF	9	0.09
11	OR	7	0.07
12	"	7	0.07
13	BUT	6	0.06
14	MY	6	0.06
15	MESS	5	0.05

These results show that 'bloody' seems to have stronger priming to co-occur with 'murder' in the blog corpus than in the magazine corpus (281 vs. 17 occurrences), which gives a log-likelihood score of 17.91. It also has a stronger priming to occur with adjectives such as 'good' and nouns such as 'hell' which it can modify in the blog corpus. Therefore, in answer to research question two, we can suggest that 'bloody' is more likely to act as a modifying adverb or adjective in the blog corpus and more likely to act as a descriptive adjective in the magazine corpus.

RQ3. To what extent do the common patterns with 'bloody' have a clear semantic prosody in the blog corpus?

To analyse this, we examined concordance lines for 'screaming bloody murder' in the blog corpus and where needed, clicked on the larger context from which the concordance lines were taken. We did this to understand whether this pattern was generally positive, negative or neutral. The majority of examples of this pattern seemed to show a negative shading rather than a purely descriptive, neutral one. It tends to be associated with negative events or criticism which bloggers are reacting to or describing. Some examples of this can be seen in Figure 9.6.

1	again disfigured (poor Emily	**screaming bloody murder**	) or Margaret catching sight
2	Media establishments would be	**screaming bloody murder**	. South Carolina wins by
3	My middle guy is	**screaming bloody murder**	. It sounds horrible, but
4	Immediately lept backwards while	**screaming bloody murder**	and in that time
5	my right knee started	**screaming bloody murder**	for relief, I said
6	and will probably be	**screaming bloody murder**	in a corner somewhere
7	running down the street	**screaming bloody murder**	, or too frightened to
8	of a sudden you're	**screaming bloody murder**	because your 350 lb
9	old standing beside me	**screaming bloody murder**	lol. I can say
10	sat outside the bathroom	**screaming bloody murder**	if they couldn't come

Figure 9.6 'Screaming bloody murder' in a blog corpus

9.5 Conclusion

In this chapter, we have attempted to show how simple research can be undertaken using corpus data and corpus analysis tools. We have presented a research cycle which could inform your practice and shown the simple application of this in three small-scale studies. It is important to remember that *all* research has limitations and while it can be exciting to uncover some answers, we must always temper this with an awareness that these answers are always limited to the particular context and study we are undertaking.

Further practice

1   Think of an area you would be interested in researching. Follow the research cycle we have suggested and try to undertake the research, even if it is only on a small scale.
2   How do you need to limit the conclusions that can be drawn from the findings?
3.   Use the cycle above to evaluate published research you are reviewing. To what extent does this research seem to follow such a cycle?

References

Carter, R. and McCarthy, M. (1999). The English get passive in spoken discourse: description and implications for an interpersonal grammar. *English Language and Linguistics*, 3, 1, 41–58.

Carter, R. and McCarthy, M. (2006). *Cambridge grammar of English*. Cambridge: Cambridge University Press.

Davies, M. (2004). *BYU-BNC* (based on the British National Corpus from Oxford University Press). [Online], Available: http://corpus.byu.edu/bnc [20 October 2013].

Dayter, D. (2014). Self-praise in microblogging. *Journal of Pragmatics*, 61, 91–102.

Fulcher, G. (1991). Conditionals revisited. *ELT Journal*, 45, 2, 164–68.

Grundy, P. (2008). *Doing pragmatics*. London: Routledge.

Hoey, M. (2005). *Lexical priming: a new theory of words and language*. London: Routledge.

Hong, M. (2008). 'Where the bloody hell are you?': bloody hell and (im)politeness in Australian English. *Griffith Working Papers in Pragmatics and Intercultural Communication*, 1, 1, 33–39.

Jones, C. and Waller, D. (2011). If only it were true: the problem with the four conditionals. *ELT Journal*, 65, 1, 24–32.

Kestner, J. (1997). *Sherlock's men: masculinity, Conan Doyle and cultural history*. Farnham: Ashgate.

Langlotz, A. and Locher, M.A. (2012). Ways of communicating emotional stance in online disagreements. *Journal of Pragmatics*, 44, 12, 1591–1606.

Longman (2014). *The Longman dictionary of contemporary English*. [Online], Available: www.ldoceonline.com [1 April 2014].

Macmillan (2014). *The Macmillan Dictionary*. [Online], Available: www.macmillan-dictionary.com [1 April 2014].

Mahlberg, M. (2007). Corpus stylistics: bridging the gap between linguistic and literary studies, in M. Mahlberg and W. Teubert (eds.) *Text, discourse and corpora. Theory and analysis*. London: Continuum, 219–246.

Mahlberg, M. (2013). *Corpus stylistics and Dickens's fiction*. London: Routledge.

Maule, D. (1988). 'If he comes, I go': teaching conditionals. *ELT Journal*, 42, 2, 117–23.

O'Halloran, K. A. (2007). The subconscious in James Joyce's *Eveline*: a corpus stylistic analysis which chews on the 'fish hook'. Language and Literature, 16, 3, 227–244.

Project Gutenberg (2014). *Project Gutenberg*. [Online], Available: www.gutenberg.org [10 April 2014].

Research and Development Unit for English Studies, Birmingham City University (2014). *WebCorpLSE*. [Online], Available: www.webcorp.org.uk/live/wlse.jsp [12 February 2014].

Spencer, H. (2011). *Semantic prosody in literary analysis: a corpus-based stylistic study of H.P. Lovecraft's stories*. Unpublished MA by Research thesis. [Online], Available: http://eprints.hud.ac.uk/12904/1/hspencerfinalthesis.pdf [10 April 2014].

Stubbs, M. (2008). Conrad in the computer: examples of quantitative stylistic analysis, in R. Carter and C. Stockwell (eds.) *The language and literature reader*. London: Routledge, 230–243.

Suggested answers

Try it yourself 1.1

Suggested answers

1   You would need samples of lectures from across disciplines and in seminars/tutorials. A million words would lead to a small but probably effective sample as this would be fairly focused, although this would take a considerable amount of time to collect and transcribe. A much smaller sample could be used if the lectures were from a single subject discipline.
2   You would need samples from most or all of Dickens' work to make statements about this as a whole. A million words are likely to be effective.
3   You would need samples of requests by email and this would need to represent colleagues across an institution. The focus is quite restricted so perhaps 50,000 words would suffice.

Try it yourself 1.2

Answers (number of occurrences per corpus shown in brackets)

   These answers are from the BYU-BNC corpus (http://corpus2.byu.edu/bnc).

Table 10.1 Occurrences of opinions and judgement patterns in four corpora

Pattern	Fiction corpus	Spoken corpus	Newspaper corpus	Academic English corpus
We can assume that ...	2 (4)	3 = (0)	3 = (0)	1 (13)
I'd say that ...	2 (10)	1 (13)	3 (3)	4 (2)
You can be sure that ...	2 (3)	3 (2)	1 (4)	4 (1)

Each pattern is of low frequency in each corpus but shows us that there is a clear difference in usage. We can see, for example, that there is a clear preference for the first pattern 'we can assume that' in academic texts.

Try it yourself 1.3

Suggested answers from the BYU-BNC http://corpus.byu.edu/bnc.

Table 10.2 Frequency of modal verbs in three BYU-BNC corpora

	Frequency order (1–4) Shown for each corpus type in turn		
Question	General spoken	Academic English	Fiction
Do I have to . . . ?	2	4	2
Must I . . . ?	4	2	3
Should I . . . ?	1	1	1
Do I need to . . . ?	3	3	4

Try it yourself 2.1

Suggested answers

Answers:

1 I mean **nice** that it was a good storyline (spoken).
2 By the way, there are a lot of things in Belgium that are very **nice** (spoken).
3 It was **nice** seeing you again, she said softly (fiction).
4 This place offers clean bathrooms, hot showers, a **nice** and reasonably priced restaurant (magazine).
5 A **nice** balance is two parts calcium to one part magnesium, says nutritionist Shawn Talbott (magazine).
6 I'm just being **nice** (spoken).

Try it yourself 2.2

Suggested answers

1. Ideational

The text expresses the idea that there is a family who exist, are poor and are faced with a decision about how to survive. It does so with simple sentences in present form and with one declarative clause. This creates an 'immediacy' which suits the beginning readers who are the intended audience of this text.

2. Interpersonal

Although there is a distance between the reader and writer, the use of 'this is' and 'here are' attempts to speak directly to the reader and get them interested in and aware of the characters.

3. Textual

Sentences are linked together through the use of repetition of key noun phrases such as 'Hansel and Gretel'. The noun phrases are also used to refer backwards and forwards in the text. For example, 'The stepmother' refers back to the stepmother just introduced; 'This is' refers forwards to characters being introduced. The use of 'the woodcutter' suggests he was introduced previously.

Examining a corpus of similar texts aimed at beginning readers would give us more definitive answers about whether these patterns can be generalised across texts such as these.

Try it yourself 3.1

Suggested answers

Table 10.3 'For example' in larger patterns in the BYU-BNC spoken corpus (http://corpus.byu.edu/bnc)

Verb + for example	* + verb + for example
Say for example (11)	I mean for example (7)
Take for example (7)	
Mean for example (7)	
Is for example (5)	
Can for example (5)	

Try it yourself 3.2

Suggested answers

Table 10.4 Log-likelihood scores for 'I mean' in a fiction and spoken corpus (http://corpus.byu.edu/bnc)

Fiction corpus (15,909,312 words)	Spoken corpus (9,963,663 words)	Log-likelihood
2634 occurrences (165.96 per million words)	20355 occurrences (2042.92 per million words)	25042.34

As we would expect, the chunk 'I mean' occurs with much greater frequency in this spoken corpus and this is highly significant at the level of p<0.0001.

Try it yourself 3.3

Table 10.5 T-test for 'I mean' in three written and three spoken corpora

Written corpora Occurrences per million words	Spoken corpora Occurrences per million words
65.56 (BYU-BNC fiction)	2,042.92 (BYU-BNC spoken)
43.10 (BYU-BNC magazine)	970.50 (COCA spoken)
7.26 (BYU-BNC newspaper)	1,116 (HKCSE)

p<0.05 (the greater occurrence of 'I mean' in the three spoken corpora is statistically significant). These results show that (as we would expect) 'I mean' is more common in spoken corpora than written ones, and the difference in frequency in this case was significant. This means that we can state with some confidence that 'I mean' is far more frequent in the types of spoken language represented in these corpora.

Try it yourself 3.4

Suggested answers

Table 10.6 Collocates for 'You want to go + collocate' in the BYU-BNC and COCA

Collocates	Number of occurrences	Mutual Information score
BYU-BNC To	352	5.23
COCA To	2013	5.13

This suggests that 'to' is very likely to co-occur with this pattern and that this is slightly more frequent in the BYU-BNC. The results also show that this is not a chance co-occurrence so we can suggest that 'you want to go + to + verb' is a more likely pattern than 'you can go + v + ing' in these corpora.

Try it yourself 3.5

Suggested answers

Table 10.7 Frequent patterns with 'have and past participle' in the BYU-BNC spoken and magazine corpora

	BYU-BNC spoken corpus	BYU-BNC magazine corpus 7,261,990 words
Have and past participle	Most common two forms = 1. 'Have been' (4541 occurrences, 455.76 per million words) 2. 'have got' (1411 occurrences, 141.61 per million words)	Most common two forms = 1. 'Have been' (4824 occurrences, 664.28 per million words) 2. 'have had' (494, 68.03 per million words)
* have and past participle * pattern	Most common patterns = 1. 'would have been a' (60 occurrences, 6.02 per million words) Examining the concordances, we can suggest that 'Noun phrase + would have been a + Noun Phase' is the most common larger pattern 2. 'would have thought that' (48 occurrences, 4.82 per million words) Examining the concordances, 'I would have thought that + clause' is the most common larger pattern	Most common pattern = 1. 'would have been a' (40 occurrences, 5.51 per million words) Examining the concordances, we can suggest that 'Noun phrase + would have been a + Noun Phase' is the most common larger pattern 2. 'to have been a' (23 occurrences, 3.17 per million words) Examining the concordances, 'Verb phrase + to have been a + noun phrase' is the most common pattern. Very often the verb phrase is modal in meaning, expressing some form of deduction e.g. 'There seems to have been a hierarchy of colours'

Try it yourself 4.1

Suggested answers

Table 10.8 Frequency of 'I must go' in spoken and written corpora

Corpus type	Spoken (9,963,663 words)	Fiction (15,909,312 words)	Magazine (7,261,990 words)	Newspaper (10,466,422 words)	Academic (15,331,668 words)
Total number of occurrences	19	218	3	6	0
Occurrences per million words	1.91	13.70	0.41	0.57	0

This results in a log-likelihood score of 115.95 (p<0.0001), which suggests that 'I must go' occurs with significantly higher frequency in the fiction corpus. If we compare this to the internet search we performed at the start of the chapter, we can see that this kind of information about frequency can be more helpful. We now know that 'I have to go' and 'I must go' occur with the most frequency in the fiction corpus we have examined. We also know that if we compare the frequency counts for each pattern in the fiction corpus then 'I must go' is more frequent, which is the opposite of the result given by a simple internet search.

Try it yourself 4.2

Suggested answers

Statements 1, 2, 3 and 5 use variations of the word *advice*, making a direct connection between the function and form of the statement. Statements 4, 6, 7 and 8 use the imperative form to provide strong advice. We can see from this example that any exploration of corpora data using frequency also needs to consider text type and purpose in the examination of language, but also that frequency searches on their own can be a little limited in scope when one considers all the different ways in which functions or modality can be expressed.

Try it yourself 5.1

Suggested answers

Frequent chunks in the HKCSE and BNC spoken corpus. The total occurrences for chunks in the BNC are followed by the number of occurrences per million words.

Table 10.9 Frequent chunks in the HKCSE and the BYU–BNC spoken corpora

	HKCSE (907,657 words)	BNC spoken corpus (9,963,663 words)
1	Hong Kong (2364)	Don't know (9034: 906.69)
2	Don't know (710)	Oh yeah (3636: 364.93)
3	Okay so (321)	One two (373: 37.44)
4	Oh yeah (180)	Okay so (332: 33.32)
5	Right yeah (86)	Right yeah (200: 20.07)
6	One two (66)	Know so (101: 10.14)
7	Okay yeah (53)	Okay yeah (47: 4.72)
8	Know so (42)	So yeah (63: 6.32)
9	Know yeah (42)	Hong Kong (43: 4.32)

Although it is not a surprise that 'Hong Kong' features so strongly in the HKCSE, what is also of note is the chunks with similar frequencies in both corpora and also those with slight differences. 'Don't know' occurs with a similar frequency in both sets of data, for example, while 'okay so' occurs with a higher frequency in the HCKSE, if we consider the number of occurrences per million words. Checking the log-likelihood confirms this as the score is (+) 746.92, which indicates that the greater number of occurrences in the HKCSE is statistically significant.

Try it yourself 5.2

Suggested answers

Table 10.10 The most common four-word chunks in a corpus of EastEnders scripts

Rank	Chunk	Number of occurrences
1	ALL RIGHT ALL RIGHT	19
2	WHAT DO YOU THINK	16
3	WHAT DO YOU MEAN	13
4	YOU WANT ME TO	13
5	CAN I GET YOU	12
6	IN THE FIRST PLACE	12
7	A BIT OF A	10
8	I DON'T WANT TO	10
9	NOTHING TO DO WITH	10
10	HAVE A WORD WITH	9

Try it yourself 5.3

Suggested answers

Table 10.11 Three and four-word chunks used in Ed Milliband's conference speech 2013

Three-word chunks	Four-word chunks
Better than this (25) (BNC spoken corpus = 14)	Race to the top (16) (BNC spoken corpus = 0)
Race to the (25) (BNC = 2)	A race to the (12) (BNC = 0)
To the top (16) (BNC = 126)	Do better than this (12) (BNC = 2)
A race to (12) (BNC = 0)	The race to the (10) (BNC = 0)
Do better than (12) (BNC = 9)	
I want to (11) (BNC = 1285)	
The voices of (11) (BNC = 1)	
Going to be (10) (BNC = 2106)	
The race to (10) (BNC = 1)	
Win the race (10) (BNC = 1)	

It seems clear from this that the chunks 'race to the top' and 'better than this' and variations of these occur with the most frequency in this speech.

Try it yourself 6.1

Suggested answers

We can see that examples 1, 2 and 4 are likely to be criticism of a particular piece of behaviour. The use of the structure may be to avoid using overly strong language (i.e. if you were to rephrase sentence 1 without using the negative you might be left saying 'it's horrible to do that'). Sentences 3, 4 and 5 are used to give opinions on a particular phenomenon, but the speakers are dis-preferring the use of a negative adjective in favour of a positive adjective with a negative structure. Again, this may be a strategy to avoid overly strong language which may either invite contradiction or seem over the top (sentence 4 for example, if it were rephrased with a negative adjective such as 'terrible', 'awful' or 'bad').

Try it yourself 6.2

Suggested answers

There are of course many reasons why a particular form might be chosen and the passive has a number of reasons for being used, some of which are to do with maintaining text coherence. Sentence 1 above is just such an example; the use of the passive avoids a repetition of the subject ('where she met . . . '), but it is also true that the sentence comes from a British news broadcast so it is unsurprising that the focus should be on the British Queen and not on the Greek Cypriot President, whose identity may be unknown to many viewers in the UK.

The second example is an example of blame avoidance. It comes from a speech by former US President Ronald Reagan who was accounting for actions in his presidency which many saw as being illegal. He very clearly avoids saying that the mistakes were his, or identifying anyone who might be to blame for them.

Sentence 3 uses the passive form because it is clear from the context who has done the sentencing (only a member of the judiciary in the UK has such power) and the focus in the sentence is on the train robbers rather than on the actual sentencing. This is similar to sentence 4 where the information about the party and its very young participants is the focus of the sentence.

Sentence 5 uses the passive form because the identity of the assailants is presumably unknown, but also because the speaker is emphasising the close relationship with the victim (my own son).

Sentence 6 is another example where the event is being portrayed as more important than the agent, but as we have seen above, it might be asked why it was not written 'For the first time ever in Britain, police fired CS gas at rioters'. One could argue that there is little change in propositional meaning, but perhaps the change in emphasis detracts from the emphasis on the importance of the action, or could be construed as being critical of the police.

Try it yourself 7.1

Suggested answers

Some possibilities for using these materials could include identifying the most common pronouns that come before and after 'must' and 'should' ('we' and 'be') and why that may be the case in this context, classifying the uses of 'must' and 'should' into those expressing some form of possibility and those expressing some form of obligation, and finally learners could contrast and discuss the different levels of obligation implied by 'somebody must sort them' vs. 'I don't think we should give her too long'.

Try it yourself 7.2

Suggested answers

A quick search on the BYU-BNC corpus for 'j* + chaos' shows us that all of these words are represented. 'Ensuing' has the most instances of any in the list (seven) and there is an example of it in the longer chunk of 'in the [aj*] chaos'. 'General' has four instances of use while 'huge' and 'resulting' have two. There are no instances of 'continuous chaos' which suggests that this answer can be eliminated. When we look at the examples of 'huge' chaos, we can see that there are two uses:

a) is how to bring them to regard life as anything but a huge chaos. The confusion
b) Azhag was confronted by a huge Chaos Troll. Azhag fought the troll

This might make us think about whether we would accept 'huge' as an answer, and corpora will not always provide a clear example, but at least we can see that there is one use of 'huge' which is comparable to the use in our gap. Since an important feature of standardising open cloze tests is ensuring that learners are not penalised for answers that are potentially correct, a corpus can at least provide us with some information that can help to inform the decisions we make. In the case of this particular test, all of the answers bar 'continuous' were accepted.

Try it yourself 8.1

Suggested answers

We would argue that lines 1, 3, 4, 5 and 6 are all instances of 'we' as the speaker and the party. This can be identified either from the concordance line (in line 1, the speaker addresses the mark to 'friends' which presumably is those in the room) but for 3, 4, 5 and 6 we had to look at the instances in the full context to identify the reference. Lines 2, 7 and 8 are 'we' as a country.

Try it yourself 8.2

Suggested answers

Category A ('we' as party): 1, 3, 4, 5, 6, 8, 9
Category B ('we' as country): 10
Category C ('we' unclear): 2, 7, 11
As in the previous examples, where the meaning is unclear there is often a reason for this. In line 2, the 'we' who have to build the railway is partly the country as a whole but also the politicians who are championing it. Lines 7 and 11 are both potentially unpalatable messages but by conflating who is being spoken to, both groups are included without being singled out. We were tempted to include line 11 in category B, but the context is quite vague about exactly who is being addressed.

Try it yourself 8.3

Suggested answers

You may have come up with a number of hypotheses related to the two terms, which may include the following:

a)   The British people: There will be attempts by the speakers to identify themselves strongly with this group.
b)   The party of: This phrase will almost certainly be followed by a noun phrase and it will be abstract in nature (e.g. education). The speaker will also attempt to associate their own party with this phrase.

Now look at the concordance lines and consider these hypotheses as well as any you have generated before you go back to the continuing discussion in Chapter 8.

1	Whether or not we have another coalition is determined by	**the British people**	– not me, not you, the people. And if that
2	Labour or the Conservatives. All of the sacrifices made by	**the British people**	– the pay freezes, the spending cuts, the
3	needs to do. Now look around you, you know the problem is	**the British people**	are paying the price of this government's
4	through tough times too. So let us take our example from	**the British people**	as together we embark on the journey ahead
5	than this. NHS Nowhere do we need to put the values of	**the British people**	back at the heart of our country than in
6	remember. The posters. The sound bites. David Cameron knew	**the British people**	did not trust the Tories with our NHS. So
7	truths. All of my adult life, whatever the difficulties,	**the British people**	have at least been confident about one th
8	and co operation. That is the magic of the NHS; that is why	**the British people**	love the NHS and I'm afraid the Tories
9	we face, we must rediscover that spirit. That spirit	**the British people**	never forgot. That spirit of One Nation
10	no. The radiologists said no. The patients said no. And	**the British people**	said no. And what did he do? He ploughed
11	what we will do... ... and at the end of it yes we will give	**the British people**	their say in a referendum. That is our
12	people to give you a blank cheque. You can sit and wait for	**the British people**	to come back to you, but don't hold your
13	us. We succeeded because of us, us the British people, us	**the British people**	who welcomed the athletes from abroad,
14	ploughed on regardless. He broke his solemn contract with	**the British people**	, a contract that can never be repaired.
15	strength of us as a country. You see the problem isn't	**the British people**	, just think about the Olympics and
16	believe from our conversations over the past year that you,	**the British people**	, know it. You've seen a series of crises
17	and flinging it into the crowd, expecting adoration from	**the British people**	, like he did recently on holiday. Maybe I
18	we succeeded because of us. We succeeded because of us, us	**the British people**	, us the British people who welcomed the a
19	have been: in power; in the liberal centre; in tune with	**the British people**	. And every day we are showing that we can
20	to me, he said, were N H S. It was a solemn contract with	**the British people**	. And then what did he do? He came along a
21	relationship with the other parties, but our relationship with	**the British people**	Imagine yourself standing on the doorste
22	The people who have done the most to get us this far. You.	**The British people**	. Never giving up. Working those extra hou
23	I am interested in the Government doing the right thing by	**the British people**	. So there is a big choice facing the coun
24	tell you what I'm interested in. Winning back the trust of	**the British people**	. Winning the next general election. My me
25	You can't trust the Tories with the NHS. And let me tell	**the British people**	: If you want someone who will rip up the
26	have no right to be here in the first place? I say this to	**the British people**	: you have every right to be angry about a

Figure 10.1 Concordance lines for 'the British people' in a political speech corpus

1	in a home of their own. That is what we're about. And this,	**the party of**	aspiration is going to finish the job we've sta
2	that is why this party has always been and must always be	**the party of**	education. Because just as there can be no real
3	as we journey from the party of opposition that we were, to	**the party of**	we are becoming. But before we head
4	without any help for their parents? 33 years old. We are	**the party of**	home ownership – we cannot let this carry on. S
5	to us to stand up for the national interest: we will be	**the party of**	In. I am an internationalist – pure and simple;
6	er it's: borrow more money. Borrow, borrow, borrow. Labour:	**the party of**	one notion: more borrowing. I sometimes wonder
7	as those in poverty. There is no future for this party as	**the party of**	one sectional interest of our coun-try. But so t
8	to stop looking in the rear view mirror as we journey from	**the party of**	opposition that we were, to the party of govern
9	the way we win the race to the top. One Nation Labour	**the party of**	small business, cutting small busi-ness rates wh
10	as the home help strug-gling against the cuts. We must be	**the party of**	south just as much as the party of the north. A
11	ducation system. . . a coun-try for the few built by	**the party of**	the many. and Labour: we will never let you for
12	in the value of work. Labour. Think about that word.	**The party of**	work. Now under my leadership, we will be the

Figure 10.2 Concordance lines for 'the party of'

Try it yourself 9.1

Suggested answers

You should get results such as those in Figure 10.3. These are just ten examples.

1	12 hour stomach bug.	**If I do, I get**	a small break and
2	Comfort in this book.	**If I may, I would**	like to recommend another
3	dollar in the world.	**If I had, I should**	not feel that I
4	or give any offense.	**If I have, I**	. But if my tax
5	obligations to my student.	**If I don't, I wouldn't**	have been in this
6	of any such accident.	**If I had I shouldn't**	in advance have had
7	a truck I think.	**If I could, I would**	say the title. Anyway,
8	outrageous charge. Ms Harney;	**If I could, I would**	, but I cannot do
9	being happy at Bolton."	**If I said I would**	be here for sure
10	or hold a seminar.	**If I don't, I won't**	. It's basically relaxed." Essentially,

Figure 10.3 Sample patterns with 'If I + verb, I + verb' from a web corpus

The variety of patterns on display here and the prevalence of those that do not fit into the four often identified by textbooks would seem to indicate that our concern was justified.

Try it yourself 9.2

Suggested answers

1 If they'd done that, they would have won the Championship (Unreal past. If + past perfect, would have + past participle).
2 If you wanted to know the answer . . . you had to keep zapping from channel to channel. (Real past. If + past simple, past simple).
3 If we could get three or four items, that would be very nice (Unreal non-past. If + could, would).
4 If I'm making a film of myself . . . , I can pass or fail . . . (Real non-past. If + present continuous, can).

Figure 10.4 Concordance lines for conditionals

Glossary

This glossary is intended as a quick reference to some of the key terms that are used in the book. More precise definitions can be found in some of the texts which we have referenced at the end of each chapter.

Aspect The simple, perfect and continuous element of the verb that informs us about how the speaker views an action in time. Actions may be viewed as being complete (e.g. 'I went to the shops'), in progress (e.g. 'I'm reading a good book at the moment') or connecting two points in time (e.g. 'He'd never been to Birmingham until last November'.

Chunk A unit of lexis that includes word partnerships (**collocations**) such as 'make a sandwich' as well as longer stretches of pre-fabricated lexis such as fixed expressions ('Happy birthday', 'How do you do') and semi-fixed expressions ('Would you mind . . . ?'). Chunks also include colligation. Chunks often carry their own in-built grammar (e.g. 'I know what you mean' is far more likely to occur than 'I knew what you meant').

Clause A stretch of text that has to include a verb. A clause may either be part of a sentence or constitute a sentence on its own. Clauses may be viewed as being main or subordinate.

Colligation The grammatical patterning or structure that accompanies a particular word or chunk including its preferred position in a sentence or **utterance**.

Collocation Word partnerships that include a number of different forms (such as verb + noun e.g. 'take a photograph'; adjective + noun e.g. 'significant likelihood'; adverb + verb e.g. 'run quickly'). These partnerships are not random but reoccurring patterns in use.

Concordance lines Pieces of text extracted from a corpora often with the key word in context highlighted at the centre of each concordance line.

Co-occurrence A feature of collocation: the probability that two words will appear close to each other within a text.

Descriptive A descriptive view of grammar looks at examples of language in use (often in a corpus) to understand how the language works in practice. Descriptive grammars are often contrasted with **prescriptive** ones.

Discourse   Language in **texts** which is longer than a sentence or a single **utterance**.

Discourse marker   A signal in a **text** that the speaker or writer is carrying out a particular function such as gaining time to think (e.g. 'Well . . . '), reformulating what has just been said (e.g. 'I mean . . . ') or signposting within a longer text (e.g. 'I'm going to start by . . . and then . . . '). Discourse markers may either be single words or longer chunks (e.g. 'as I was saying').

Entailment   Utterances or sentences that convey an automatic message (e.g. 'the train has been delayed' contains the entailment that the train is late). Entailment is distinct from **implicature**.

Form   The construction of a particular phrase/clause or utterance (e.g. 'I smoke' = Pronoun + Lexical Verb. The pronoun is a Noun Phrase and the 'smoke' is a Verb Phrase).

Function   The meaning of a phrase/clause or utterance in context (e.g. 'I smoke' = 'I' as subject and 'smoke' as predicator').

General reference corpus   Often a large corpus used as a point of reference when checking the importance of **keywords** within a smaller corpus.

General Service Lists   Lists of lexis constructed according to word frequency from the West Corpus often used as the basis for constructing English language learning materials such as graded readers.

Ideational metafunction   A principle from the functional analysis of English established by Halliday. The ideational metafunction is the use of language to represent the world external to the text and the writer's/speaker's ideas.

Idiom principle   A principle described by Sinclair (1991) which suggests that much of the language we use comprises pre-fabricated chunks that we learn and use just as we would idioms. This concept stands in contrast to Sinclair's **open choice** principle.

Implicature   Where a meaning is not necessarily explicit (e.g. 'the train may be late' suggests that the speaker believes there is a possibility that the train will be delayed).

Interpersonal metafunction   A principle from the functional analysis of English established by Halliday. The interpersonal metafunction relates to the way that speakers or writers build and maintain relationships with their audience in a text.

Keyness factor   The number accompanying each word representing the number of times more frequently a term is in your corpus compared with a **general reference corpus.** The higher the number, the more 'key' the word is. Chung and Nation (2004) suggest that words with a 'keyness' of fifty or above are likely to be of importance.

Key word in context (KWIC)   In **concordance lines** the key word in context is the term that has been searched and is highlighted normally in the middle.

Keywords   Words that occur many more times in your data when compared with a **general reference corpus**.

Lexico-grammar   Lexico-grammar is a term coined by Halliday whereby grammar and lexis are not viewed as discrete and separate but rather part of a single system for constructing meaning.

Log-likelihood   A way of calculating statistical significance between occurrences of language in corpora of different sizes.

Mono-modal   A corpus that stores texts in only one medium, usually written text.

Morphology   A part of grammar concerned with the structure of words and phrases such as the formation of different word classes. For example, the verb 'rely' becomes an adjective by adding the suffix 'able' and a noun by adding 'ability', forming 'reliable' and 'reliability'.

Multi-modal   A multi-modal corpus stores texts in more than one medium, for example a video may accompany the transcript of a particular recording.

Mutual Information (MI) score   A score produced indicating a pattern of co-occurrence between two words. For example, the relationship between the phrase 'I was wondering' and 'if' could be checked using this score to determine how high the chance of co-occurrence is. The higher the score, the greater the chance.

N-Gram   A two, three or four (or more) word combination that occurs in data. N-Grams can produce recognisable chunks (e.g. 'I know what you mean') or string of words that co-occur ('It was a').

Open-access   A corpus or web-resource that is freely available for use by any individual.

Open choice   A concept described by Sinclair (1991) which takes the view that people can use grammar to create unique utterances, sentences and clauses.

Pragmatic   Appropriacy of a piece of language for use in a particular context.

Prescriptive   A prescriptive view of language is one in which rules are formulated (often based on intuition). These rules are then set as a standard with deviations regarded as being largely incorrect.

Primed   Hoey (2005) suggests that words are primed for particular collocations and colligations so that hearing or reading a word in a particular context brings with it particular and predictable patterns of use.

Qualitative   A type of research that centres on non-numeric data. Qualitative research is often used to try and generate an in-depth understanding of a particular sociological phenomenon.

Quantitative   A type of research in the form of numbers or statistics usually carried out to test hypotheses using empirical data.

Register The use of language appropriate to a particular setting which includes an awareness of the language forms and the sociolinguistic requirements for conventions such as politeness.

Semantic prosody The concept that certain forms of words carry with them positive, negative or neutral shadings.

Sentence-level pattern A grammatical pattern that occurs at the level of a clause or sentence.

Statistical significance A measure of whether two variables can be considered to have a relationship that is not purely the result of chance. The usual convention is that a statistical score of 0.05 or lower is statistically significant.

Syntax The way in which words are arranged into sentences and texts.

Tense Tense locates the time when something happens within a text. This is indicated by an inflection of the verb. In English there are only two tenses (past and present).

Text A stretch of written or spoken language which is usually longer than a speaker's single turn or than a sentence in writing.

Textual metafunction A principle from the functional analysis of English established by Halliday. The textual metafunction relates to the way that speakers/writers construct their text and maintain cohesion.

Token Individual words in a text. For example, the sentence 'I saw him yesterday when I was at the office' contains ten tokens.

Turn A basic unit of conversation (Carter and McCarthy, 2006). Speakers take turns as part of the co-construction of conversation.

Type A unit for counting the number of words in a text by which each new word is counted but re-occurrences of types are not. For example, the sentence 'I saw him yesterday when I was at the office' contains ten **tokens** but only nine types because the word 'I' occurs twice.

Utterance A unit of speech that is meaningful and complete.

References

Carter, R. and McCarthy, M. (2006). *Cambridge grammar of English*. Cambridge: Cambridge University Press.

Chung, T. M and Nation, P. (2004). Identifying technical vocabulary. *System*, 32, 251–263.

Hoey, M. (2005). *Lexical priming: a new theory of words and language*. London: Routledge.

Sinclair, J. (1991). *Corpus, concordance, collocation*. Oxford: Oxford University Press.

Index

Note: Page references in **bold** are to the Glossary; those in *italics* are to answers to exercises.